Jewish Eating and Identity Through the Ages

D1589991

This book explores the history of Jewish eating and Jewish identity, from the Bible to the present. The lessons of this book rest squarely on the much-quoted insight: "you are what you eat." But this book goes beyond that simple truism to recognise that you are not only what you eat, but also how, when, where and with whom you eat. This book begins at the beginning – with the Torah – and then follows the history of Jewish eating until the modern age and even into our own day. Along the way, it travels from Jewish homes in the Holy Land and Babylonia (Iraq) to France and Spain and Italy, then to Germany and Poland and finally to the United States of America. It looks at significant developments in Jewish eating in all ages: in the ancient Near East and Persia, in the Classical age, throughout the Middle Ages and into Modernity. It pays careful attention to Jewish eating laws (halakha) in each time and place, but it does not stop there: it also looks for Jews who bend and break the law, who eat like Romans or Christians regardless of the law and who develop their own hybrid customs according to their own "laws," whatever Jewish tradition might tell them. In this colorful history of Jewish eating, we get more than a taste of how expressive and crucial eating choices have always been.

David C. Kraemer is Professor of Talmud and Rabbinics at the Jewish Theological Seminary, where he has taught since 1979. Over the course of these 25 years, he has contributed to the training of thousands of rabbis, cantors, Jewish educators and others, many of whom are now active as leaders in Jewish communities across the country and abroad. He has published six books on topics as varied as Rabbinic understandings of human suffering, beliefs concerning death and the afterlife in Rabbinic Judaism, and the Jewish family. His intellectual history of the Babylonian Talmud, *The Mind of the Talmud*, was named an "Outstanding Academic Book of 1991" by Choice (May 1992). Kraemer has also published hundreds of articles, columns and opinion pieces, both scholarly and popular.

Routledge Advances in Sociology

Jewish Eating and Identity Through the Ages

David C. Kraemer

Routledge
Taylor & Francis Group

LONDON AND NEW YORK

First published 2007
Paperback edition first published 2009
by Routledge
270 Madison Avenue, New York, NY 10016

Simultaneously published in the UK
by Routledge
2 Park Square, Milton Park, Abingdon, Oxon, OX14 4RN

Routledge is an imprint of the Taylor & Francis Group, an informa business

© 2007, 2009 David C. Kraemer

Typeset in Sabon by
Taylor & Francis Books
Printed and bound in Great Britain by
CPI Antony Rowe, Chippenham, Wiltshire

British Library Cataloguing in Publication Data
A catalogue record for this book is available from the British Library

Library of Congress Cataloging in Publication Data
A catalog record for this book has been requested

ISBN 10: 0-415-95797-4 (hbk)
ISBN 10: 0-415-47640-2 (pbk)
ISBN 10: 0-203-94157-8 (ebk)

ISBN 13: 978-0-415-95797-7 (hbk)
ISBN 13: 978-0-415-47640-9 (pbk)
ISBN 13: 978-0-203-94157-7 (ebk)

To the Memory of my Father, Paul Kraemer (1930–2006)

Contents

Acknowledgments

This book, a project that grows out of my love for both cooking and the study of Judaism, has been in process for many years. Early readers might no longer recognize the versions they read and critiqued. Nevertheless, their contributions are found throughout the book. As a consequence of their comments and suggestions, the version now offered is far better than it might have been. To these readers I extend my heartfelt thanks:

Chapter 2: Steve Geller, Professor of Bible at the Jewish Theological Seminary (JTS)

Chapter 3: Seth Schwartz, Professor of Ancient Jewish History at JTS

Chapters 4–6: Ross Kraemer and other respondents at a session of the Society of Biblical Literature convention devoted to ancient Jewish foodways.

Chapter 7: Israel Francus, Professor of Talmud at JTS and Elisheva Carlebach, Professor of History at Queens College (CUNY).

Maria Diemling, of Trinity College, Dublin, drew my attention to six-teenth-century German works that were essential for the histories recounted in chapters 7 and 8. Mary Helen Dupree helped me with the translations of those works.

Susan Braunstein, Curator of Archaeology and Judaica at The Jewish Museum (New York), provided me with references to eighteenth through nineteenth century kosher dishes in the Museum's collection.

Nancy Sinkoff, Professor of Jewish history at Rutgers University, also read sections of chapters 7–8 and provided me with important references.

Participants in the biannual retreat of the American Academy of Jewish Research (New York, 2006) offered helpful critiques of my interpretations in chapter 10.

Jacob Neusner, Research Professor of Religion and Theology at Bard College, read an earlier version of this manuscript and offered many impor-tant suggestions. To him, in particular, I want to express my appreciation for his enthusiastic support of this project.

To these and others I owe many of the better parts of this work. Errors of fact and judgment are my own.

An earlier version of chapter 5 appeared in *The Review of Rabbinic Judaism*, vol. 8 (2005): 35–54. The present version has been revised slightly. An earlier version of chapter 8 appeared in *Food and Judaism*, edited by Leonard J. Greenspoon, Ronald A. Simkins, and Gerald Shapiro (Omaha, NB: Creighton University Press, 2005), pp. 235–256. It has been corrected and revised significantly for inclusion here.

Source: Meshal Hakadmoni (Brescia: ca. 1491), f. 55v. Courtesy of The Library
of The Jewish Theological Seminary.

1 Introduction

Tell me what you eat and I will tell you what you are.

Anthelme Brillat-Savarin, *Physiologie du Goût*, aphorism n. 4

Cooking is a language through which that society unconsciously reveals its structure. . . .

Claude Lévi-Strauss, *The Origin of Table Manners*[1]

Cooking is a language through which a society expresses itself . . . .

Jean Soler, "The Semiotics of Food in the Bible"[2]

[Food is] a system of communication . . . food signifies

Roland Barthes, "Toward a Psycho-Sociology
of Contemporary Food Consumption"[3]

If food is treated as a code, the messages it encodes will be found in the pattern of social relations being expressed.

Mary Douglas, "Deciphering a Meal"[4]

You know that what you eat you are . . . .

George Harrison, "Savoy Truffle"

As these collected quotations make clear—and many more could be compiled from the writings of scholars and others who study human foodways—it is widely assumed that peoples' eating habits somehow express who they are. Common experience supports this notion. We know we would probably be correct in guessing that an immigrant living in New York in the early twentieth century who regularly ate noodles dressed in tomato-based sauce and olive oil was Italian. By the same token, a young person living in early twenty-first century America eating rare, peppercorn-crusted tuna and drinking fine wine is likely to be an urban-dweller with an upper-middle-class salary. In fact, with just a little information concerning what a person habitually eats, it is often possible to venture a rough, stereotyped portrait of who they are—and chances are, that portrait will be relatively reliable.

To illustrate this reality before a college class, in the early 1990s in New York City, I placed side-by-side on a table two salads: one made with iceberg lettuce and bottled creamy French dressing and the other with assorted baby greens dressed in a light mustard vinaigrette. I then asked the class to tell me as much as they could about the people who were likely to eat each salad. Remarkably, before too many minutes had passed, the board in front of the class was filled with two groups of lists—one for each salad—suggesting not only where these people lived and their socioeconomic level, but also the books they were likely to read, the cars they were likely to drive, the films they were likely to view, and so forth. All those participating in the exercise recognized that, as with all stereotypes, there were limits to the accuracy of what we were proposing, particularly when applied at the level of the individual. But we also understood that a great many of the generalizations we offered were relatively accurate, that is, they were likely to be true for a significant majority (70%?, 80%?) of the people who preferred each salad. If this is what one can say on the basis of a salad, imagine what be said on the foundation of large-scale patterns of the foods a people eats *and the ways they eat them.*

This latter addition is crucial. While it is true that if you "tell me what you eat . . . I will tell you what you are," food choices are only one of several factors relating to eating that communicate volumes concerning a peoples' identity. As important as *what* they eat are *how, when* and *with whom* they eat it. Italians living in Italy may eat Italian food of one region or another, but they might also eat French or Moroccan or Korean food, at home or in a restaurant, in the company of family, friends, or business associates, on a regular basis or only on special occasions. And each of these choices in combination with others, if frequent enough to establish a pattern, will display the identity of the eater to the discerning eyes of the interpreter who interprets carefully.

To illustrate with a "Jewish" example: A Jew living on the Lower East Side of Manhattan in the early twentieth century who chose to eat Italian food—combining meat and cheese—in a nearby restaurant would most likely have been declaring his "emancipation" from the strictures of the religion of the "old country." At the same time, a neighbor who ate black bread and borsht, whether at home or in a small local restaurant, would "merely" have been eating "as he always had." But a Jew living on the Upper West Side in the late twentieth century who chose to eat Italian food at an upscale restaurant would most likely have been enacting her well-established and long-taken-for-granted cosmopolitan identity, while her neighbor who ate chicken soup with matzo balls would have been identifying with a "lost," traditional culture, perhaps one she experienced in her own mother's kitchen. Of course, these combinations and others like them are only the beginning of what we might note and interpret.

To offer another example: Over the course of history, pork was, from the perspective of the Jew (and often from the perspective of the neighboring gentile), a non-Jewish food. A Jew who ate pork in private was a transgressor and in public, in the company of non-Jews, an apostate. But in the Muslim world, where pork was similarly forbidden to most of a Jew's neighbors (Christian neighbors might well have partaken), pork would not have distinguished Jew from non-Jew. In such a setting, pork was not a "non-Jewish" food, at least not obviously so. In this context, one would have had to look for subtler evidence of a Jew's eating practices, such as the separation of meat and dairy. But if both meat and dairy were relatively uncommon, because bread, vegetables and oils constituted the bulk of most common meals, then how would one have known the Jew? He might have recited certain characteristic blessings before eating, or drunk wine, which many Muslims deemed forbidden. But, for the most part,[5] there was no particular food one could identify as "Jewish"—Jews in Muslim lands did not eat gefilte fish or pastrami on rye. So, in settings such as this, one might have to look hard to find distinguishing foods or eating practices, and work even harder to understand their meaning.

Despite such difficulties, we may safely assume that there will always be some practice or pattern or choice that distinguishes the eating of one coherent culture (or subculture) from another. It will, therefore, always be possible to identify something in the eating practices of Jews in a given place and period that distinguishes them from their neighbors—and from Jews in other places and periods as well. When we do identify such distinctive practices, we shall be able to interpret them as signs of current Jewish identity. We will understand that Jews who refuse to eat pork are different, in significant ways, from their gentile neighbors who celebrate their festivals over pork chops, or that Jews who insist on commencing their sacred days with a cup of wine are different from their neighbors who deem all alcoholic beverages taboo. But we will also understand that Israelites whose rules require only the shunning of "impure" animals are different from Jews who also refuse to cook meat and cheese together, and Jews who merely refuse to cook meat and cheese together are different from those who organize their kitchens into separate "meat" and "dairy" domains. With the recognition that these differences matter, we will have insights into the identities of Jews through the ages that have previously been unrealized.[6]

My purpose in this book is to present a history of Jewish eating practices through the ages and to interpret those practices as expressions of Jewish identity. I wish to emphasize that my subject is eating practices in general, not food choices in particular, though the latter is certainly subsumed in the former. Still, it is crucial to recall that it is not necessarily the food as such that represents particularly Jewish choices. Jews have often eaten exactly (or, more often, almost exactly) the same dishes as their neighbors. How and with whom they ate them was often their most notable choice.

Some few authors have addressed isolated chapters in the history of Jewish food-ways in earlier work, most of it quite recent.[7] The bulk of attention has been turned to modern cases, and some of this scholarship is superb. But aside from writings dedicated to the subject of "kashrut"—a subject that generally stands outside of time, with little recognition of its contexts, developments and nuances—very little has been written on Jewish eating between the Bible and modernity. This is the first book to attempt a (selective) history of the whole, from biblical roots through ancient and medieval developments and on to the modern world. It is also, therefore, the first to interpret Jewish eating practices in these many ages as keys to understanding current Jewish identities.

Needless to say, a history of Jewish eating is potentially voluminous, the topic encyclopedic in scope. Yet this book is of relatively modest length. So I must explain the choices I have made: which chapters have "made it in" and which have—so to speak—yet to be written? My first criterion for selection was that a particular eating practice (or cluster of practices) constitute a major new development in the history of Jewish eating. I have no interest in describing the practices of a given period for their own sake. I have sought out changes or developments that represent new directions in the eating practices of Jews, in a given age and often for centuries to come. This explains my (re-) consideration of the biblical laws of permitted and prohibited animals; no future Jewish eating system would fail to define itself, somehow, in relation to these laws. They are the foundation on which everything else rests. This criterion similarly explains my devotion of three entire chapters to the founding and development of the meat-dairy prohibition in its various aspects; the invention of this prohibition in the early rabbinic age provides significant evidence for early rabbinic identity, and developments relating to this prohibition in the subsequent centuries would be among the most distinctive of Jewish eating practices throughout the ages.

My second criterion for selecting a particular focus was that a phenomenon persists and remains central throughout the centuries. Certain phenomena or trends transcended specific ages or locales, and tracing them from one period to another provides an opportunity to consider both what changed and what remained the same. This criterion is behind my choice to trace the phenomenon of "transgressive" Jewish eating—eating that pushes or breaks through the boundaries—from the early Middle Ages to modernity. It also motivates my examination of contemporary "kashrut wars" in the final chapter; though that chapter addresses only the contemporary expression of this phenomenon, I have found that, throughout the ages, Jewish eating practices have as often distinguished Jew from Jew as they have Jew from non-Jew.

The first five chapters (following this one) examine Jewish eating practices periodically, the first in the pre-exilic (Torah) period, the second in the so-called Second Temple period (fifth century BCE–early first century CE), and the latter three in the rabbinic period—the first five centuries of the common era, during which time the rabbis emerged as the most significant religious leadership in the Jewish world. Thereafter, I devote several chapters to phenomena that describe a trajectory of development from the earliest post-talmudic centuries—that is, the early Islamic period—to the dawn of modernity and beyond. The first of these examines the development of practices to create a separation between the consumption of meat and dairy, the second uncovers the history of maintaining "separate dishes" in observant Jewish households, and the third considers transgressive Jewish eating, as described already above. The final chapter, as already indicated, considers Jewish eating practices that divide Jew from Jew, in recent decades but also, by implication, throughout history.

Ultimately, the theme of this book is one that, perhaps naively, I had not anticipated when I began. Jewish eating is and has always been a "negotiation," that is, a struggle on the part of individual Jews and the community over where the boundaries of Jewish identity should be laid. The questions asked during this unending struggle have been questions such as these: How distinct are Jews from their neighbors? How high must the boundaries between Jew and non-Jew be? In what ways am I, a Jew, the same as or similar to my non-Jewish neighbor? In what ways am I the same as or similar to my Jewish neighbor? How does my identity relate to that of my parents and grandparents? In what ways am I different? And so on.

Though it is easiest to express these questions in terms of binary oppositions ("same-different"), it is essential to bear in mind that the answers need never be dichotomous. The answer is almost never "I am totally unlike my gentile/Jewish neighbor" or "I am totally like my Jewish/gentile neighbor." The answers to the above questions are always matters of degree, and the precise placement of a boundary along the spectrum from totally x to totally y will always be a consequence of negotiations—negotiations that are often, though not always, internal, and of which the party or parties to the negotiation are often unaware. For example, when a Jew in the second century privileged the eating of bread and wine (along with olive oil) by making their consumption occasions for the recitation of special blessings, he was actually privileging *Jewishly* foods that already enjoyed a pride of place on the Roman and Mediterranean tables. But when a Jew, following the dictates of the rabbis, refused to eat exactly these foods if produced by gentiles, she was refusing to join the common Roman table. Well, were these practices statements of a Jew being "like" or "not like" her gentile neighbor? Taken together, they were statements of both. The actual eating practice, whether following rabbinic prescriptions, adapting them in part, or ignoring them completely, was the outcome of a negotiation between contrary considerations and attractions. The struggles of Jewish identity in the age in question could not be more eloquently expressed than in the "mute" form of new customs around the table.

Before we commence our study, it is necessary to say some words about the nature of the evidence we will use and the obstacles to interpreting that evidence.

Much—though by no means all—of the evidence we will draw upon is the literary record of laws or other kinds of legal discourse. This is true, obviously, of the biblical eating regulations, as well as of the many rabbinic writings—classical, medieval and modern. Using such records to draw historical conclusions is fraught with problems, some of them insoluble.

Beyond the obvious problems confronting someone who tries to use any centuries-old source (How was the tradition transmitted? How did it change in the course of transmission? What is the quality of the manuscript record? What is the nature and meaning of manuscript variants? And so forth.), legal sources are affected by a set of additional difficulties. The simple fact is that we will never be able to determine fully the relationship between the laws recorded in the book and the practices of the society these laws seek to regulate.

To begin with, we must ask whose opinion the laws represent and the relationship of the writer(s) to the society at large. For example, many of the Torah's laws, including the eating laws, speak for and represent a priestly perspective. But what is the relationship between the literary priestly record—separated, in the form we preserve, by perhaps centuries from the circle in which it originated—and the actual practice of that circle? Moreover, did Israelites outside of the priesthood observe these laws and to what extent? Archaeology may provide some answers to such questions, but its record, too, is subject to significant interpretive difficulties, so many of these questions will remain, at best, only imperfectly answered.

Second, we must ask what kind of legal system the apparent legal system actually is. For example, the Mishnah, the first record of rabbinic law (c. 200 CE), is, in many respects, a very odd compilation, one that has challenged interpreters to come up with an adequate definition of its identity and purpose. It has most often been understood as a "law code," both traditionally and by modern interpreters. But if it is a law code, why, in the year 200, does it describe at length laws relating to the Jerusalem temple and its practice; the temple had been destroyed by the Romans 130 years earlier! Or why does it fail to provide comprehensive laws for the writing of a Torah scroll, the production of phylacteries, burial and mourning practices, and other presumably central and ongoing Jewish practices? As a consequence of such difficult-to-explain qualities, some have come to the conclusion that the Mishnah is a kind of utopian document. But, if that is so, then a history of the practices it describes will be a very peculiar kind of history.[8]

Furthermore, in recent decades, scholarship has come more and more to recognize that the rabbis in late Antiquity were a small and, to a large extent, elitist group whose ideas and practices were hardly shared by Jews at large. During the first five or so centuries of the Common Era, most Jews in Palestine and elsewhere either continued to observe customs learned from scripture and tradition or to adopt "pagan" practices that were common in the environs in which they lived.[9] In either case, they did not, for the more part, follow rabbinic practices. So when we read the Mishnah or other rabbinic documents, we must ever be mindful of the fact that, whether fact or fiction, the record is the fact or fiction speaking for a very small group and not for Jews more generally. How this particular history relates to the more general history will never be easy to determine.

The Talmud, perhaps the rabbinic text *par excellence*, is in many ways even more difficult to interpret in this context. In addition to the obstacles already enunciated (its speaking for an elite, etc., not to mention questions of transmission, manuscripts, and the like),[10] the Talmud is characterized by contradictory tendencies that make its evidence particularly opaque in a context such as this. On the one hand, the Talmud regularly relates stories that *seem* to describe actual events. On the other hand, large swathes of the Talmud are clearly theoretical in nature, and theory often seems to be its primary concern in any case. Are the stories recorded in the midst of theoretical deliberations to be taken at face value? Is the theory just theory or might it preserve some record, however indirect, of at least rabbinic practice? Judgments will have to be made—and I will make them—but significant questions will remain.

The Medieval rabbinic literature will, depending upon its sort, be characterized by similar and related problems.[11] Of this literature, apparently the most useful for writing a history of "real life" is the responsa literature, questions addressed to well-known rabbis followed by their detailed answers, usually justified theoretically by reference to the received rabbinic tradition. To be sure, this literature has been used richly to document parts of the history of Jews throughout the Middle Ages and beyond. But its usefulness for such purposes is neither obvious nor transparent. The questions recorded in this literature seem to emerge from "real life." But this is only sometimes the case. In some instances, it is obvious that the scenarios described in the questions are invented to represent a theoretical category. In other instances, possibly real circumstances are rendered generic because of certain conventions (e.g., actual names are typically rendered as "Shimeon" and "Levi" or other standard biblical names); is the reality behind the generic real, or is it similarly standardized or otherwise fictionalized? This literature, so potentially rich for our purposes, must, like the rest of rabbinic literature, be used only with extreme caution.

Fortunately, beyond the rabbinic legal literature, there are many other sources available to draw upon—archaeology, histories, legends, memoirs, polemical literature, material culture, and so forth. And while every category of evidence will have its own problems for purposes of a history such as this, every category will also have something to contribute. We will assemble the pieces, compare the evidence, and seek to interpret the whole. Needless to say, it is the interpretation itself that is the most difficult step in this process. It is the interpretation, based upon a thick description of evidence that has been subject to critical analysis, upon which the results of this inquiry will stand or fall.

A crucial question of interpretation must also be addressed here. As I said earlier, this is a book about Jewish eating and its relationship to Jewish identity. Obviously, eating is not the only lens through which one may seek to understand and interpret identity. There are many such perspectives, all of which, individually and in combination, may contribute to our understanding of Jewish identity (plural). Recent studies, focusing on such matters as purity,[12] sexuality,[13] and the like, have enhanced our understanding of the history of Jewish identities in important ways. By focusing on eating, I do not mean to suggest that this is the best lens through which to examine the question, nor that it stands in isolation from other practices. But it is a perspective that has been neglected, and for that reason it merits an extended and dedicated study.

Is it reasonable to conduct such a study in relative isolation from these other studies, with their important lessons for understanding Jewish identity? The answer, it seems to me, is an unqualified "yes." The danger of interpreting the evidence of eating practices by constant reference to other practices (say, sex practices, which similarly rely on the body for their performance) is the temptation to interpret the former—the study being conducted now—in light of the latter—the study conducted earlier. In my mind, it is better to gather this evidence, formulate defensible interpretations, and then compare this to that. This way, we will be in a better position to trust mutually reinforcing parallels and in a better position to challenge particular interpretations—on either side of the comparison—when they appear to be in tension or outright conflict. This job of comparison will be the job of every interested reader or student.

In conclusion, I want to repeat my earlier claim, one that seems to me unassailable: it has been the case in all ages that Jews, like others, have expressed their identities—with their questions and ambivalences—through their table habits. Our task in the following chapters is to identify and interpret the eating habits that have somehow borne the burden of expressing the identities of Jews in each subsequent age. To the degree that we succeed, we will gain fresh insights into the complexities of those identities, sometimes understanding them as they have never before been understood.

2 The biblical period
Our animals, their animals

The history of Jewish eating practices must begin with the ancient biblical laws pertaining to permitted and prohibited foods. Technically speaking, of course, the Torah's eating laws are not, in their origin, "Jewish." The name "Jewish," or even "Judahite," did not identify the people of the bible until the return from the Babylonian exile (sixth–fifth century BCE). But these people—ancient Israel—were the ancestors of the people who would later be known as Jews, and, more importantly, their eating laws would regulate the eating practices of Jews for all centuries to come. It is thus unimaginable to begin this history anywhere else.

But as we begin this history—a history that seeks to interpret the connections between Jewish eating and Jewish identity—we immediately confront an obstacle. Obviously, such a history requires that we identify the historical context in which the given set of practices was current. But there is considerable debate concerning the dating of biblical (including Torah) texts and the practices they elaborate, and the disagreement is particularly profound with respect to the book of Leviticus, in which the Torah's eating prohibitions are described in the greatest detail. Stated succinctly, since the ground-breaking work of J. Wellhausen in the nineteenth century, biblical scholarship has mostly assumed that "P"—the priestly code including the great bulk of the books of Leviticus and Numbers—is post-exilic (sixth or fifth century BCE). But others have argued for an earlier dating of the Priestly code, contending that the evidence suggests that the laws of P predate those of Deuteronomy—commonly understood to have originated in the seventh century BCE. The most persuasive exponent of this latter position is Jacob Milgrom, and this writer finds Milgrom's arguments convincing.[1] But even if Milgrom is right, this does not solve the problem for present purposes.

The scholarship that argues for this or that dating of the documents from which the Torah was composed assumes, with those who promulgated the "documentary hypothesis," that the Torah was indeed shaped from pre-existent documents—that is, written scrolls. But this working hypothesis is built on a metaphor—one which imagines that Torah traditions were actual documents. Unfortunately, little evidence of such documents actually exists—aside from the Torah itself—and the Torah is, in its present form, a much later cultural artifact. More recent scholarship has reminded us that the Torah came to shape in a manuscript—and therefore largely *oral*—world, and it is thus unreasonable for us to imagine discreet bodies of "published" tradition at the foundation of the Torah text. Traditions circulated in oral and written forms—each influencing the other—and we must therefore imagine a long history for the development of any given set of laws. And even if there was a documentary record, this does not mean that that particular documentary version was authoritative.[2]

There is still another important obstacle to dating the Torah's eating laws. If we were able to date a given set of laws, we still would not know for whom (or *to* whom) those laws spoke. Just because a class of priests accepts or promulgates a set of laws does not mean that those who avail themselves of the priests' cultic services will observe those laws. Indeed, even if God did reveal the Torah as a whole to Moses at Sinai in the thirteenth century BCE (as later Jewish tradition would have us believe), this does not mean that the people accepted or observed the laws of that Torah. In fact, the Bible's own history suggests definitively that the People of Israel did not observe the Torah's law during virtually all of the centuries the first Jerusalem Temple was standing. Rather, it seems clear that the Torah and its laws were accepted as authoritative by most of this people only after the Babylonian exile. So, when we ask about the relationship of the eating practices described by the law and the identities of the people who observed the law, of whom are we speaking? Of the priests who were more likely to have observed the law? Of the idealized audience who was supposed to have observed the law? Of the real people, who probably did not accept this law until centuries after it was first articulated (in whatever form)? Obviously, we will have to answer these several questions before we can begin.

In the discussion below, I follow Milgrom in dating the law of Leviticus to a period before the promulgation of Deuteronomy. This means that the setting for the laws we will study is Israel of the eight–seventh century BCE. I do not assume that the law, as recorded, speaks for the practices of all of Israel at this time but, given the parallel record in Leviticus and Deuteronomy, it is reasonable to conclude that, by at least the mid-seventh century, the eating regulations had spread beyond priestly circles (Deuteronomy is not a priestly book). Still, this does not mean that the practices described in the law were yet observed by most of Israel. So, I will speak of Israel as a whole only when referring to the post-exilic period, the period during which, according to scholars of the biblical canon, the Torah was first accepted as the authoritative constitution of the nation as a whole. Ironically, this was the very period that ancient Israel was giving birth to the people we call Jews.

The Torah's eating laws are comprised of three categories of regulations: those defining the animals which may or may not be consumed (Lev 11 and Dt 14), those prohibiting the consumption of blood (Lev 17), and those prohibiting the cooking of a calf in its mother's milk (Ex 23:19, 34:26, Dt 14:21). These laws—especially those defining the pure and impure animals—have been subjected to various and repeated interpretations, and it would serve no purpose to review the extensive scholarship on this subject. Rather, I will first describe the most influential approaches to the interpretation of this material and then turn to our immediate subject: the relationship of these laws, however interpreted, to the identities of the people who observed them.

The laws pertaining to permitted and prohibited animals, as spelled out in Leviticus, chapter 11, are these:

These are the creatures that you may eat from among all of the quadrupeds on the land: any quadruped that has hoofs, with clefts through the hoofs, and that chews the cud—such you may eat. The following, however, of those that chew the cud or have hoofs, you shall not eat: the camel—although it chews the cud, it has no hoofs: it is impure to you; the rock badger—although it chews the cud, it has no hoofs: it is impure to you; the hare—although it chews the cud, it has no hoofs: it is impure to you; and the pig—although it has hoofs, with the hoofs cleft through, it does not chew the cud: it is impure to you. You shall not eat of their flesh or touch their carcasses; they are impure for you.

These you may eat of all that live in water: anything in water, whether in the seas or in the streams, that has fins or scales—these you may eat. But anything in the seas or in the streams that has no fins and scales, among all of the swarming creatures of the water and among all of the living creatures that are in the water—they are an abomination to you and an abomination for you they shall remain: you shall not eat of their flesh and you shall abominate their carcasses. Everything in the water that has no fins and scales shall be an abomination for you.

The following you shall abominate among the birds; they shall not be eaten, they are an abomination: the eagle, the black vulture, the bearded vulture, the kite, and falcons of every variety; all varieties of raven; the eagle owl, the short-eared owl, and the long-eared owl; hawks of every variety; the tawny owl, the fisher owl, the screech owl, the white owl, and the scops owl; the osprey, the stork, and herons of every variety; the hoopoe, and the bat.

All winged swarming creatures, that walk on all fours, shall be an abomination for you. But these you may eat among all the winged swarming creatures that walk on all fours: all that have, above their feet, jointed legs to leap with on the ground. Of these you may eat the following: locusts of every variety; all varieties of bald locust; crickets of every variety; and all varieties of grasshopper. But all other winged swarming creatures that have four legs shall be an abomination for you.

And you shall make yourselves impure with the following—whoever touches their carcasses shall be impure until the evening, and whoever carries any part of their carcasses shall wash his clothes and be impure until evening—every quadruped that has hoofs but without clefts . . . .

The following shall be impure for you from among the creatures that swarm on the earth: the rat, the mouse, the large lizards of every variety; the gecko, the spotted lizard, the lizard, the skink and the chameleon. Those are for you the impure among all the swarming creatures; whoever touches them when they are dead shall be impure until evening . . . .

All creatures that swarm upon the earth are an abomination; they shall not be eaten. You shall not eat anything that crawls on its belly, or anything that walks on all fours, or anything that has many legs, comprising all creatures that swarm on the earth, for they are an abomination. You shall not defile your throats with any creature that swarms. You shall not make yourselves impure therewith and thus become impure, for I the Lord am you God. You shall sanctify yourselves and be holy, for I am holy. You shall not contaminate your throats with any swarming creature that moves upon the earth. For I the Lord am he who brought you up from the land of Egypt to be your God; you shall be holy, for I am holy.

These are the instructions concerning quadrupeds, birds, all living creatures that move in the water, and all creatures that swarm on the earth, for discriminating between the impure and the pure, between creatures that may be eaten and creatures that may not be eaten.[3]

There are differences between the laws enumerated above and those spelled out in Deuteronomy—differences of detail, terminology and style. But most of these differences are relatively insignificant, and the categories of inclusion or exclusion are identical. No one, in fact, would fail to recognize the close relationship between the two records, even if they might dispute which version is dependent upon the other (and the vast majority of scholars agree that there is some sort of interdependence). For purposes of interpretation, therefore, we may assume the identity of the two.

The most influential of modern interpreters of these laws is Mary Douglas, whose *Purity and Danger* (1966) elaborated a comprehensive interpretation from an anthropological perspective.[4] Douglas, following the anthropological tradition established by Emile Durkheim, assumes that (to borrow Milgrom's felicitous phrasing) "the customs and rituals of any society are reflections of its values." (Milgrom, 719) The categories established by the Torah's eating laws (and there are undeniably categories) must, therefore, somehow reflect the values—and even the categories—of the Israelite society in which these laws were promulgated. The key to interpreting the system is thus to discover the manner in which the animal taxonomy described in the Torah reflects the human society whose values it represents.

Douglas equates the Torah's "impure" with "dirty" (= "unclean") and defines dirt as matter (or, for present purposes, anything—including animals) that is out of its proper place. Recognizing the association of the eating laws with the creation story of Genesis 1, Douglas notes that that story describes three realms of animal creation—water, air, and land. And there are, Douglas suggests, three means of animal locomotion, each considered appropriate to its realm, at least by the codifiers behind the system of Leviticus 11. The appropriate means of locomotion are those described in the eating laws: land-dwellers must have four legs and hoofs for walking, water-dwellers require fins and scales for swimming, and birds—who both walk and fly—must have two legs for the one and two wings for the other. Any creature that does not meet these standards is thought to transgress the boundary established at creation, and any such creature is deemed "out of place" and thus impure. (The reader will recognize that this is an oversimplification, not accounting for all of the details of the law. But, for present purposes, a simplification of Douglas'—and the Torah's—system will do.)

The problems with Douglas' interpretation are several, and even she has repudiated much (probably *too* much) of what she offered in *Purity and Danger*. She commits several errors of fact, and her proposed categories fail to account for some of the details of the law. More importantly, even if all matter out of place is "dirt," all dirt does not pollute—"dirty" and "impure" are not synonymous.[5] Finally, even if, despite these flaws, there is value in Douglas's proposed interpretation (and, in the opinion of this writer, there is), ritual symbols are, by their nature, multivocal. Symbolic communications carry multiple meanings at the same time. We must, therefore, consider other prominent interpretations before we consider their relevance to the question of ancient Israelite identity.

In more recent work, Jacob Milgrom has proposed a masterful comprehensive interpretation of the Torah's eating laws. Milgrom's interpretation commences with the recognition that the Torah does justify/explain the eating laws by reference to holiness. In the words of the text quoted above: "You shall not make yourselves impure therewith and thus become impure, for I the Lord am your God. You shall sanctify yourselves and be holy, for I am holy. You shall not contaminate your throats with any swarming creature that moves upon the earth. For I the Lord am he who brought you up from the land of Egypt to be your God; you shall be holy, for I am holy." In fact, as Milgrom notes, this reasoning is offered in all of the contexts in which the prohibited foods are listed (Milgrom, 729). The insistence on offering such a rationale is highly unusual, so the author of these laws must believe that this reasoning is crucial—and that it is crucial for us to understand it. The question thus becomes: what is the meaning of "holy" in this context?

Turning a keen eye to the practice of holiness in ancient Israel, Milgrom proposes that "'Holy' is thus aptly defined . . . as 'that which is unapproachable except through divinely imposed restrictions' or 'that which is withdrawn from common use.'" He adds below that "holiness implies separation." If that which is holy is set apart, then a people who are, like God, holy, will be set apart. "Thus, the biblical laws that limit Israel's diet to only a few of the animals permitted to other peoples constitute a reminder—confronted daily at the dining table—that Israel must separate itself from the nations." (Milgrom, 730) Later in Leviticus, this purpose is made explicit: "I am the Lord your God who set you apart from other peoples. So you shall set apart the pure quadrupeds from the impure, the impure birds from the pure . . . . You shall be holy to me, for I the Lord am holy and I have set you apart from other peoples to be mine" (20:24–26). Pragmatically speaking, laws that restrict dining with one's neighbors will indeed separate one from one's neighbors. It would appear, therefore, that such an interpretation is unassailable. Moreover, given the repetition of this reasoning, it is reasonable to suppose that the people who, observing these restrictions, would have experienced such separation would also have understood that this was indeed the purpose of the law.

One could object that, if separation is the purpose, any arbitrary set of legislated differences would have done the trick. We are still left with the question: why these differences and not others? The law could have demanded that Israelites eat while reclining. It could have prohibited fowl and wine. What, if anything, can we say about the meaning of these *specific* regulations? Milgrom, at least, is not satisfied with a merely pragmatic answer. He goes further in proposing a very specific interpretation of "holiness" and its meanings.

Milgrom's more comprehensive interpretation begins with the proposition that "holy" is the antonym not of "profane," as is commonly assumed, but of "impure." The two categories, holy and impure, are, he shows, "antagonistic, totally opposite." (Milgrom, 732) Thus, if "impure" means one thing, "holy" will mean its opposite. And it can readily be demonstrated that "impure" is associated in biblical law with the forces of death. Carcasses/corpses are impure, genital discharges are impure, and scale disease ("leprosy")—representing the deterioration of the flesh at death—is impure. Therefore, if that which is "impure" represents death, that which is holy must represent life. The eating laws, which demand that Israel be holy by separating herself from that which is impure, must be an affirmation of life and a repudiation of death.

But how, precisely, is this so? To begin with, it will be recalled that the Torah's eating laws do not begin and end with the list of pure and impure animals. Rather, the first of these laws is the blood prohibition, a prohibition deemed so important that it is incumbent upon all of mankind, not just upon Israel. It is enunciated, in fact, near the beginning of the Torah, on the occasion of Noah's exit from the ark. There, God revises the vegetarian diet of Eden to permit, for the first time, the consumption of animal flesh. But God adds: "You must not, however, eat flesh with its life-blood. For your life-blood, too, I will require a reckoning. Whoever sheds the blood of man, for that man shall his blood be shed . . ." (Gen 9:4–6). Eating flesh with blood is compared to shedding blood—to taking life. In fact, in the opinion of Leviticus, the blood *is* the life. As the text specifies, "And I say to the Israelite people: you shall not ingest the blood of any flesh, *for the life of all flesh is its blood* . . ." (17:14, emphasis added). The blood prohibition, therefore, is explicitly about life and death. Avoiding the life-blood, which is life, symbolizes the sacredness of life and the shunning of death.

The same principal, Milgrom argues, lies at the foundation of the Torah's list of permitted and prohibited animals. In this case, the sacredness-of-life-repudiation-of-death message is accomplished rather directly. The very purpose of the Torah's prohibitions is, Milgrom writes, "to limit the Israelites' access to the animal kingdom" (733). The severely restricted number of species permitted to the Israelite will limit the quantity of animals the Israelite will consume, and thus the number of animal lives he or she will take. This very restriction, together with the prohibition of ingesting blood (symbolizing life), will "teach the Israelite reverence for life . . ." (735).

But, we may wonder, how will merely limiting the permitted species control the quantity of flesh eaten? Is it not possible that the ancient Israelite would make up for the camel or pig he could not consume simply by eating more goats or sheep? There is, as Milgrom properly notes, no restriction on the quantity of permitted animals an Israelite could slaughter and enjoy.

The answer to this question lies in the economic realities of animal husbandry and consumption in the ancient world—as well as in the history of animal slaughter in the Israelite cult. Leviticus 17 (3–7) limits the consumption of animal flesh by demanding that all animals destined for the table first be slaughtered at the sanctuary. If this law is speaking for a period when local sanctuaries were still common, then the restriction of meat-eating would have been substantial but not radical. If it assumes a single, centralized sanctuary, then meat-eating would have been virtually unheard of—at least for those who observed this law. In fact, under such circumstances, the enjoyment of meat would for the most part have been limited to the pilgrimage festivals, when meat itself would have stood as a symbol of the specialness of the occasion.

Whichever the reality assumed by Leviticus 17, its restrictions came to an end with the permitting of profane slaughter—anywhere in Israel—in

Deuteronomy 12, presumably during the reign of King Josiah (mid-seventh century BCE). At that point, it became possible to consume as many permitted animals as the supply would permit. But such a liberalization could have done little to increase the quantity of meat enjoyed, for the realities of ancient life would have curtailed what the law did not. The raising of significant quantities of livestock requires vast pastures and an abundance of feed—either grains or grasses. Neither was available, except to the very wealthy, in the ancient world. Moreover, animals were of crucial importance for supplying other needs—oxen were work animals and sheep and goats provided wool and cheese. It would have been a significant decision to diminish one's small flock to eat the animal's flesh—a decision to be made only rarely. Thus, for common folk, the only occasions when meat might normally have been enjoyed were festivals and special celebrations (again, the meat would have served as a symbol of the unusual nature of the occasion). This was true not only in ancient Israel (Milgrom, 733–74) but in the ancient world as a whole. Concerning classical antiquity, Peter Garnsey writes that meat and other animal products were in generally short supply, and meat can have been of only minor importance in the diets of the majority of the population.[6] In fact, outside of a religious context, meat was hardly consumed at all (Garnsey, 86). What was true in nearby Mediterranean lands was surely true in Israel only a few centuries before. The common economic reality would have permitted no different practice in this regard. Further corroborating such a conclusion, Kaj Århem reports that, among the Massai, whose diet is ideally restricted to milk, meat and blood, meat is nevertheless an extraordinary food, consumed almost exclusively for ritual purposes in connection with a public meal.[7] Again, in the absence of modern economies and cattle-raising techniques, sufficient quantities of animal flesh were mostly unavailable for common consumption (there were historical exceptions, as we shall see in later chapters). Thus, the Torah's restrictions would only have further curtailed what was already severely circumscribed in reality.

The same, it turns out, was true for the Torah's laws restricting the permitted species of sea-creatures. Once more, in theory, Israelites could have enjoyed unlimited quantities of permitted fish. But, in practice, they can have consumed relatively little. This is so, first, because they resided primarily in the hilly central spine of the "promised land." Israel did not control the coastal plain, and their contact with it can have been only occasional. Indeed, the evidence suggests not only that Israelites were not fisherman, but also that they had "little acquaintance with marine life." (Milgrom, 660) But their lack of acquaintance was not only a consequence of political geography. As Milgrom shows, the Mediterranean adjacent to Israel was a poor environment for marine life, so fish and other marine populations must have been quite small. Hence, as in the case of land-animals, the laws prohibiting many species of sea creatures were limiting what was already severely limited. In the service of life, the taking of life was restricted still further.

If this is all true, then another of Milgrom's claims—one he shares with virtually everyone who writes about these laws—will have to be rejected. In one of his several summations of the purpose of the biblical eating laws, Milgrom writes, "Thus, the biblical laws that limited Israel's diet to only a few of the animals permitted to other peoples constitute a reminder—*confronted daily at the dining table*—that Israel must separate itself from the nations" (730, emphasis added). Of course, if both meat and fish were rare in the ancient Palestinian diet—*of whatever local people*—then the Torah's eating laws will *not* regularly have distinguished the Israelite diet from that of neighboring peoples. If sea life was unavailable, then they can have eaten no more fish than the Israelites. Likewise, if ancient ecologies and economies permitted the consumption of animal flesh only infrequently, then the "dining tables" of neighboring Canaanites (allowing for Milgrom's anachronism) will have been visited by meat barely more often than those of the Israelites. In fact, the only time the eating laws will regularly have distinguished Israelites from their neighbors is on the occasion of festivals and other cultic celebrations.

If one of the central purposes of these laws was to separate Israelites from their neighbors, it is very odd that the legislator (divine, collective or otherwise—I intend this as a metaphor) chose to restrict the laws to the foods that were eaten least often, if at all. In the judgment of John Cooper, the common diet of the ancient Israelite consisted of "barley bread, vegetables, and fruit, supplemented by milk products and honey" (he adds that "Unless a family belonged to a section of the small priestly elite or court circles, meat was rarely eaten but was consumed at festive meals or tribal gatherings . . .").[8] Laws intended to separate Israelites from their neighbors would have had to pertain to these foods, not to those rarely found on the local table. In fact, in light of these observations—and despite the explicit claim of Leviticus 20:25–6—it seems highly implausible that this was central to their purpose at all. Or, if it was their purpose, then it would appear these laws must have been a miserable failure.

Against this conclusion, Veronika Grimm writes that the Torah's eating code "presupposes a meat-eating population." She continues: "the Law appears to confront a human society that in order to obtain its necessary nutrients in a most efficient form would eat, if not regulated, just about anything that moved."[9] To be sure, this is what the law *appears* to assume. But Grimm offers no evidence for her conclusion aside from the text itself—a weak foundation on which to build an edifice. In view of the abundance of scholarship suggesting the contrary, it would be imprudent to imagine that Israel's neighbors regularly dined on the many animals the Torah prohibits. To begin with, some of the prohibited animals could have been available only irregularly to the local population—the rock badger lived in wild, craggy regions (Milgrom, 648), the species of owls enumerated were nocturnal birds who dwelled "in ruins, tombs, rocks, and thickets" (Milgrom, 663). Second, as I commented above, animals are expensive to raise and, when viewed as food (= suppliers of calories and nutrients), they must be recognized as consuming more than they produce. Moreover, the economic niche occupied by most animals would not have permitted their regular consumption; animals were primarily workers (analogous to our trucks and tractors) or producers (wool, hides, etc.). Only after these other purposes were exhausted would they have been exploited for their flesh. Zooarchaeological evidence, however spotty, supports just such a picture. For example, analysis of remains at Tell Jemmeh suggests that, in middle bronze age Syria, cattle were used for milk and traction, sheep and goats for dairy and wool.[10] Other studies suggest a similar reality. In light of these observations, it is more reasonable to assume that the "meat-eating population" the Torah presupposes is a priestly population. The Levitical law—and the Deuteronomic list which depends upon it—certainly speaks from the perspective of the priests. And these would have been the only ancient Israelites who ate meat regularly. Whether this or another explanation best accounts for the Torah's meat-emphasis, Grimm's broad conclusions are simply unsustainable.

But even if Grimm's assertion is too extreme, she may nevertheless have understood something important about the relationship of the Torah's eating regulations to the practices of neighboring peoples. To say that people residing in ancient Palestine did not *regularly* eat animal flesh is not to say that they did not eat it at all. And, particularly if animal flesh was not commonly obtainable, we may imagine that its consumption was opportunistic, that is to say, when it was available it would be eaten with an almost desperate eagerness. One day, a person might eat an injured owl, a week later, the remains of a goat carcass or an aging hare. But all would be eaten given the opportunity—because the opportunity was not regularly given.

A possible exception is the case of pig-flesh. Unlike cattle or sheep or goats or camels, pigs had no pragmatic economic function. In the absence of other roles, they were available to be exploited for their meat. In some ancient societies, this was indeed the case. Brian Hesse reports that, at Philistine Ekron, pork had an important part in the diet.[11] In the settlement represented at Tell Jemmeh, almost all of the pigs were killed for meat (Hesse and Wapnish, 88). If pork was more commonly eaten by the Israelites' neighbors, then its exclusion from the Israelite diet would have been meaningful.

Crucially, as Milgrom shows, the Levitical criteria for the inclusion/exclusion of quadrupeds were intentionally formulated to exclude pork (649). (This is not to say that pork was singled out as a uniquely abhorred animal. To the contrary, the Torah's formulation gives no hint that pork was different from any other prohibited flesh. The isolation of pork as a particularly strong taboo occurs during the Second Temple period, to be considered in the next chapter.) Milgrom explains this exclusion on the basis of several factors. First, he notes that pigs were widely reviled in the ancient Near East (650). At the same time, the pig was revered in the chthonic cults of the Philistines (652). This combination, he argues, explains why the pig was prohibited to the Israelite—though the status of the pig as a uniquely abhorred creature did not develop until later centuries. Whatever the merit of these explanations, Milgrom omits the one possibility that would most have supported his overall thesis. If, in general, the intent of the eating laws was to honor life by drastically limiting the amount of flesh Israelites could consume, then it is particularly noteworthy that the law went out of its way to prohibit the flesh of the one species that was raised for its flesh. What may have made the pig a particular problem, in other words, is precisely the fact that it, uniquely, offered a relatively ample supply of meat. If the law wanted to limit the consumption of meat, it had to prohibit pork. Prohibiting the common *meat* of the ancient world, the Torah would effectively have advanced its agenda favoring life.

All of this being said, we still cannot avoid the conclusion that the daily diet of the ancient Israelite would *not* have made it impossible to eat with his or her neighbor. Thus, the purely pragmatic explanation of the eating laws (= they are intended to separate Israel from her neighbors) cannot be upheld. On one level, these laws must be didactic—they must symbolically communicate a message. But the path to understanding that they are, say, about "life" (to follow Milgrom's proposal) is too long and convoluted. These meanings could not have been consciously available to the ancient Israelite public who respected these laws. The same would of course be true for Douglas' interpretation. For these laws to have "taught" the messages they were intended to teach, the symbolic associations would have had to be more immediate and commonly held. Only if their symbolism employed a popular idiom could they have expressed and reinforced Israelite identity in a more direct way.

None of this is to say that the symbolism of the law must have been transparent if it was present at all. Introducing his own interpretation of the pure and impure animal system, Howard Eilberg-Schwartz wisely observes,

> I take for granted that Israelites would have found implausible the kinds of interpretations offered here. In fact, they probably would have considered such interpretations quite bizarre. I take as axiomatic that individuals are not aware of all the interconnections between their practices and the various strands of thought that exist in their culture.[12]

In other words, the sorts of connections proposed by Douglas or Milgrom may well exist. But most of those who perform the practices which are the product of such connections will not recognize them. So we can imagine that in ancient Israel, a small class of priests—at most—consciously understood the meaning of these eating laws. But Israel as a whole, even if she observed the prohibitions articulated in the Torah, could not possibly have expounded the deeper message they implied.

In my opinion, it is Eilberg-Schwartz's explanation, if any, that may capture the most evident meaning of the animal categories lying at the foundation of the Torah's eating regulations. His thesis is rather simple:

> Significantly, cloven hooves and chewing the cud are precisely the traits that distinguish the kinds of animals that routinely serve as metaphors for Israelite society from those that do not. The flocks and herds which are the paradigmatic metaphors for Israelite society are also the model kind of food. Moreover, those animals that serve as metaphors for other nations, such as predatory animals, are defined as unclean. Thus the dietary restrictions carve up the animal world along the same lines as Israelite thought. In a literal sense, therefore, the dietary restrictions specify what kinds of animals are "food for thought." (125)

In other words, the permitted animals are commonly used, in biblical expression, as a metaphor for Israel and the prohibited animals commonly represent non-Israelites.

Reference to the brief list compiled earlier by Eilberg-Schwartz (he offers no support for his present assertion on the spot) shows that there is surely evidence for the associations he claims (120). Israel's neighbors are lions, vultures, asses or eagles. Israel is he-goats or the "choice of the flock." But even given the modest evidence Eilberg-Schwartz provides, it is clear that there are numerous exceptions to his rule: Israel can also be described as a lion or an ass, and Moab as a dove. Moreover, Israel can be likened to other prohibited animals, such as the camel, even if that animal is not "predatory" (it is not such qualities, after all, that render a species impure).

In fact, a more detailed examination of the animal metaphors employed in the Hebrew Bible shows that the simple equation proposed by Eilberg-Schwartz (pure animal = Israel, impure animal = foreign nation) requires some modification. While it is true that the animals do sometimes represent Israel or the nations (the sheep is a particularly frequent metaphor for Israel), they more often represent qualities or "personality traits" that can be associated with any nation, and even with God. At Jeremiah 2:23–4, for example, the restive young camel and wild ass represent the *wicked* Israel, being castigated by the prophet for her profligate ways. And the swooping eagle or predatory vulture serve as metaphors for God who will, in anger, come against the sinful in order to punish them (see, e.g., Dt 28:49, Job 9:26, and Hos 8:1). In contrast, the ox is used in Isaiah 1:3 to represent loyalty to one's master—a quality that Israel should but does not display. The sheep might represent the lost or suffering Israel or the proverbial "sheep to the slaughter," but it might also serve as a metaphor for God who will be like gentle mother sheep (Isa 40:9). More typically, Israel is the sheep and God the shepherd (see, in particular, Ez 34).

So rather than representing the nations as such, it is clear that the metaphors capture certain qualities marked as positive or negative. The prohibited animals generally (but not always) represent the negative, the permitted animals the positive. The predatory lion or vulture, or the lustful camel, embody characteristics that are evil and therefore should be shunned. The peaceful grazers embody characteristics that are good and thus should be embraced. Of course, Israel's neighbors are often associated with negative characteristics—but the same might be true of the errant Israel and even of the vengeful God. The pure, good animals—particularly the sheep—stand in for Israel or for God.

How, then, can I favor Eilberg-Schwartz's interpretation if it is inaccurate in important respects? To begin with, he remains correct in his fundamental assertion that "the dietary restrictions carve up the animal world along the same lines as Israelite thought" (125). But the lines are not primarily between Israel and her neighbors. They are between the good and the bad. More importantly, Eilberg-Schwartz's attention to metaphors provides us with an important interpretive tool. Crucially, while the animal metaphors that are central to his thesis—and now to our revised thesis—are distributed throughout scripture, they are particularly concentrated in the prophetic books. This fact suggests a solution to our problem with Douglas' or Milgrom's interpretations, described above.

The prophets offered themselves as spokespersons of God's message. While they (or their scribes or followers) obviously recorded their messages in writing, these messages were also clearly intended for oral performance (whether before or after their writing makes little difference). In fact, as Susan Niditch explains, the relationship between "the oral" and "the written" in ancient societies was so fluid that it is probably wrong to speak of each as independent forms in any case.[13] What matters is that the prophetic messages were intended for communication to an audience, one that extended far beyond the literate elite of ancient Israelite society. In order to communicate effectively—that is, to influence the people they sought to influence—the prophets must have employed language, terms and images that were accessible to the understanding of their audience. The prophets may have used language or metaphors that were "new" to their audience, but not so new that they could not be comprehended. And if the communication was effective, once used a "first" or "second" time, these "new" metaphors would have become part of a store of collective images. Prophetic metaphors, particularly those that were commonly used, therefore represent what we may describe as the "common wisdom" of the ancient Israelite audience.

In his sociological study of prophecy, modern and ancient, Robert Wilson explores the relationship between prophets and what he calls their "support groups." In connection with the prophets of the northern Kingdom of Israel, he writes:

Prophets related to the groups that bore the Ephraimite traditions used stereotypical speech patterns and employed a distinctive vocabulary.

> The prophet's use of language presumably conformed to the expec-
> tations of their support groups . . . For the most part stereotypical
> prophetic language seems to have reflected the normal speech of the
> prophet's social matrix . . . .[14]

He writes much the same thing concerning prophecy in the southern Kingdom of Judah. His study, we can see, confirms the picture proposed above.
There is a necessary relationship between the prophet, his message and his
audience. If a particular metaphor or set of metaphors is regularly employed
by the prophets, as is true of the animal metaphors, then these metaphors
must speak for the sensibilities of the society in which the prophet worked.
And these were not obscure or implicit sensibilities. They were available at
the level of explicit articulation. To state matters very simply, not only the
prophets, but the people as well, must have associated certain animals with
certain characteristics (much as we do). The people must therefore have
understood that the sheep or the ox represented ("had") desirable qualities and the vulture or aggressive eagle undesirable qualities (the eagle's
strength or majesty could be admired; see Isa 40:31 and Obadiah 1:4).

Knowing which animals could be consumed and which not, the Israelite would also have known which qualities should be emulated and which
shunned. And when she ate the meat of the sheep, she would have known
that she was to be like that which she ate. Crucially, as we have seen, such
consumption would have been relatively uncommon. Most often, therefore,
the eating practices were about what Israel could and, particularly, could
not eat—not about what they actually did nor did not eat. They were, in
other words, most often about negation—negation of certain evil qualities
and, by extension, negation of nations who displayed those qualities. As
we have seen, though, the nation whose qualities should be avoided could
be Israel herself.

It is noteworthy that the only times Israel would commonly have consumed meat were festive days—holidays, more modestly on Sabbaths and,
less frequently, clan or family celebrations. On these occasions, Israel was
celebrating her identity in multiple and various ways. What has not before
been noticed is that one of the ways she was celebrating that identity was
in what she ate. In fact, in light of what we said above, she was not only
celebrating, *but also eating*, her national identity.

All of this is not to say that this is the only possible interpretation of the
meaning of the eating laws. But it is the one that would have been available to Israel as a whole. It is the one that would both have reflected and
influenced her identity across classes and clans. Limited groups would have
shared other understandings and meanings. The priesthood, for example,
would have been particularly attentive to the category-formation at the
foundation of these laws. The priest, who would have eaten meat far more
often than the common Israelite, would have seen the eating laws divide the
animal world into pure and impure and he would have seen a perfect reflec-

tion of the priestly concern for hierarchy and order. He would have understood that, just as God divided the animal world into pure and impure, so too did God command the division between priest and non-priest, blemished and "perfect," Israel and stranger. Of course, permitted to eat only the pure, the priest would have understood his obligation of cleave to the pure and hate the impure.

Still, for the common Israelite, this world-view would have been less central and the symbol contained in the meat less immediate. For him, the permissions and prohibitions would have provided a mostly theoretical guidance—to avoid evil qualities and pursue good ones. This would have been a "torah"—an instruction—to be borne in mind from one special occasion to the next, but not one to be ritualized—*at least not in food practice*—from day to day.

In the end, it is impossible to escape the fact that these laws would not regularly have constituted an obstacle for the Israelite to break bread (and then dip it in olive oil or crushed beans) with his non-Israelite neighbor. This law is not anxious to create such a separation. (The same is true of a singular law upon which we have not commented—the prohibition of cooking a calf in its mother's milk. As Philo comments centuries later, it would have been very easy to find milk from another mother. This law could therefore have had little practical effect. It would not, in other words, have stood in the way of eating with someone who did not observe the same law. The only reason it has attracted so much comment is because of its association with the later Jewish law restricting the mixing of dairy and meat—upon which we will comment at length in chapter four.) How do we explain this reality? Why, despite frequent expectations to the contrary, does the Torah's eating law do little to separate Israelite from non-Israelite?

The answer, it seems to me, may be found in the conditions that obtained in Israel during the so-called "first Temple period." Israel, in the eighth–seventh centuries (the period offered by Milgrom for the codification of these laws), was divided into independent kingdoms, north (Israel) and south (Judah). While it is clear from biblical and archaeological sources that the population of these kingdoms during these periods contained both Israelites (or Judahites) and members of various Canaanite nations, the identities of the kingdoms *as national kingdoms* could be challenged only from the outside, not from within. Foreign armies might threaten—and they often did—but these were threats to borders and security, not to the identity of the people. The Israelite or Judahite, protected and regulated by his or her own government, might have had regular occasion to mix with "strangers" (*gerim*). But the status of the foreigner as resident stranger, and of the Israelite as citizen at home, was little questioned—at least from the perspective of the Israelite. For this reason, the eating laws exhibited little urgency. They reflected a condition of relatively congenial mixing and allowed for the possibility of such mixing. In the regular course of affairs, such associations need not have been resisted. But, significantly, when the Israelite (or

Judahite) nation gathered to observe and celebrate its particular identity, be it on a weekly or seasonal basis, then *and only then* did the law intervene to create a reminder *in practice* of what that identity was. National celebration indeed demanded separation. Life in the day-to-day did not, at least not to the same extent.

The importance of this distinction—and of its connection to national conditions—will become clear in the next chapter, when we proceed to consider the eating practices of Jews in the period of the second Jerusalem Temple. During that long period, the eating laws of Jews, at least as recorded in the literature that has survived, underwent a significant change. And the direction of the change could not be more transparent. As those several centuries progress, the Torah's laws, pertaining exclusively to food sources from the animal kingdom, will be regularly reaffirmed. But there will also be a new category—gentile food. When and how this category develops, and how it helps us understand a developing Jewish identity, we will see in the next chapter.

3 The second temple period
The food of the gentiles

The Kingdom of Israel came to an end in 722 BCE, at the hands of the Assyrian army. The Kingdom of Judah survived the Assyrian onslaught, but found itself under siege slightly more than a century later, when the Babylonian army progressed against the Judean territories. In 600–599, the first Judean exiles were removed to Babylon. Thirteen years later, the great Jerusalem Temple was destroyed and the last wave of exiles was on its way to a new, foreign home.

Some of the grandchildren or great-grandchildren of these exiles were permitted to return to their ancestral home in the latter part of the same century. Other descendants found their way back to Judea in the middle of the next century. But Jewish independence would not be recovered until the time of the Maccabees, centuries later. The territory on which these Jews lived continued to be ruled by foreigners—first Persians and then Greeks. Under foreign rule—and particularly after the Hellenization of the Near East—many foreigners made their homes along the military and trade routes that traversed the northern valleys and hugged the coast. At first, Judean territory proper remained "off the beaten track," but after Greek and Roman rulers turned their attentions to Jerusalem, even the highlands saw an influx of foreigners. Finding themselves in the regular company of foreign governors, soldiers, and traders, Jews in their own land could imagine themselves in a kind of "exile," as the book of Daniel—written in Judea but representing the experience of exile—attests. During this period, Jews in Judea and its environs were constantly being challenged to reconsider the nature of their identities in relation to their new neighbors. Jewish practice and belief were contested regularly, as Jews divided into a variety of competing parties or sects.[1]

Jewish writings from these centuries are abundant.[2] Some of these works, from the early second Temple period, in particular, found their way into the Hebrew Bible. Others were not later canonized by Jews, but were nevertheless preserved by different groups. Suffice it to say that, whether "official" or not, Jewish (and even non-Jewish) testimony to the beliefs and practices of Jews during this lengthy era is more than ample.

Unfortunately for our purposes, the testimonies to Jewish eating practices cluster toward the latter half of this period. This is apparently coincidental; there is no reason to conclude that Jews in the early second Temple period were less concerned with eating regulations than those in later centuries. It would probably be correct to say, in fact, that the best testimony to Jewish eating practice in the early second Temple period is the Torah itself. It was, after all, not long after Ezra's return from Babylon, in the mid fifth century BCE, that the Torah was accepted as authoritative in Israel (Schwartz, 19–22). This acceptance would naturally have included the Torah's food laws. But the literature that begins speaking in the late third century and beyond makes it clear that there is more to contemporary eating customs than the Torah.

THE LITERARY HISTORY[3]

The Book of Daniel is, of course, a biblical book, though a very late one. In its present form, it dates from the early Maccabean period (c. 165 BCE). But its first several chapters apparently preserve stories of a traditional hero by the name of Daniel, which may have originated centuries before the final redaction of the book.[4] These same chapters claim to relate events that occurred in exile, during the reign of Nebuchadnezzer.

In the first chapter of this book, we read of Nebuchadnezzer's attempt to collect wise youth from among his subject peoples, including Israel, to offer wisdom and instruction in the royal court. Included in the group are Daniel and three colleagues. When the king's deputy, the chief eunuch, seeks to feed Daniel and his Jewish companions from "the king's portion" and "his drinking wine," they refuse, asking that they not be thus defiled. Instead, Daniel asks that they be provided with vegetables and water.

Daniel's request is not expressed neutrally. He asks, specifically, that he not be "defiled" by being forced to eat the royal food. The term translated here as "defile" is not a technical term, not a synonym for "impure." It conveys a sense of disgust. Moreover, while it might be possible to interpret Daniel's entreaty as an appeal to avoid consuming the biblically prohibited foods, this is neither the necessary nor the most natural interpretation. "The king's portion" may or may not include meat, and it is also likely to include bread and other non-meat items. Moreover, even if "the king's portion" might include biblically prohibited substance, it is impossible to interpret "wine" in the same fashion. Wine, of course, is produced from fruit, and only animal substance is restricted in the Torah's law. Thus, the author of this text clearly wants to extend Jewish eating restrictions beyond what the Torah would require.

In a later period, rabbinic law will prohibit the wine of gentiles for two reasons—first, because it may have been "poured out" in the service of idol worship and, second, because of fear of "marriage" with them (that is, if you drink with them, you might develop more than cordial relations with them, and this might lead to marrying them). The latter factor is certainly not relevant here, for the narrative scenario does not allow for friendly fraternizing. On the other hand, there may well be concern that the wine was used in foreign "worship;" rituals are enacted in many public, and especially royal, settings, as the author and his characters surely knew. But, even if correct, this explanation does not stand alone, because it doesn't explain the avoidance of the other royal foods. For this reason, the simplest explanation of the present taboos seems to be that the proffered meal, food and wine alike, was prepared in the king's kitchen and not by Jews. The author evidently wants to mark as prohibited both food cooked in the foreign court and wine produced in foreign vats. Vegetables, unaffected by and therefore unmarked by foreign culture, remain permitted.

Another Jewish book written in roughly the same period supports and clarifies the same taboo. The book of Tobit tells the story of another Jewish exile, the namesake of the book, who finds himself exiled in Nineveh. Recounting his experience there, Tobit reports, "All my relatives and my race ate gentile food; however, I myself scrupulously avoided eating gentile food. And because I was mindful of my God with my whole being, the Most High granted me favor and good standing with Shalmaneser..." (1:10–13). Here we read the story of another Jew in exile who has (or, in the case of Daniel, develops) a relationship with the king (Tobit goes on to report that he was the royal purchasing agent). And this Jew also has concerns about the food he and his brethren eat in this exilic environment. His concern is described rather explicitly: he wants to avoid *gentile* food. He condemns his compatriots for eating *gentile* food (the Greek and other ancient versions of Tobit have not "food," like the Latin Vulgate, but "bread," in which case his intent cannot be biblically prohibited food as such). So the trouble is not with the substance of the food, but with the fact that the food is the food of gentiles. Merely because it is the food of gentiles, Tobit believes Jews should avoid it. True, Tobit reports that his compatriots fail to observe his eating piety, suggesting that he stands apart in his avoidance. But other books from this same general period make it clear that Tobit—or the pietistic author who represents him—does not, in fact, stand alone.

Jubilees, a book which typically retrojects contemporary pious practice into the lives of the biblical patriarchs, has Abraham command Jacob upon the former's deathbed: "Keep yourself separate from the nations, and do not eat with them; and do not imitate their works nor associate yourself with them; for their works are unclean and all their ways polluted..." (22:16).[5] One could hardly imagine the equation stated more directly: the works of the gentiles are polluted and you must maintain your distance from them. You must, therefore, never eat with them, because eating together is the opposite of distance. Unlike what we read in Daniel, there is no indication that their food *as such* is polluted. But the leap is not a big one.

In the Book of Judith, when Holofernes sought to express his pleasure at the heroine's presence by ordering his servants "to set a table for her with some of his own delicacies, and with some of his own wine to drink," Judith responded by saying, "I cannot partake of them, or it will be an offense [Greek: *skandalon*]..." (12:1–2). Remarkably, Judith is not concerned that she might give "offense" to the foreign general. She is more anxious to avoid Holofernes' food. The context does not permit us to determine exactly what might have been among the delicacies that Judith was offered. But one thing is clear: she does not see fit to pick among the options. And, as we imagine the ancient context, it is inconceivable that there would not have been any food acceptable to a pious Jew following the law of the Torah. So Judith's concern, like those of Daniel, Tobit and Abraham (in Jubilees), seems to have been the fact that the food was that of a foreigner. For that reason, alone, its consumption would be considered an offense.

The practice of avoiding gentile food, attested in these several works, is an extremely significant development. The taking of food, it has often been noted, is far more than an act of mere self-sustenance. It is, at the same time, a social act—an act that creates and cements bonds between those who share a meal. If I eat with you, I declare that I am socially involved with you in a way that is far more profound than, say, the exchange of words in the marketplace. Moreover, if I take your food, I indicate thereby that I am willing to place myself—symbolically and even literally—in your debt. Thus, to say that a Jew should not eat gentile food is to declare that certain kinds of vital social relations between Jew and non-Jew must be avoided. And to say that a Jew should not partake of gentile food even in the absence of the gentile—that is, merely because he has provided it—is to declare that social indebtedness to the gentile must be shunned.

The message of avoidance contained in the law may be supplemented by another, less pragmatic communication. The language of Daniel suggests that a Jew who partook of the king's food—which I understand to be the contextual equivalent of gentile food—would be "defiled" or rendered disgusting. This is, at first blush, rather a startling claim: that the food of gentiles is defiling or disgusting merely because it is their food—because they have prepared it or served it. This is effectively to say that the gentile is defiling and by virtue of having prepared a food-substance she or he has caused it to be defiling. It is as though there is a gentile "miasma" which can be communicated to food, and that food is in turn hateful because by ingesting it the Jew would ingest the same miasma. A Jew who believed and observed this would be significantly restricted in the sorts of relations he could have with his gentile neighbor. And, even when involved with his neighbor, he would understand that that neighbor, like any gentile, is a potential source of defilement.

If there is "gentile food," there must also be—by implication, at least— "Jewish food." And if laws marking the food of the "other" as "gentile" would encourage avoidance of the Jew's gentile neighbor, laws restricting the Jew to "Jewish" food would reinforce his or her own "otherness" (= Jewishness) in the gentile context. They would say, in effect, that the Jew must eat what she is—Jewish food for the Jewish person. The Jew, observing these restrictions, would see herself as somehow apart, living among gentiles, perhaps, but not fully part of them. And the gentile observer would understand the same message: the Jew who refuses to eat my food remains somehow foreign, despite his being my neighbor.

How are we to understand the development of these practices (the marking of gentile food as "Gentile food" and the utter avoidance of that food) and their implicit meanings (the gentile is a source of defilement; he or she is to be avoided)? As far as we can discern, the works reporting this development came to formation, mostly if not exclusively, in Judea in the second century BCE. Their setting, therefore, is a territory with an increasingly significant Hellenistic presence, where "foreign" (= non-Jewish) populations are more and more present and inherited Jewish identities are regularly challenged. Archaeology has shown how ubiquitous was the cultural presence of Hellenism during this period, even, ironically, under restored Jewish hegemony. Indeed, the books that bear the names of these new Jewish rulers, Maccabees I and II, testify unambiguously to the profound Hellenization of the Jewish elite.[6]

We must imagine that, under such conditions, a "traditional" Jewish identity was an increasingly vulnerable construct. The temptations of the "other"—an other who was the Jew's neighbor and trading partner—must have been constant and unavoidable. How, in such an environment, could a Jewish identity be maintained? One answer, it seems clear, is the new eating regulations attested in these contemporary documents. The writers of these documents—pietists all—sought to create a bulwark against incursions on Jewish identity by declaring all gentiles defiling and all gentile foods prohibited. The Jew who fully observed these new restrictions would, of course, be practically separated from intimate contact with gentiles and more dependent upon the graciousness of Jewish friends and neighbors. Moreover, if he absorbed the attitude implicit in the practice, he would have avoided gentiles merely because they were gentiles. Sources of defilement are, after all, to be shunned.

But we must be cautious in judging the actual consequences of these developments. These books may speak for only small numbers of particularly pious (in their own eyes) Jews. We can have no idea of how widely these new restrictions were observed. We might suppose that the various claims of Jewish "misanthropy," beginning with Hecataeus in c. 300 BCE and continuing throughout this period, testify to the refusal of many Jews to eat with their gentile neighbors.[7] But many other Jewish practices, if scrupulously observed, would separate Jews from their neighbors, and few of the "misanthropy" accusations—and none from this period—speak of a misanthropy expressed in the refusal to eat with non-Jews.[8]

In fact, the testimony of Tobit, quoted above, suggests that, at least as far as that author knows, Jews did *not* refuse to eat the food of gentiles. On the contrary, they seem to have enjoyed such food with great regularity. (This is not to say that these same common Jews ate biblically prohibited foods. In reality, they may have refused such foods when presented with them—which would have occurred infrequently—and still enjoyed food prepared by their non-Jewish neighbors.) Moreover, even the pious few, reported to be avoiding all gentile foods, were at the same time represented as involved in important contacts with their gentile hosts or neighbors. Consider, for example, the fate of Daniel, who became a confidant of the court, or of Judith, who partook of her meal in the intimate privacy of Holofernes' tent. Thus, whatever the symbolic or pragmatic implications of the gentile food restrictions, it is evident that even those who observe them can build significant ties with the non-Jews amongst whom they live. Indeed, we may wonder whether, in reality, it is those Jews who have the opportunity to cross cultural or national bridges who are most in need of the boundary reinforcements that these restrictions constitute. Being drawn into the gentile sphere with one hand, they seek to distance themselves with the other.

All we can be sure of in evaluating this evidence is that some Jews during this period, aspiring leaders, effective or not, sought to protect Jewish identity by prohibiting the food of the non-Jew. In their judgment, marking the food of the gentile as taboo, as defiling, would encourage Jewish avoidance of him and his ways. That their success was partial is proved by the increasingly Hellenized Jewish population that would be found in Palestine in the centuries to follow.

THE PROBLEM WITH PORK

The other major development in Jewish eating practices between the Bible and the rabbis is the emergence of pork as a uniquely abhorred substance. While it may be true that, as Milgrom argues (see p. 649), the Torah's law was consciously and specifically formulated to outlaw the flesh of swine, this fact is in no way obvious to the reader of that law. Rather, in the Torah's enumeration, the pig appears side by side with other prohibited animals, marked by no highlighting formulation or pride of place. It is but one of many outlawed species. But in the latter part of the period at hand—that is, by the early first century CE, at the very latest—the pig has become the hated species *par excellence*. This development, which has long attracted comment and interpretation, is worthy of further attention.

Gentile writers are perhaps the first to notice—in writing, at least—the unique place of pork in the Jewish system of eating taboos. Thus, Josephus notes that the Jew-hater, Apion (early first century CE), denounces Jews for refusing to eat pork.[9] Petronius, in the same century, speaks of Jews as worshipping a "pig-god" (Stern, 444), evidently assuming that their refusal to eat it is evidence of its divine status in their eyes. Epictetus, who lived in the latter half of the first century until 130 CE, also knows of the Jews particular avoidance of swine flesh (Stern, 542). And his contemporary, Plutarch, writes of the Jewish avoidance of pig at length (Stern, 554–57).

Early Jewish sources are somewhat less yielding in their testimony to this new reality. The first writings to speak of swine—in isolation from other animals—as a hated species are I and II Maccabees (both written, at approximately the same time, in the latter part of the second century BCE). II Maccabees records two related, gruesome stories in which the pious heroes (either the scribe Eleazar or the mother and her seven sons; see chapters 6 and 7) demonstrate their steadfast commitment to the faith by refusing to eat swine's flesh. In both cases, the text indicates that the king's men sought to force our heroes to eat this meat as a means of compelling them to transgress their ancestral law. What is unclear is whether swine already had a specially abhorred status or whether swine's flesh was simply the available prohibited meat. At a parallel point in the narrative of I Maccabees, the king seeks to force Jews to adopt Hellenistic practices by having them, among other things, "sacrifice swine and other unclean animals" in the Temple (1:47). Again, it is not clear whether swine is singled out in this statement because of its already established status as particularly hated, or this was merely the flesh which, in the awareness of the author, was preferred for gentile cultic slaughter. This lack of clear developmental direction has even lead some to propose that it was the use of pig flesh in these persecutions that propelled pig to its unique status in the first place (Milgrom comments that pig "did not become the reviled animal par excellence until the eating of its flesh became a test of the Jews' loyalty in Hellenistic times (2 Macc 6:18)").[10] Whether or not we are inclined to accept this overly credulous reading of the Maccabee narratives, it is evident that they themselves do not yet give clear evidence of the uniqueness of pork in the Jewish psyche. But sometime between 100 BCE and 100 CE, this transition undoubtedly took place.

Rabbinic sources, beginning with the Mishnah (200 CE), are well aware of the unique status of the pig. Mishnah Baba Qamma 7:7, for example, instructs that "[Jews] should not raise pigs in any place." To explain this ruling, the Talmud quotes a tradition that relates the "history" of the internecine battles of the Hasmonean dynasty. Reportedly, during the war between Hyrcanus and Aristobulus, one party encamped within the Temple compound in Jerusalem while the other attacked—at first unsuccessfully—from the outside. Conquest came only when those in the Temple were tricked into raising pigs into the Temple compound (or, to be more specific, half way up the surrounding wall). Because of this abomination, they then declared "cursed be the man who raises pigs" (B.Q. 82b, with parallel at y. Ta'anit 4:5, 68c).

If we are dubious about the "historical" explanation, whether offered by Milgrom or the Talmud, the question nevertheless remains: how are we to understand the transformation in the status of the pig during this period—a transformation that would affect the symbolism of Jewish eating to our own day? An early rabbinic midrash unwittingly suggests an answer. Explaining the meaning of Leviticus' command, "you shall observe my ordinances" (18:4), the midrash comments, "these are the things concerning which the Evil Inclination offers a retort, and concerning which the nations of the world... offer a retort, such as [the prohibitions upon] eating pork or wearing linen and wool together..." (Sifra, *Acharei Mot*, ch. 13). Why, in the rabbis' world, would both a Jew's non-Jewish neighbors and his or her own transgressive urge mock the prohibition of pork, in particular? Certainly, the prohibition of pork is no more arbitrary or illogical than the prohibition of other animals! The answer must be that pork was the prohibited meat that was actually available to lust after. Otherwise, there would be no reason to imagine that the "evil urge" would be attracted to this meat in particular. If we assume that pork was *their meat*, that is, the meat commonly enjoyed by gentile neighbors of the Jews and therefore *identified with them*, then this midrash will make immediate sense. So too, of course, will the place of pig as the uniquely reviled species of their day.

Indeed, pig was *meat* in classical antiquity. Writing of the Mediterranean region in the Greco-Roman period, Peter Garnsey reports that "meat and other foods of animal origin were relatively speaking in short supply, and therefore of minor importance in the diets of the mass of the population." The raising of livestock was uneconomical and unpractical. Oxen were primarily work animals, sheep and goat were kept for wool and cheese. "Pigs alone," he emphasizes, "were kept basically for meat," this because they had no other economic function and could well be sustained even on garbage rather than valuable grains or grasses.[11] Notably, centuries later in Byzantium (again the Mediterranean region), the same considerations continued to be influential: cattle were still working animals, while pigs, along with likewise abundant sheep and goats, were killed for their flesh.[12] Even in medieval Europe, pork was the only flesh regularly consumed by the masses (Flandrin and Montanari, 273, 307), and until the Black Death—which precipitated profound changes in the European economy—pigs were the only animals kept entirely for meat.[13]

The archaeological evidence for Palestine in the period that concerns us supports this picture of meat consumption for the local non-Jewish population. Bone samples taken from Ashkelon of the Classical period (as well as the Byzantine and Islamic periods) "indicate that pork was a mainstay of the diet."[14] The same is indicated by findings in Anafa, leading Hesse and Wapnish to conclude that "urban-pagans were eating pigs in the Hellenistic period...," or, again, that "enormous numbers of pigs were being eaten in (Late) Hellenistic times" in urban settings in Palestine.[15] Thus, the abundance of evidence, both direct and indirect, supports the same conclusion:

when the common Palestinian Jew viewed the common gentile eating meat at her or his table—in the first century BCE or the first century CE—that meat was far more likely to be pork than anything else. In other words, of all of the species marked as off-limits by the Torah's legislation, the only one concerning which this would make a difference on a regular basis was the pig. The rest were primarily of academic interest, the pig was a presence and potentially a temptation. But it was also, crucially, *their* meat—ubiquitously so. And thus, it was taboo—taboo because the Torah outlawed it, taboo because it was so readily associated with "the other." It emerged as the abhorred symbol par excellence because it was available to serve in that capacity. No other species on the Torah's list could do the same.

As we discussed earlier in this chapter, Palestine, in the second century BCE, saw rising numbers of Hellenized soldiers, traders and other residents within its territories. Notably, pork was a mainstay of the Hellenistic—and later, Roman—diet. By contrast, in the centuries before the Hellenistic conquest, local peoples in Palestine rarely consumed pork (Hesse and Wapnish 1997, 253, 262). What this means is that in the Hellenistic period, for the first time, Jews observing the Torah's prohibitions would have had increasing opportunity to witness their neighbors regularly consuming a particular prohibited flesh: pork. As this awareness grew, pork could grow into a symbol—it could be viewed more and more prominently as the food of the other. At the same time, during the persecutions of Antiochus, pork was used as the test of Jewish loyalty. In the larger culinary context, this surely would have helped push Jews to avoid pork with a particular passion. If this is the food that represents acceptance of Hellenistic cultural hegemony, then—in the minds of the pious—this is the food that must be shunned at all costs. As a marker of cultural identity, standing at the boundary between "Hellenist" and "pious Jew," pork will have been a uniquely effective tool for fighting the battle between "us" and "them." It was precisely at this stage, therefore, that pig ceased to be merely pig, and became (to engage in a conscious anachronism) *"hazir,"* the forbidden meat *par excellence* (supporting this same interpretation, see Hesse and Wapnish 1997, 263).

THE PERSISTENCE OF THE BIBLICAL LAW

What is perhaps most notable about the literary record concerning Jewish eating practices during the period of the second Jerusalem Temple (fifth century BCE–first century CE), beyond the developments discussed above, is its conformity to the laws of the Torah. The literature from this period suggests that, with small sectarian peculiarities, the Jewish eating laws, observed or not, were those spelled out in Leviticus and Deuteronomy. The only question for contemporary Jews—at least of the intellectual, Hellenized variety—was how these laws were to be interpreted.

For example, the author of the "Letter of Aristeas," writing in the second century BCE (Nickelsburg, 168), seeks to illustrate the superior wisdom of the Torah's law by interpreting the eating laws as a symbolic philosophical discipline. The general purpose of these laws is, he writes, to assure that Jews will not mix with other nations and thus remain pure in body and soul (139). More specifically, he claims that the birds permitted to Jews are domestic and distinguished by their purity, and they eat only grains and vegetables (145). In contrast, the prohibited birds are wild, they eat flesh, and they "oppress" others by force in order to obtain their prey (146). They also steal small animals (kids, lambs) from their rightful owners. Needless to say, Israel is to emulate the qualities of the permitted birds and shun those of the birds labeled "impure."

He also interprets the qualities that distinguish the permitted quadrupeds as instructive symbols. The requirement of a split hoof he understands to represent the division between good and evil, and the recommendation that Israel aspire to be righteous. It also symbolizes the separation of Israel from the nations—desirable because of the impurity and corruption of those nations. Concerning the other quality that characterizes the permitted animals—their chewing the cud—he suggests that such chewing represents the importance of memory (cud = that which is regurgitated, that which "comes up again"). Memory, of course, is crucial for the educated man, the man who will be characterized by the qualities of the philosophical Greek.

Writing approximately two centuries later, Philo of Alexandria suggests similar interpretations:

> ...for as the animal which chews the cud, while it is masticating its food draws it down its throat, and then by slow degrees kneads and softens it, and then after this process again sends it down into the belly, in the same manner the man who is being instructed, having received the doctrines and speculations of wisdom in at his ears from his instructor...still is not able to hold it firmly and to embrace it all at once, until he has resolved over in his mind everything which he has heard by the continued exercise of his memory....But as it seems the firm conception of such ideas is of no advantage to him unless he is able to discriminate between and to distinguish which of contrary things it is right to choose and which to avoid, of which the parting of the hoof is the symbol (The Special Laws, IV, 107–8).[16]

He suggests analogous interpretations of the other permitted and prohibited animals (including birds and sea creatures), all understood to recommend the good life as it might be understood by a contemporary (Hellenistic) philosopher.

But the point of all this is not to examine the interpretations of these authors. It is to observe that, as far as they know, the only laws regulating

Jewish diet are those found explicitly in the Torah. Upon reflection, that this should be the case is not surprising. The so-called "Second Temple period" was, as I hinted earlier, the *biblical* period proper. This was the period when, after centuries of formation and accretion, the Torah, along with the historical and classical prophets, had achieved their canonical form. This was the period when these books were accepted as authoritative by the majority of Jews. This was the period when the laws they describe defined the life of Jewry, individually and as a nation.

In fact, the agreement of these two authors, one living in the late-second century BCE, probably in Alexandria, and the other in the early first century, also in Alexandria, attests to the reality of biblical authority. Despite the passage of centuries, despite the long influence of Hellenistic culture, both understand that to be a Jew means to observe these laws regulating diet. And both understand that the single authoritative source of such laws is the Torah, as recorded and available to Israel as a whole. Interpretations might vary—the culture that influences these interpretations might change as well—but the Torah defines the unity of Israel, across time and (we must assume) across space.

The persistence of the biblical law throughout this period is noteworthy precisely because of its persistence, that is, because of the apparent absence of developments relating to the biblical law itself. True, some Jews tried to outlaw all gentile food, but it is difficult to ascertain how widely this taboo was observed. Besides, this represented a new category, one not connected to the Torah's law as such. And, as we saw, pig attained a special status as prohibited flesh, but this was a matter of rebalancing, not a genuine innovation. Aside from these two developments — undeniably significant as they are — Jewish practices seem to have remained static, at least so far as they are reflected in the literature. The significance of this stasis will be evident only in the next chapters, describing developments during the rabbinic period. When seen in the mirror of difference, the relative sameness of the Second Temple period will be striking.

To appreciate the coming change, it is necessary to note often overlooked testimony to what, until at least the early first century of the Common Era, remained the same. I am speaking of the odd and inexplicable biblical ordinance which prohibits the cooking of a kid in its mother's milk. At a later time, this law will undergo a change so significant that it will, in its new form, come to constitute the centerpiece of Jewish eating practice for centuries to come. But now, the Torah's law is the law, and it is understood to mean (for the most part) precisely what it says.

In this matter, the record of Philo is probative. In his essay "On the Virtues," Philo describes a number of biblical laws relating to animals that embody, in his mind, the quality of compassion. One of these is the law just mentioned—"Thou shalt not seethe a lamb [or "sheep;" Greek: 'αρνα] in his mother's milk." (Philo relies here on the Septuagint; see Milgrom, 742) Expanding upon this Torah law, Philo writes:

For he looked upon it as a very terrible thing for the nourishment of the living to be the seasoning and sauce of the dead animal, and when provident nature had, as it were, showered forth milk to support the living creature…that the unbridled licentiousness of men should go to such a height that they should slay both the author of the existence of the other, and make use of it in order to consume the body of the other. And if any one should desire to dress flesh with milk, let him do so without incurring the double reproach of inhumanity and impiety. There are innumerable herds of cattle in every direction, and some are every day milked by the cowherds, or goatherds, or shepherds, since, indeed, the milk is the greatest source of profit to all breeders of stock, being partly used in a liquid state and partly allowed to coagulate and solidify, so as to make cheese. So, that, as there is a great abundance of lambs, and kids, and all other kinds of animals, the man who seethes the flesh of any one of them in the milk of its own mother is exhibiting a terrible perversity of disposition.... (143–44)

Philo is here interpreting and justifying the law of the Torah which he, like others, understands to obligate Israel, not the nations. When he speaks of "anyone," therefore, he means "any Jew" (though he would argue that the same good qualities ought to direct the behavior of other peoples as well). And what he says about what the law of Moses does or does not require is perfectly clear. In Philo's understanding, the law prohibiting the cooking of a lamb in its mother's milk is meant to teach and symbolize compassion. Because milk, the first sustainer of young life, represents life, it must not be used to prepare the dead flesh of the former life it was meant to sustain. Such a combination would be perverse not only because of its symbolism but also because it is so easy to avoid this combination. (In fact, one would almost have to go out of one's way to cook the flesh of the young animal in the milk of its very own mother.) There is milk available in abundance from the multitude of flocks that are found in any civilized dwelling place. If one—a Jew—wants to cook the flesh of a slaughtered young animal in milk, he can easily find milk with which to do so, milk that does not come from the mother of the same animal. *Crucially, there is no problem with cooking flesh in milk*—let alone with eating meat and dairy together. The only known prohibition is the one the Torah expresses explicitly, and it, like most of the Torah's eating regulations (at least in an earlier period, before "there [were] innumerable herds of cattle in every direction"), has little regular consequence. Its symbolism speaks louder than its practical application. (Despite Philo's testimony to the abundance of herds of cattle, goats, and sheep around contemporary Alexandria, it is notable that they are raised, in his experience, primarily for their dairy production. This suggests that the consumption of quantities of meat was not an accepted cultural practice, and thus the judgment that the Torah's eating laws had little regular application requires little modification.)

It was Philo's record of laws like these, so different from the familiar Judaism of later centuries, that long caused scholars to judge Philo's a heterodox Hellenistic brand of Judaism. But such a conclusion was founded on the opinion that rabbinic Judaism represented "normative Judaism" and any Judaism that strayed from the standards and opinions of the rabbis was virtually sectarian. This view has been subject to challenge for decades and it is now deemed insupportable.[17] If any Judaism is, during this period, more normative than another, it is the Judaism that hews more closely to the Judaism of Hebrew Scriptures, and to the law of the Torah. It is reasonable to conclude, therefore, that Philo's record of early first century Jewish practice is reliable testimony to the practice of most God-fearing Jews. In all probability, observant Jews did not cook young animals in the milk of their own mothers. But they ate meat prepared with dairy without compunction.

By way of conclusion, we return to a characterization suggested earlier. A Jew in the late second Temple period was a person whose unique identity was defined by the law of the Torah of Moses. Her festivals were centered in the Temple, as the Torah commanded. His Sabbaths were shaped by the Torah's simple command ("thou shalt do no labor"), as elaborated in Jeremiah and Nehemiah (Jer. 17:21–22, Neh. 13:15–22). And her diet was circumscribed by the pure and impure species list of Leviticus-Deuteronomy, by the prohibition of consuming blood, and by the thrice-repeated prohibition concerning the mother and the kid. Of course, we do not know how completely the masses of Jews observed these ordinances. But even when they observed them completely and meticulously, the limitation they imposed was relatively narrow. As we observed in the prior chapter, it was possible for one who respected the eating regulations to share considerable social intercourse—even over food—with his non-Jewish neighbors. Some Jews, therefore—again, we cannot know how many—instituted more extreme restrictions, prohibiting any and all "Gentile food." These Jews exhibited the full anxiety of an exilic condition. Seeing the temptations of foreign cultures as a threat, they sought to build a high wall, one that made intimate contact impossible. But surely not all Jews agreed with this strategy, and many must have been perfectly at home sharing food with Greek or Roman neighbors. Such were condemned by the likes of the author of Tobit. But theirs was a different path.[18]

So we see in the eating practices of these generations of Jews the emergence of the first genuinely Jewish (as opposed to Israelite) identity, one centered on the Torah and its practices. But we also witness the beginning of a debate for that identity, one that asks two questions: What should be our relationship to our neighbors? And when and to what degree can we supplement the law (the Torah) that serves as our constitution? These were good, crucial, abiding questions, questions that would continue to command Jewish attentions for centuries to come.

4 The rabbinic period
"Thou shalt not eat a calf with a mother's milk"

Judaism in the late Second Temple period was characterized by variety. In addition to the identified and well-known sects—Pharisees, Sadducees, Essenes, etc.—there were many and various permutations of Jewish national and cultural identity, a confused mixture of choices competing for the loyalty of each and every Jew. This was the world into which Jesus was born, into which Rome stepped in her arrogant glory. No one living in the early first century could have imagined how events would conspire to confuse matters still further—and to challenge Jewish identity as it had never been challenged before. And no one living at the same time could have imagined what would be identified as Judaism only a few centuries later.

Roman administrative incompetence accompanied by a powerful Jewish spirit of independence led to revolt and war. In the year 70, Jerusalem was captured and the Temple destroyed; the last battle of the war came but a few years later. The Jewish identity that, motivated by Deuteronomy, saw the Temple as the necessary center, refused to yield to the new reality. In dreams and prayer, Jews hoped for restoration with the rebuilt Temple standing in all its glory. For the non-Jew, it must have been impossible to appreciate how powerful this hope was. The Romans, certainly, misjudged drastically, and two generations later found themselves engaged in a bitter war with "Messianic" Jewish troops under the leadership of Bar Kokhba. The war was arduous, and the Romans (along with the Jews) suffered great losses. But never again would Rome misjudge the Jewish capacity for spirited resistance. To suppress the Jewish hope, Rome razed Jerusalem and replaced it with a Roman encampment. Those Jews who survived were forbidden to remain in Judea, and the Galilee became the undisputed center of the Jewish population in Palestine. It was in this Galilee, a multi-cultural territory with a mixed population, that successor Judaisms, whatever they might be, would have to emerge.

The complexity of the Galilee in the second century would be a powerful contributor to the dynamics of identity in this next period.[1] Through the Galilee passed important roads from the north and east—that is, from Syria and Persia—to the coastal plain and beyond. As a consequence, this territory was the home, whether short or long term, of multiple foreign populations and cultures. Its cities were genuinely cosmopolitan; Sepphoris is only one of many good examples of this reality. This meant that, outside of isolated villages in the hills and valleys, it was impossible to escape exposure to—and the influence of—the multifarious cultures of the region. The record of archaeology leaves no room for question in this regard. Each population adapted from the forms of its neighbors. Hence, for example, synagogue floors were decorated with conventional Roman icons, and Jewish burials were characterized by many typical Roman forms and rituals. Who was a Jew and what were to be his or her practices?—these were real and at least partially open questions. And, against all this, the traditional center, commanded by the Torah, lie in ruin, the traditional leadership, now without a base, was rendered impotent. These were confusing times, when the future of Jewish form and expression could not be known.

It was in the context of this Galilean mixture that a new community of religious adepts, the rabbis, began to formulate and promulgate their version of Judaism. Their first formulation, already a massive, meticulous work, was the Mishnah—a corpus of law and opinion intended to shape the practices of Jews in their mundane and not-so-mundane lives. The Mishnah does, naturally, define many of the laws shaping Jewish eating practice—according to rabbinic understanding, in any case. But before we examine those laws, we must first understand for whom they were relevant. Whose identity, in other words, is reflected in the practices to which the Mishnah gives voice?

The rabbis began as a small group of scholars in master-disciple circles sometime in the first century. By the late second century, the rabbis themselves still amounted to a small number of individuals, certainly no more than a few hundred. They surely had followers, other Jews who were attracted by rabbinic discipline or reputation. But altogether, the rabbis can have served as authorities for a small percentage of the local population—and for almost no one beyond the Galilee itself.[2] Thus, when we consider the Mishnah, we must understand that it was, in its own context, little more than a sectarian document. We learn little about the identity of second-third century Jews in general from its pages. But we do gain significant insights into the identity of the rabbinic movement itself—the movement that would, after the passage of several centuries, come to define virtually all of Judaism, in Palestine, Babylonia, and far beyond.

The eating laws of the rabbis are divided primarily between three Mishnaic tractates. In one, Hullin ("[the slaughter of] profane [animals]"), we find laws pertaining to slaughter, prohibited substance (blood, suet, the meat of improperly slaughtered or prohibited animals) and the prohibition of mixing dairy and meat. In the second, Avodah Zarah ("foreign worship"), we find restrictions concerning the consumption and use of gentile food. And in the third, Berakhot ("blessings"), we learn of the system of blessings that are to be recited before and after enjoying different sorts of foods and meals.

We will begin our examination of the rabbis and their rules with tractate Hullin and, more particularly, with the regulations concerning dairy and meat. There, in the middle of the Mishnah's exposition of the food system, we read the following apparently casual—but actually quite stunning—delineation of what a rabbinically observant Jew may or may not do at his table:

> It is forbidden to cook any flesh with milk, with the exception of the flesh of fish and grasshoppers, and it forbidden to bring it up on the table with cheese, with the exception of the flesh of fish and grasshoppers... (8:1)[3]

Here, in stark simplicity, is the first expression of the prohibition of mixing dairy and meat. The Mishnah's formulation takes the prohibition for granted. It provides no source for the prohibition nor seeks to justify it in any other way. It simply states the restriction and adds a regulation apparently intended to distance a person from transgression (don't place it upon the same table lest you eat it together). The structure it is necessary to define, the foundation is simply taken for granted.

The newness of this rabbinic prohibition becomes apparent not only against the background of Philo and other Second Temple witnesses (none of which knew of this prohibition, as we saw in the previous chapter), but also upon examining the confused state of pertinent regulations even in centuries to come. It is in the gemara—the rabbis' discussions of the Mishnah and other early rabbinic law over the course of the third through fifth centuries—that we find this evidence preserved. By virtue of the later rabbinic habit of seeking consistency in this authoritative source of Jewish law, the reality of this confusion has mostly been overlooked.

The relevant gemara (beginning at Hullin 104b) comments upon the following Mishnah:

> Fowl may be placed on the table with cheese but may not be eaten [with it]—these are the words of the school of Shammai. But the [masters of the] school of Hillel say: It may not be placed nor eaten.

The dispute recorded in this Mishnah is the reflection of a larger disagreement: Does fowl, which produces no milk, count as "meat" for purposes of these laws or not? At this stage of the development of the law (and continuing for several centuries) the law is not yet decided. Fowl therefore demands separate scrutiny, and possibly different practices and restrictions, in the earliest talmudic deliberations. The gemara's discussion of this Mishnah includes the following sequence:

1. Agra, the father-in-law of R. Abba taught: "Fowl and cheese may be eaten with abandon." He taught it and he explained it: "[This means] without washing the hands and without wiping the mouth."
2. R. Yitzhaq the son of R. Mesharshya went to the house of R. Ashi. They brought him cheese and he ate, [then] they brought him meat and he ate, and he did not wash his hands!
3. They said to him: But did not Agra, the father-in-law of R. Abba teach: "Fowl and cheese may be eaten with abandon"—[implying] fowl and cheese, yes, [but] meat and cheese, no?
4. He said to them: These words [apply] at night, but during the day I can see.

This is, from the perspective of later Jewish practice, a rather puzzling exchange, one that has provoked a good deal of learned commentary. But if we make no assumptions about what each step must mean or about what each person must be saying, we actually learn quite a bit about the (then) contemporary state of practice concerning the separation of meat and dairy.

In step 1, we learn that, in the opinion of Agra, the flesh of fowl may be eaten before or after cheese without taking any additional steps or precautions. Merely refraining from eating fowl and cheese at the same moment is sufficient to fulfill the requirements of the law. Having finished one, a person may eat the other without waiting and without doing anything else to establish separation. In step 3, those residing in the house of R. Ashi understand Agra's teaching to imply that what is not required for the flesh of fowl is required for other meat. In other words, if washing one's hands and wiping one's mouth is not required between eating fowl and cheese, it must be required between eating meat and cheese. R. Yitzhaq, who ate one after the other without doing so, must, therefore, have acted improperly. But R. Yitzhaq explains his actions (in step 4): this is all true only at night, when one cannot see what is still on one's hands. But during the day, when one can see if any food substance is still on one's hands, if nothing remains, one may proceed from one food to the other without any additional steps.

Notably, the order in which one eats these foods seems not to be a factor in this discussion. In steps 1 and 3, flesh is mentioned first. In step 2—the story of what transpired in R. Ashi's home (or school)—cheese is mentioned first. The talmudic exchange attributes no significance to this distinction. In fact, if order mattered, then we would have expected R. Yitzhaq to respond (in step 4), "but I ate cheese first!" If order mattered, then this would have been the most natural defense of his actions. So, it seems clear, what this deliberation says about requirements for separation applies whatever the order of the consumption of the food. If meat and cheese may be eaten at night providing that the hands are washed and the mouth wiped, then this is true even if the meat is eaten first. And if meat and cheese may be eaten during the day when the hands are clean, then this is true even if the meat is eaten first. Taken at face value, this text seems to describe a state of affairs according to which requirements for separating meat and dairy are minimal and the law in general is quite lenient.

The next brief exchange, while proposing other methods of separation, supports the conclusion that separation is actually rather a simple affair:

1. It is taught: The School of Shammai say "wipe" and the School of Hillel say "rinse."
2. What is "wipe" and what "rinse?"
3. If you say [it means] "The School of Shammai say wipe and rinsing is not required" and "The School of Hillel say rinse and wiping is not required,"
4. So, that which R. Zeira said, "wiping the mouth may be done only with bread," like whom [would his teaching be]? Like the School of Shammai! [This is implausible because the halakha is known, in general, to follow the School of Hillel] . . .
5. Rather, the School of Shammai say "wipe, and the same holds for rinsing" and the School of Hillel say "rinse, and the same holds for wiping," and the [one] master said [it] one [way] and the [other] master said the other [way], yet they do not disagree. (104b–105a)

The argument recorded here, between the two early schools of rabbinic disciples, concerns what must be done to one's mouth before proceeding to eat the other kind of food. According to the first record of their opinions, the School of Shammai prefers (or, according to one interpretation, allows) wiping (with bread, using a neutral food to eliminate the remains of the prior, categorized food) and the School of Hillel prefers rinsing with water. We do not learn why each party prefers the stated method. But, in the end, it doesn't matter, because the gemara concludes that there is no actual dispute and all agree that both methods are equally effective. Wiping or rinsing will both suffice.

The question, of course, is "between what?" Between the eating of which foods must a person wipe or rinse her mouth, and does the time of day matter (as it did in the prior exchange)? In view of the fact that this deliberation follows immediately in the footsteps of the one examined earlier, it would be reasonable to conclude that this debate pertains to making a separation between dairy and meat when eaten at night, in whatever order. But even if we want to argue that this section is adding to the terms of the prior discussion, by suggesting, perhaps, that the mouth must always be cleaned in one way or another (even during the day), we still have no reason to imagine that such a cleaning is effective only if the foods are eaten in one order but not another. Rinsing and wiping appear to be offered here as effective means of cleaning one's mouth whenever a person wants to eat meat and dairy, one after the other. This exchange, therefore, would serve to support our reading of the prior one, giving evidence that the lenient positions articulated there are supported by the opinions of earlier authoritative parties.

The open and even confused state of the halakha at this stage of its development becomes especially clear in several of the next quoted traditions. The crucial passages are these:

1. R. Asi asked R. Yohanan: How long must one wait between [eating] meat and cheese?
2. He said to him: Not at all.
3. Is this so? But did not R. Hisda say: If one ate meat, he is forbidden to eat cheese, [but] if he ate cheese, he is permitted to eat meat.
4. Rather [R. Asi, in step 1, must really have asked]: How long must one wait between cheese and meat?
5. He said to him: Not at all . . . .
6. Mar Ukba said: I, in this matter, am like "vinegar the son of wine" (when compared with my father), for father, when he would eat meat today would not eat cheese until the next day at the same hour, whereas I would not eat at the same meal but I would eat at another meal.[4]

This exchange is particularly interesting because of its apparent confusion with the traditions it records (what is the correct version of R. Asi's question?) and because of its lack of clear connection with the brief deliberations that precede it. We must address both matters simultaneously in order to ascertain the state of the law.

In the first steps, R. Asi asks how long one must wait after eating meat before one may eat cheese. His question seems to take for granted that one must wait some period of time, though he does not know precisely how long. But this assumption is not an obvious one. The Mishnah knows nothing of such a waiting period. The only separation of which it explicitly speaks is physical separation; individuals eating meat must not sit at the same table as those eating dairy. But how far a single person must go to separate the two, one following the other, is a question not commented upon. Neither do the sages whose opinions are recorded earlier in this gemara know anything about waiting. For them, separation is accomplished either by checking to assure the absence of the offending substance or by cleaning it from one's hands and mouth. This discussion of waiting, therefore, introduces a new method for accomplishing the desired end. How are these different methods to interrelate? As yet, we do not know.

But from the variety or proposals we have seen, it seems clear that the very notion of "separation" is a fluid one, even for the final, edited gemara. That this is so will be no surprise if we consider the source of the requirement to separate dairy and meat *as the rabbis themselves understand it*. In the view of the rabbis, the mixing of meat and dairy is scripturally prohibited only when it happens "*derekh bishul*"—by way of cooking (Sanhedrin 4b). This is because, for the rabbis, the prohibition of mixing meat and dairy derives from the biblical verse, "thou shalt not *cook* a kid in its mother's milk"—the Torah explicitly prohibits cooking, and the rabbis, though interpreting the Torah's law in what we might call an expansive manner, respect at least this part of the simple meaning of the verse. Of course, the rabbis, on their own authority, also extend the law well beyond what they understand the Torah to require. We have seen some elements of this extension already in the Mishnah. But they do continue to distinguish between the rabbinic elements of the law and what they claim to be the scriptural elements of the law.

It is, needless to say, impossible to "cook" food in one's mouth. Thus, according to the rabbis' understanding of the Torah's law, one would be forbidden to eat meat and dairy that had previously been cooked together in the same pot but he or she would not be forbidden to eat cold meat together with cold cheese. The prohibition of doing the latter is a rabbinic injunction, one which only the rabbis can define, in all of its details. Clearly, they want to demand the "separation" of dairy and meat. But exactly how is this separation to be accomplished? Waiting a day, or even several hours, would certainly constitute a separation. But so, reasonably, would rinsing or wiping one's mouth. And so might merely finishing one sort of food before going on to the other. In fact, at least one medieval commentator admits that Mar Ukba's "another meal" (step 6) could mean reciting the blessing after the first (meat) meal and then proceeding immediately to the next (dairy) meal.[5] Symbolically speaking, a concluding blessing followed by a new breaking of bread would certainly represent a separation.

So when R. Asi asks how long one must wait between meat and dairy, and R. Yohanan answers "not at all," this is a perfectly reasonable answer. The answer could be "not at all" if some other act, aside from chronological distance, marked the required separation. Admittedly, the gemara, by raising R. Hisda's opinion in opposition to R. Yohanan's answer, does not want this simple conclusion to stand. Based upon R. Hisda's contrary view, the gemara revises the original conclusion and leaves us with a law which demands chronological separation between meat and dairy while requiring none between dairy and meat. But even with this revision, two observations are called for. First, if they had judged the first quoted version of R. Asi's question to be thoroughly and obviously incorrect, the authors of the gemara could simply have quoted a "corrected" version along with R. Yohanan's answer. For some reason, they wanted us, the gemara's students, to know the original "incorrect" version and evaluate it on its own terms.[6] Above, we did so from a theoretical perspective and saw that there is nothing unreasonable in what it assumes. From a systemic perspective, as well, the first version could well be maintained. The gemara revises R. Asi's question as a consequence of the opinion of R. Hisda. But R. Asi, R. Yohanan, and R. Hisda are all sages with exactly the same level of authority. If R. Yohanan and R. Asi want to disagree with R. Hisda, they are entitled to do so, and we as students know that. This is particularly so because R. Asi and R. Yohanan are Palestinian rabbinic sages, while R. Hisda resides in

Babylonia. So what we witness here may well be regional differences in the rabbinic approach to separation, with the Babylonian Talmud seeking to privilege the view of one of its own sages. But it does not hide the alternative from us, its students.

Moreover, even if we accept the Babylonian revision here, the practical consequences may be relatively minimal. For it is possible—perhaps even probable, given the "jumbled" state of affairs in this gemara—that this "chronological" solution to the problem of separation is meant to be only one of several acceptable solutions. This gemara may best be understood as a series of brief deliberations each of which addresses an *alternative* means of establishing a separation between meat and dairy. So washing one's hands or rinsing one's mouth may alone be adequate, and perhaps even unnecessary during the daylight hours. Alternatively, rinsing or wiping one's mouth after eating one type of food may suffice. Or, finally, in the absence of any bread with which to wipe or water with which to rinse, waiting some period of time—and doing nothing else—will establish the separation that the law, at its rabbinic foundation, demands. Surely, this text imposes no final agreement after reviewing these various methods. And, if we read this as a strongly formulated composition, this lack of conclusion may be intentional. If, on the other hand, the "sloppiness" of the gemara here reflects the unfinished state of affairs, we are in essentially the same position. As the evidence of this sequence attests, in the centuries following the rabbinic declaration that meat and dairy have to be separated, the community of rabbis could not yet decide how this separation should be accomplished.

So, what we discover in these texts—the Mishnah and accompanying gemara—is the early history of a new Jewish eating practice, one invented by the early rabbis and elaborated, slowly and variously, by generations of their disciples. As I remarked earlier, the rabbis claimed to derive this practice from the Torah's "thou shalt not cook a kid . . ." prohibition. But such an extension clearly goes well beyond any simple reading of the verse, and no earlier Jewish party records such a reading (or practice). Thus, our question must be, why did the early rabbis (or, if you prefer, "proto-rabbis") invent this practice? Why, in the first century of the Common Era, did a small group of Torah scholars living somewhere in Palestine decide that, to eat as a proper Jew, one had to maintain a separation between dairy and meat?

To answer this question, we begin with the observation that, despite lack of biblical precedent, rabbinic Jews are by no means the only people to separate dairy and meat. Louis Evan Grivetti surveys the numerous peoples and tribes world-wide (but particularly in Africa) who practice such separation.[7] Many forbid the eating of meat and dairy on the same day, including the Kipsigi, Nandi, and Massai peoples, all of east Africa. In a notable parallel to the position of R. Hisda quoted above, the Huma permit the consumption of meat shortly after drinking milk but require a wait of twelve hours if meat comes first (Grivetti, 207). Thus, we see, for some reason, certain peoples and societies express or codify underlying beliefs or social assumptions in the separation of milk and meat. The rabbis are far from alone.

In a close analysis of the separation practices of the Massai, Kaj Århem suggests several overlapping interpretations of the symbolic meanings of milk and meat in Massai culture.[8] He begins by observing that, in the Massai diet, milk is ordinary food—the staple—while meat is extra-ordinary food, consumed only occasionally in the context of public rituals and meals. Women collect the milk, which they distribute on a regular basis, while meat is slaughtered, prepared and distributed (again, in public, ritual contexts) by men. Of course, milk is derived from live cows, while meat is the flesh of dead animals. But the roasting of meat is understood to remove its "death" from it, and therefore serves as a kind of rebirth. Furthermore, roasting transforms the dead flesh into human food—a cultural state— whereas milk remains in its natural form. In summation, milk is associated with the common (domestic), the natural, life and women, whereas meat is associated with the uncommon (public, ritual), culture, death yielding rebirth, and men. These associations are powerfully opposed and should not be easily mixed, even symbolically. Life must be separated from death, the common from the special and sacred, nature from culture and the masculine from the feminine. Milk, culturally inscribed with the meanings on one side of these oppositions, must therefore be separated from meat, culturally inscribed with the meanings on the other side.

What is the value of these interpretations for the rabbinic development? Notably, shortly before the rabbis, Philo interpreted the "thou shalt not cook a kid . . ." prohibition by associating milk with life and the cooking of meat with death, as we saw in the prior chapter. Jacob Milgrom follows Philo explicitly in his own interpretation of the kid-in-milk prohibition.[9] Thus, one of the associations witnessed among the Massai finds significant support among interpreters of the biblical law, ancient and modern. Can the rabbis' expansion of the biblical law be understood as an intuitive elaboration of these symbolic associations? Admittedly, no explicit evidence is available. But the parallel Massai practice, despite the absence of any conceivable historical connection, is sufficient to support such an interpretation.

What of the other associations proposed above? As in earlier times, meat was not a common food in the societies in which the early rabbis resided. The Tosefta (Pe'a 4:10) relates the case of a man who would daily consume a quantity of meat to illustrate "luxury" or "extravagance." Commenting on this story several centuries later, the writers of the Yerushalmi declare, "Is it possible?!" Evidently, in Palestine, whether in the second–third century (the Tosefta) or the fifth (the Yerushalmi), meat was sufficiently rare— and expensive—that regular consumption merited surprise. Of course, the rabbis regularly associate meat with special occasions. They comment, for example, that "there is not joy without meat" (b. Pesachim 109a). The "joy" referred to here is the joy of festival celebrations, and the quoted statement is understood, in context, to refer to the era when the Temple was still standing. In the Temple, there can be no doubt, festivals were marked by the abundant consumption of flesh, and the Passover was not the only occasion on the ancient Jewish calendar when this consumption was biblically commanded. The rabbis, clearly, continue to associate meat with special "appointed times," and meat thus became a significant marker of the coming of the Sabbath or a Festival. Dairy, on the other hand, was a more common, everyday food. Cheese—not milk (note the Mishnah and gemara, which always refer to the former and not the latter)—was an easily renewed resource, in abundant supply, and thus could be enjoyed regularly.

Indeed, cheese was a customary part of the Near Eastern diet, as the rabbinic record itself attests. Therefore, the second association noted earlier (dairy//meat = common//uncommon) would have pertained in the rabbinic context as well. On the other hand, if dairy, in the rabbinic system, was cheese and not milk, then the natural substance, milk, will not have served as a regular signifier. Cheese, of course, is not a substance in its natural state. It is, rather, milk culturally transformed. There is, therefore, no natural-cultural symbolism available in these foods, and this binary will not serve to explain, even in part, the rabbinic impulse to separate dairy and meat.

In contrast, the next Massai association, equating meat with male and milk with female, may well be supported in rabbinic cultural constructions. Male-female is a strong rabbinic opposition, and it is codified in new and powerful ways in rabbinic documents. The Mishnah devotes an entire order to the legal disposition and categorization of women, and femaleness is a significant factor for determining status throughout the rabbinic system. By and large, women are codified by the rabbis as private persons, restricted primarily to the domestic realm. Men, by contrast, are public citizens, active in public ritual and assumed to bear communal and civic responsibilities. Many of the details that the rabbinic system defines find no precedent in earlier Jewish records, and even if the rabbis inherited significant elements of their notions of maleness and femaleness, they give definition to this opposition as did no Jews before them.

But can this opposition have found symbolic representation in dairy and meat foods? The association of milk, and hence dairy, and femaleness is perhaps "natural" in any culture. It is females who produce milk and hence milk may readily stand in for "female." When we recall that the Torah prohibits the cooking of a kid in its "*mother's* milk," this association will be admitted as all the more natural in a Jewish context. Even if milk, in its natural state, was not the common dairy food of the early rabbinic era, this connection is sufficiently powerful for this cultural significance (dairy = female) to be sustained.

The association of meat and maleness will derive from the fact that meat was a relatively rare food, consumed primarily on special, public occasions. In the pre-rabbinic era, when the Jerusalem Temple stood at the center of the Jewish nation and its religio-cultural consciousness, meat was associated, first, with formal sacrifices, and the sacrificial system was controlled by men. Men (priests) slaughtered the animals and men (priests) were qualified to eat greater portions of the sacrificed animals. Certain sacrificial products, particularly the meat of the Paschal Lamb, could be consumed by women, but even in this case, it was male heads-of-household[10] who determined the groups in which the Paschal meal would be enjoyed. In the post-Temple era, the reality of men controlling the occasions when flesh was consumed cannot have changed much. Meat-eating was still primarily restricted to Sabbath and festival meals, and these meals, as formal and often communal occasions, were still largely directed by the male characters in the ritual drama. As an occasional, festive food, meat will have been more associated with men than with women, and it is no stretch, therefore, to imagine the meat-dairy opposition as encoding a parallel male-female opposition. Such a symbolic dichotomy would have been quite natural in the early rabbinic context.

So reference to interpretations of the practice of separating milk and meat in other cultures provides us with some tools for understanding the rabbinic practice. Still, we must ask whether other interpretations serve equally well in the rabbinic context, interpretations that reflect realities particular to the early rabbinic condition.

The first such possibility, I want to suggest, emerges from the historical context that gave birth to the rabbinic movement, and from the impact of the destruction of the Jerusalem Temple in particular. As we have said, for Palestinian Jews of the first century, meat was inevitably associated with the Temple's sacrificial system. But as the rabbis began to form as a group, the Temple was destroyed, and the Judaism the rabbis sought to promulgate was formulated largely in response to that destruction. Still, the centrality of the Temple, symbolically at least, did not quickly wane. Common Jews expressed their hope for its restoration in the symbols that decorated their synagogues and tombs. The rabbis, too, devoted considerable attention to preserving its active memory in their extensive codification of Temple and sacrificial laws. And they insisted that Jews mourn the destruction actively. Notably, one such sign of mourning, proposed but deemed too extreme in the rabbinic estate, was the avoidance of meat (b. Baba Batra 60b). Why this proposal? Because, as we said, meat was the stuff of animal sacrifice, and if the sacrifice could no longer be offered, meat—so closely associated with the sacrifices—should also be shunned. Meat served as a powerful reminder of and symbol for the Temple, and in the Temple's absence meat could never fully escape its role as mournful reminder.

Dairy, on the other hand, is the only food that had no place in the Temple service. Grain, wine and oils were all part of the regular offerings. First fruits and tithes, which included grains, vegetables and fruits, were all brought to the Temple on an annual basis. But there was no place for milk or cheese, either alone or in combination with other ingredients. Thus, dairy, of all foods, would well serve as the symbol of "non-Temple." If meat represents Temple and dairy non-Temple, then this food opposition will effectively stand in for an ancient and crucial cultural opposition. It was always true, and should continue to be true, that Temple and non-Temple do not mix. Did meat and dairy—and the prohibition of mixing them— symbolically enact the Temple centered world, now lost? Did Jews after the destruction seek to preserve the former opposition in the substance of Temple food and non-Temple food? While we could never be sure of such an interpretation, we must admit that it is suggestive.

In all of the discussion until this point, we have explored various possible symbolisms of the milk-meat prohibition, and sought to understand how these symbolisms give expression to underlying religious and cultural values and structures. But while pursuing this line of interpretation, we have failed to observe what is perhaps the most powerful—and therefore meaningful—consequence of the new rabbinic prohibition. On a purely pragmatic level, if the milk-meat prohibition is an innovation, promulgated by the rabbis and accepted only by those who followed them, then this enactment will effectively have separated rabbinic from non-rabbinic Jews on significant occasions. Presumably, non-rabbinic Jews continued to eat like pre-rabbinic Jews. That is, if they respected Jewish custom at all (and the evidence suggests that many did), they will have avoided the animals proscribed by the Torah. But thy needed have no concern for the mixing of meat and dairy. The small rabbinized population, by contrast, will have distinguished themselves from the general Jewish population by creating separations between meat and dairy. The new rabbinic prohibition, in other words, separated Jew from Jew (at least on certain occasions) and set off rabbinic Jews as the keepers of what was then a more esoteric law.

This, indubitably, will have been the pragmatic consequence of the new laws. But how are we to understand this development in context? It seems to me that the meaning of this development comes into focus when we recall the sectarian atmosphere of the late second Temple period. This period was, as we commented earlier, the most sectarian in all of Jewish history (until modernity, that is).[11] During these centuries, Jew was divided against Jew with disturbing frequency. The religious landscape was marked by numerous sects, the Pharisees, Sadducees and Essenes being (by virtue of Josephus's attentions) only the best known. Scribes also may have formed a distinct social group as, obviously, did early Christians. And, in the face of the war with Rome, Jew literally battled Jew, with different generals gathering their own forces and fighting jealously not for the Jewish nation but for their own superiority. In this respect, though, nothing was new; the same condition characterized the earlier war with Hellenistic Syria, when different Jewish parties fought one another as much as they did the Syrians. The Maccabees who emerged as national champions from this war stimulated only further internal Jewish divisions. Jewish sectarian strife—centuries old—continued until at least the late first century CE.

Admittedly, the evidence for continuing divisions after the destruction is less clear. But this is only because the record is so sparse and one-sided. The record of the post-war years comes to us primarily from the rabbis, who were in any case uninterested in what we would call history. Still, if Jewish identity was contested and confused before the destruction, this cannot have changed quickly after the war. It may be true that Pharisees and Sadducees disappeared as distinct parties,[12] but Priests surely survived as a group, and others, too, certainly vied for positions of leadership and power. In the absence of given structures and directions, the question of "where do we go now?" must have been acute. So different parties, with competitive visions, certainly continued to compete for the soul of the people.

The rabbis were but one of these groups, and a rather small one at that. So the rabbis, to constitute themselves as an effective force, had to be identifiable. They had to mark themselves off from common, non-rabbinic Jews. They did this in numerous ways, in fact. One such way was by adopting new and distinct eating practices.

The pragmatics of separation are reinforced by the symbolism of separation. The prohibition of mixing dairy and meat is very different from the ancient biblical prohibition upon animals identified as "impure." In the biblical system, there is an inside and an outside, a permitted and a forbidden. And this marked dichotomy appears to represent (as suggested in chapter two) Israel and the nations. Israel is inside, permitted and pure, the nations are outside, forbidden because impure. The world structured by the food laws echoes the world of Israelite experience—or, at least, the world the way the Israelite elite would have it experienced, that is, a world of "us" and "them."

But the rabbinic law focuses its concern on two *permitted* foods. Both milk/dairy and the meat of pure animals are positively configured in the biblical and rabbinic systems. It is only the mixing of these foods that creates a problem. If we seek a reflection of the social order in the practices of a people—here, *rabbinic* people—we will quickly observe that the gap between rabbinic and non-rabbinic Jews nevertheless still separates the inside from the inside, the pure from the pure. It may be better, in rabbinic opinion, to observe Jewish law according to rabbinic directive and interpretation. But a Jew is still a Jew, and the Torah is still—one way or another—the Torah. So if the dairy-meat prohibition separates Jew from Jew, it does so by declaring, symbolically at least, that both sides are on the inside, both are fundamentally pure. It may be necessary to distinguish rabbinic identity through the promulgation of distinct rabbinic practices. But these practices encode the opinion that, though separation is desirable and mixing problematic, this is true on only limited occasions. Otherwise, a Jew is a Jew.

Again, when we consider the realities of the ancient cuisine, we will quickly recognize how limited the practical—and therefore symbolic—scope of these rabbinic innovations. If meat was consumed by most people on only limited and special occasions, then this law will infrequently have been called upon. At a common meal, the question of separation will simply not have arisen. Thus, in the regular course of things, a rabbinic meal will have been identical to a non-rabbinic meal, and rabbinic and non-rabbinic Jews could have eaten together without restriction. Only when gathering for the Sabbath or other festive occasions would meat be present and the concern for separation therefore arise. The rabbis evidently judged that on these occasions for the celebration of identity, it was better for rabbinic Jews to celebrate in their distinct groupings. In this manner they would enact the opinion that "we are the same, but also different."

First century Palestine was also, culturally speaking, Hellenistic. In an article entitled "Eaters of Flesh, Drinkers of Milk," Brent Shaw documents a Hellenistic cultural prejudice against "eaters of meat" and "drinkers of milk."[13] The people who regularly ate meat and drank milk, in the ancient Greek and Hellenistic experience, were pastoral nomads, that is—from the perspective of civilized Greeks—*barbarians*. This prejudice goes all the way back to Homer, who described the savage Cyclopes as eating wild flesh and drinking milk (Odyssey IX, 190–91, 219–25, 244–49). Herodotus described Scythian nomads as "eaters of meat"—often raw—and "drinkers of milk," and he viewed them as barbaric, much in contrast to the civilized farmers of his own nation (cited in Shaw, 13–14). He wrote the same about African pastoralists in general (IV, 186.1). Aristotle, too, saw pastoralism as primitive, because hunting and gathering demand no cultural transformation of the food. He wrote: "pastoral nomads . . . their means of subsistence is derived from domesticated animals and is gained without any labour and at their leisure" (see Politics 1256a.29–40 and 1256b.1–2; Shaw, 18–19). In other words, they are lazy. Civilized Greeks, by contrast, work to produce their food. So Greek culture, and the Romans who inherited its prejudices, associated milk and meat eating with pastoral nomads, that is, with barbarians (Shaw, 26).

There can be no question that some Palestinian Jews in the ancient period knew Greek and Hellenistic culture and literature; even the rabbis refer to "the books of Homer" (m. Yadaim 4:6). Jews in the ancient world in general—both Palestinian and non-Palestinian—participated in Hellenistic-Roman culture and often aspired to emulate its values and mores.[14] And Jews, like others, partook of a typical Roman-Mediterranean cuisine—the triad comprised of bread, wine, and olive oil. In recognition of this fact, it comes as no surprise that it is precisely bread and wine that attract unique blessings in the rabbinic system. They are, after all, the most important components of the ancient Mediterranean (= Hellenistic and Roman) diet. Thus, the prejudices that privileged bread, wine, and olives, and shunned flesh and milk, must have been known to Palestinian Jews as well. Crucially, the Hellenistic peoples of antiquity continued to eat meat in religious contexts,[15] and cheese too formed part of the diet (Garnsey, 16). The same pattern typifies Jewish eating, as rabbinic literature testifies. So the Hellenistic-Roman cuisine and its prejudices were adopted by Palestinian Jews. But what, you may ask, does this have to do with the rabbinic prohibition?

By avoiding the simultaneous consumption of meat and dairy, a Jew would be distancing herself from the very combination that, in Hellenistic prejudice, would mark her as a barbarian. The combination of these foods had a symbolic power, and by avoiding the symbol one would avoid its connotations. Was a Jew a barbarian? Assuredly not. Should a Jew, like a barbarian, regularly eat meat and drink milk? Again, certainly not. Some meat on special public and ritual occasions, or cheese in its proper place? Surely. But this was a civilized Roman practice. What the milk-meat prohibition assured is that the Jew would not be able to eat like the barbarian. Instead, he would eat like a cultured citizen of the Roman Empire.

Is it possible that this ancient prejudice contributed to the development of the new rabbinic law? By itself, certainly not. But, in combination with other cultural and symbolic forces, reasonably yes. As I commented above, there is no question that Palestinian Jewry was highly acculturated, and most surely viewed the civilized elements of Roman culture as worthy of emulation (while still shunning offensive religious or cultural expressions). Of course, they might not have been consciously aware of these motivations, no more than they were of the other cultural and historical forces and associations which impelled the generation of these new practices. But people are often unaware of the forces that motivate them to construct rituals and other cultural expressions.[16] This makes such explanations no less likely. In the combination of forces we have discussed—some if not all of them—we may discover the impetus for the development of this significant and radical new eating practice.

The Talmud (Hullin 108a) calls the prohibition upon mixing meat and dairy a "*ḥiddush*," literally, an innovation. It is unlikely that this means to admit what I have claimed above—that the prohibition is a rabbinic innovation. The common interpretation of the Hebrew term, in context, is "anomaly" or something of that sort. In other words, the prohibition is recognized within the system as being different, unexpected, even "weird." What does this weird new law tell us about the identity of the rabbis who adopted it?

Accepting, for the moment, the interpretations considered above, it tells us that they continued to be concerned for the powerful biblical opposition between life and death, and they saw these as realms that should not be promiscuously mixed. It tells us that they saw human society as divided between male and female domains, and similarly judged that these should not mix. Also to be kept separate were the world of the Temple and the world beyond its walls, and, at least on special occasions, the world of the rabbis and the world of non-rabbinic Jews. Finally, those foods which represented the barbarian were, at least in their combination, to be avoided by Jews. Jews may be distinct from other citizens of the Roman Empire, but they do participate in that civilization. God forbid they should be seen as the barbaric outsider.

Of course, we cannot be sure of any of these interpretations, and no one of them suffices to explain the development of this "weird" new prohibition. But that is precisely the crucial point. Ritual practices and symbols never mean just one thing. Their power is in their ability to embody and communicate multiple meanings and messages. And the more such social and religious meanings may be inscribed upon a single practice or ritual act, the more powerful it will be and the more likely to be accepted by significant segments of a society. So, while we may not be sure of any of the meanings proposed earlier, the fact that they may, in their multiplicity, be "discovered" in the practice of separating dairy and meat, goes a long way toward explaining not only why this practice developed but why it was ultimately adopted by the vast majority of practicing Jews. By respecting the prohibition of mixing these foods, they declared that they were the sort of Jews the rabbis desired them to be. Knowing that "dairy" and "meat" were meaningful categories, they entered the world of rabbinic Jewish identity.

It is significant that the subject of this new law is "mixing." Mixing was perhaps the single most important Jewish identity question from the late second Temple period through at least the first several centuries of the Common Era. With whom may a Jew mix? To what extent may he or she mix with non-Jews? When may such mixing take place? When not? And may a rabbinic Jew mix with a non-rabbinic Jew? When? How significantly? For what purposes? Most crucially, what mix of the elements of ambient identities—traditional Jewish and new Jewish, Jewish and civilized Roman—should the "good" Jew seek to achieve? Mixing, not mixing, and how mixing are the issues. In this chapter we have examined one way that questions of mixing were embodied in the law. In the next chapter, we will consider how mixing, as a more general question, became central to rabbinic discussions and practices, and how this focus gave way to new applications which also served to express the direction of ancient Jewish identity.

5 The rabbinic period
Problematic mixings

The moment certain foods are designated as prohibited, the question arises: What must one do if a forbidden food comes to be mixed with permitted foods? There are a variety of ways to imagine the realities that would lead to asking this question. In the rabbinic context, what should one do if a drop of milk is accidentally dropped into a pot of meat? What should a Jew, rabbinic or not, do if a piece of prohibited meat comes to be mixed with permitted meat? What if some other prohibited substance comes to be mixed in with permitted foods? The ways such a problem might arise are endless, and it is impossible for a system of eating regulations to exist in reality unless solutions to such problems are available.

Of course, the nature and frequency of these problems will differ depending upon the context in which the observing Jewish community dwells. If Jews lived only amongst themselves, having little or no regular contact with non-Jews, then they would have little cause to worry about the possible intermixture of prohibited flesh, and they would similarly have little reason to concern themselves with problems relating to "gentile" foods. They would, in the case of an irresponsible butcher or slaughterer, have to worry lest improperly slaughtered meat find its way into their home (the rabbis and possibly Jews before them required animals for profane consumption to be slaughtered in a fashion analogous to sacrifices). And they might more regularly confront the problem of bits of meat or dairy falling into foods of the other category. By contrast, if Jews lived with non-Jewish neighbors—shopping at many of the same shops and trading together on a regular basis—then prohibited foods would be ever-present and the question of what to do in the case of mixtures would be more frequently asked. Needless to say, if Jews enjoyed regular social contact, and even friendly relations, with those non-Jewish neighbors, then the question of how complete the separation from prohibited foods must be would be urgent. In fact, considering the problem this way, we quickly realize that regulations concerning mixtures and separations are intimately bound with questions of socializing with those who consume what is prohibited. Legislating one will inevitably regulate the other.

Yet, despite the obvious relevance of these questions, no pre-rabbinic text suggests a solution to the prohibited mixture problem. Nowhere do we learn what to do if prohibited substance is mixed with permitted substance. We might surmise a continuity between rabbinic regulations in this matter and earlier Jewish practices, but his would be mere surmise. For all we know, in the pre- and non-rabbinic worlds, the smallest quantity of prohibited food would render an entire mixture forbidden. There is certainly nothing in the pre-rabbinic record to suggest that this was *not* the case. When we approach the rabbinic record, then, we stand without a basis for comparison. We simply cannot know whether rabbinic regulations concerning mixtures are significantly innovative or completely traditional. It seems to me that the absence of any prior record suggests the former is more likely than the latter. Yet, whether this is the case or not, rabbinic laws of mixtures do, nevertheless, provide an important window into rabbinic Jewish identity in the first centuries of the Common Era.

The earliest rabbinic statements concerning mixtures are scattered through the Mishnah. The most pertinent are the following:

1. A thigh which was cooked with the sciatic nerve [forbidden in Gen. 32:33], if it [= the prohibited nerve] *gives taste* [to the thigh flesh], it is prohibited. How do we measure it [given the fact that the taste of the nerve and the flesh in which it is imbedded is the same]? As though it were meat in turnip stew.

   If the sciatic nerve was cooked with other sinews, *if it is distinguishable*, [the prohibition begins] at the *giving of taste*. But *if not*, all [of the sinews] are prohibited, and the gravy [is prohibited] when taste is given. And so, too, a piece of prohibited meat and so too a piece of impure fish which were cooked with other pieces, *when they are distinguishable*, [the prohibition begins] at the *giving of taste*. And *if not*, they are all prohibited. But the gravy [is prohibited] when taste is given. (M. Hullin 7:4–5)

2. A drop of milk which fell on a piece [of meat], *if taste has been given* to that piece [it is prohibited]. If he stirred the pot, *if taste has been given* to the pot [as a whole, it is prohibited]. (M. Hullin 8:3)[1]

3. Wine that has been poured out [in the worship of idols] is prohibited, and it prohibits [substance with which it has been mixed] in *the smallest measure*. Wine [mixed] in wine, and water [that has been used in idolatrous worship] in water, [prohibits] in *the smallest measure*. [But] wine in water or water in wine, [prohibits only] *when it gives taste*. This is the general rule: something mixed in its own kind [prohibits] in the smallest measure, but [if mixed] not in its own kind [it prohibits] when it gives taste. (M. Avodah Zarah 5:8)

4. Wheat leavening [that has been separated as the priestly portion] which fell into [common] wheat dough, and there is a sufficient quantity to leaven [the dough], whether or not there is *a quantity of 100 to 1* [of

dough relative to leavening] it is prohibited [despite the general rule of priestly gifts, according to which the priestly portion will be annulled by 100 measures of common substance]. If there is not a quantity of 100 to 1, whether or not there is a sufficient measure to cause leavening, it is [according to the normal rule] prohibited [because there is not a sufficient quantity to annul]....

Beans [that have been separated as the priestly portion] that were cooked with [common] lentils, *if they give taste*, whether or not there is a quantity of 100 to 1 [of lentils relative to the beans] it is prohibited. *If they do not give taste*, whether or not there is a quantity of 100 to 1 [of lentils relative to the beans] it is permitted. (M. Orlah 2:6–7)

5. [Sacrificial] blood [meant to be poured on the altar] which was mixed with water, if it has the *appearance* of blood, it is fit [to be poured]. If it was mixed in wine, we figure it as though it [= the wine] is water. If it was mixed in the blood of a domestic animal [not meant for the altar] or a wild animal [not fit for the altar], we figure it as though it is water. R. Judah says: blood cannot annul blood. (M. Zevahim 8:6) (All emphases in the above translations are added.)

First, an observation relating to all of these texts: the first three all, in effect, ask a common question—at what point does the in-mixing of a prohibited substance make the mixture prohibited? The fourth Mishnah, from Orlah, also asks this question, but the way it expresses the question (its reference to the 100 to 1 proportional measure) makes it clear that there is another way to ask, that is, when has the prohibited substance been *annulled*? This way of conceptualizing the process is explicit in the last quoted Mishnah, from Zevahim. Despite these two different ways of expressing the question, it is clear that these are really two sides of the same coin. When one asks about the minimum quantity at which the prohibited substance will render the whole prohibited, one assumes that anything less than that measure will have no consequence. The substance will, for practical purposes, be annulled. By the same token, if one says that a prohibited substance is annulled if it is equivalent to one in one-hundred or less, one is at the same time saying that a lesser quantity will not cause the whole to be prohibited. In these respects, these texts are asking a common question.

But there are also obviously significant differences between them. The first three texts discuss mixtures of prohibited foods, though the nature of the prohibition in #3 is different from that in the first two. These first two, from adjacent chapters in the tractate discussing laws of *kashrut*, are consistent with one another. Assuming the prohibited substance either can be removed or disappears from sight (because the foods have been stirred together), the mixture will be prohibited only if the forbidden substance imparts taste to the mixture as a whole. If no taste has been imparted—or no taste would be imparted if the substances in question had distinguishable tastes (see #1)—the mixture is thoroughly permitted and forbidden substance, if present, is as though naught.

How is the imparting of taste to be determined? The Mishnah doesn't say, presumably because it doesn't consider this a serious problem. May a Jew taste the mixture to ascertain whether taste has been imparted? Perhaps. To justify this, we would merely have to assume that the mixture is not technically prohibited until taste has been determined. Would it be better to ask a non-Jewish neighbor to taste the mixture to make this determination? Perhaps. The crucial point is that such a determination can be made and prohibited substance may, in fact, have no consequence.

The Mishnah from Avodah Zarah (#3) seems to demand a more stringent standard, prohibiting at least certain mixtures however minute the quantity of prohibited substance present. As we read the first part of the Mishnah, we might surmise that this is because we are now talking about foodstuff used in the service of idols—a taboo of the highest order. But, surprisingly, the rule found at the conclusion of this same Mishnah suggests that the issue is not idolatry but the relationship of the foods that have been combined. If they are of the same kind, no nullification of the prohibited substance is possible, but if of a different kind, then the prohibited food may, given an adequate quantity of permitted food, be nullified, just so long as its taste has not been imparted. Presumably, the same is not possible is the case of a mixture of like kinds because their tastes are identical and it is impossible, therefore, to determine whether the taste of the prohibited food may be detected. Admittedly, in the case described in #1, the Mishnah allows for the nullification of a food with the same taste (the sciatic nerve), but this may be because the nerve is of a different "kind" than the flesh of the thigh.

The setting changes in the next two quoted Mishnahs, but the first of them (#4), at least, still respects the importance of the imparting of taste. This Mishnah, discussing the obligatory agricultural gifts to priests (*terumah*), knows that, as a general rule, misplaced priestly portions can be nullified in a ratio of 100 to 1 (see M. Orlah 2:1). But if the priestly portion has a particularly strong effect upon a mixture—if it causes it to leaven or spices it—then the rules are more stringent. Simply put, in this case, the outcome generally depends upon the rule already spelled out in Avodah Zarah: are we talking about same kinds or different kinds? If same kinds, we take the most stringent position available. If different kinds, then the "giving of taste" principal takes precedence over the "100 to one annulment" principal. Taste remains important—these portions will, after all, be eaten by the priests—but it does not stand alone. Uniquely, and for the first time, a specific measure is also relevant to the adjudication of mixtures.

The last quoted Mishnah, the first discussing a mixture that will not be consumed as food, is also the first in which taste is not a factor when judging the status of the mixture. The reason for this shift is perhaps obvious: the subject of the Mishnah's discussion is sacrificial blood to be poured on the altar of the Temple (the discussion, therefore, is purely theoretical), and sacrificial blood is not "tasted." The principle the rabbis define is whether or not the mixed liquid has the appearance of blood. If it does, it is considered blood and therefore may be poured, if not, it is unfit for pouring.

So regulations concerning mixtures are appropriately adapted for their particular context. And, appropriately, whenever the mixed substances are foods and might be eaten, the determining factor is whether the taste of the prohibited food is evident. Significantly, this measure is a subjective one. It is also, it seems to me, a relatively lenient one. Both realities merit comment.

"The giving of taste" is not a universal standard. Persons' tastes differ, and a flavor that may be evident to one person may be imperceptible to another. Nothing in these various Mishnahs attempts to deny or overcome this fact. Thus, when we ask how the imparting of taste is to be determined, we must bear in mind the subjective nature of the determination. If what matters is how the mixture tastes *to you*, then we must assume that *you* are the one who will taste it. You will approach the forbidden substance and judge its status, in a personal and even intimate way. It is your relationship with the forbidden, in other words, that is determinative.

This same subjective measure is also, arguably, rather lenient, though this judgment requires explanation. In theory, at least, making taste—as opposed to substance—the determining factor leads to a possible stringency: even if the substance is physically removed, if taste remains, the mixture is forbidden. Similarly, if taste cannot be determined—such as when like is mixed with like—then the mixture must be prohibited. But compare the contrary. Let us suppose that what matters is the presence of the prohibited substance. This would mean that, whenever forbidden matter is present in the mixture, even if it cannot be seen or tasted, the mixture is prohibited. Such an approach would obviously allow for far less flexibility, for this would render nullification of prohibited matter impossible. The alternative approach declares, by contrast, that if you cannot taste it, it is not there—a radical claim indeed.

The principal of "giving taste" introduces a standard where one was not previously known. Such a standard, subjective though it may be, is typical of the world constructed by the rabbis and, like standards in general, it makes possible what earlier might not have been. This dynamic—how the introduction of new standards potentially creates new leniencies—has not been sufficiently appreciated, but it is easily demonstrated. In my study of a historically analogous case, that of labors prohibited on the Sabbath, I found that the single prohibition that is agreed upon by all sources after the Torah is the one concerning carrying. Every literary record which testifies in any way to ancient Sabbath practice includes, in its testimony, a prohibition directed against carrying from the public to a private domain, or vice versa. But no source suggests how the difficulties created by this prohibition might be overcome—until the rabbis. By defining, in a precise way, what constitutes a public or private domain, and by creating, as a matter of definition, domains which are counted as neither of the above, the rabbis allow for the transformation of "public" into "private" and for the ultimate elimination of the public domain as a meaningful factor.[2] The introduction of definitions—of standards that did not previously exist—makes the law not more onerous but less. By knowing precisely what is forbidden, you also know what is permitted.

The same, I want to argue, may be true in the case of food laws. As I said earlier, we have no record of how the cases discussed in the Mishnah might have been handled during the Second Temple period (or by Jews who did not accept rabbinic standards). But it is possible to imagine the following scenario: let us suppose I am sitting in my market stall enjoying my afternoon meal—a soup made from vegetables boiled with bones left from the lamb I had enjoyed with my family the prior Sabbath. Past my stall walks the local butcher—a non-Jew—carrying scraps he will sell for soups or stews. As he stops to chat briefly, he mistakenly drops a small scrap of pig fat into my soup. What am I to do? Well, what choice do I have? There is a piece of pig fat—of impure animal—in my food. If I am to follow the Torah's law prohibiting the consumption of such impure substance, I must discard the soup. Anything less would be an impious compromise.

Of course, the next time my non-Jewish neighbor stops by to chat while I am eating, I will be wary; what if he drops something again? And if this sort of thing happens more than once, I will be apt to avoid his company, at least when there is food around. Moreover, if the prohibited food is identified as "gentile food"—that is, if the food represents the person—then the anxiety which leads to the avoidance of the food will ultimately teach avoidance of the person. In the absence of rules of nullification, the company of the gentile is rendered both pragmatically and symbolically problematic.

But then the rabbis come along and define a minimum threshold. At what point does the intermixture of prohibited food render the entire mixture forbidden? When it imparts taste. Less than this quantity is of no concern. Thus, to return to the same market stall, if my neighbor mistakenly drops a piece of pig fat in my soup, I have to ask whether the taste of that fat is likely to be detectable. If the answer is obviously no, I may go ahead and partake of the soup without hesitation—and without having committed an impiety. If I do not know the answer, then I might take a small taste of the soup to ascertain whether taste has been imparted. Or, if I am afraid that the taste of the pig fat might be present, I might ask that same gentile butcher to taste the soup for me. He, in other words, might now be instrumental in the operation of my law. The consequences of this shift, both pragmatically and symbolically, are immense. Under the conditions established by the rabbinic regulations, it will be quite a bit easier for me to live in close proximity to my gentile neighbor. If there is a mishap in the market or at the table, the outcome might not be as grave. I might well find that the prohibited food is nullified, that what was a moment before taboo is now permitted. Furthermore, by lowering the degree of fear and avoidance of gentile food, the law intimates that the fear and avoidance of the gentile is less severe a concern. He or she remains the source of potential problems, to be sure, but modest mixing—mixing that will not leave its "taste" behind—is allowable.

Matters change significantly when we turn to the subsequent rabbinic record, the gemara. Here, for the first time, we witness an attempt to introduce a standard measure for the nullification of prohibited substance. The most direct statement of this position is this: "R. Hiyya b. Abba said that R. Joshua b. Levi said in the name of Bar Kappara: All substances forbidden by the Torah [are nullified] by a measure of sixty [to one]....R. Asi said that R. Joshua b. Levi said in the name of Bar Kappara: All substances forbidden by the Torah [are nullified] by a measure of one hundred [to one] (Hullin 98a)."

Both traditions, the gemara claims, derive their measurement from a common source—the Nazirite offering. According to the Torah (as understood by the rabbis), following the period of a Nazirite vow, the Nazirite must bring a ram as an offering. The shoulder of the ram, the portion for the priest, is to be cooked together with the ram, the remainder of which will be eaten by the former Nazirite (see Numbers 6:13–21). If the Torah permits the portion of the Nazir (assumed to be a common Israelite) to be eaten after it has been cooked with the priest's portion, then the remains of this portion must somehow have been nullified. In the gemara's telling, this must have been a result of the "overwhelming" quantity of the ram relative to the shoulder portion, estimated differently (60 to 1 or 100 to 1) by the sages whose opinions are recorded.

The claim that the named authorities actually derive their measurements from the stated source is obviously tendentious. Even Rashi, the well-known medieval commentator, admits that this is so. Clearly, the gemara wants to establish an accepted standard measure, and it will go to considerable lengths to insist upon such a standard. Even the Mishnah from Orlah which, in the case of diverse kinds, declares that taste takes priority over numbered measurement, is made to support one or the other (sixty or one hundred) universal standard (see Hullin 99a–b). In the end, it is the one-in-sixty standard that is accepted, and it serves the gemara through a variety of discussions. Not surprisingly, once this measure is standardized, the Mishnahs quoted earlier must be reinterpreted in often novel ways.

Once the one-in-sixty standard is introduced, the question of how different methods of nullification should be applied arises. Proposed solutions appear in two contradictory teachings, both attributed to the prolific sage, Rava. In the first, Rava is quoted as having said:

> The rabbis said "taste" and the rabbis said "with a [gentile] cook" and the rabbis said "in a measure of sixty." Therefore, [in a case of] diverse kinds each of which is permitted [to at least some Jews, such as priests], rely on taste. Diverse kinds that are prohibited [such as milk and meat],

rely on [the tasting of] a [gentile] cook. And [a mixture] of the same kind, in which case you cannot rely on taste, or diverse (prohibited) kinds when there is no [gentile] cook [available], rely on a measure of sixty [to one]. (Hullin 97a–b)

In the second, Rava is quoted as having said:

The rabbis said "taste" and the rabbis said "with a majority [quantity of the permitted substance]" and the rabbis said "according to appearance." [In a case of] diverse kinds, rely on taste. [In the case of a mixture] of the same kind, rely on a majority measure. Where appearance is what matters, rely on appearance. (Zevahim 79a)

Needless to say, these two traditions are at odds with one another in significant ways. In a mixture of diverse kinds, the second tradition directs us to rely only on taste; in the first tradition, it depends upon whether the mixed kinds are permitted or prohibited. If prohibited, then we are directed to allow a gentile cook to taste the mixture—still a determination of taste, and so still in agreement with the second tradition. But where there is no gentile cook on whose taste to rely, the first tradition directs that we determine whether there is a 60 to 1 proportion of permitted to prohibited substance, a measurement which the second tradition seems not to know. And even if we want to claim that 60 to 1 is the proportion in which, it is estimated, taste will be given (as Rashi, in his commentary, wants to claim), we still have to admit that we are in the presence of a significant development: if ratio = taste, then what was earlier subjective and variable (it would depend, after all, on the taste of the foods involved) is now "objective" and inflexible.

Moreover, the rules for like kinds are obviously contradictory: the first tradition suggests that a prohibited food mixed in permitted food of its same kind (such as improperly slaughtered beef in kosher beef) will be nullified by a measure of 60 to 1, while the second tradition requires a mere majority. These are radically different measures, and the law as lived will be different in the extreme, depending upon which is accepted. Needless to say, the subsequent tradition saw a need to reconcile this contradiction and (based upon a hint found in the gemara at Hullin 98b) proposed that a "majority" is what the Torah would require whereas 60 to 1 is a rabbinic stringency.

Whatever the internal workings of the talmudic tradition, it is the overall significance of these developments that concerns us here. How are we to understand the transition from taste to measure?

The first factor contributing to this transition may be a more general phenomenon, of no particular pertinence to the eating laws as such. Though principles are implicit throughout the Mishnah, and explicit on rare occasions, the Mishnah's law is generally characterized by its tendency to locate its rulings in "real life" (actual or imagined). In matters of measurement, this means the Mishnah will use the experiential or subjective measures of a prestandardized world, commonly associated with the body or natural phenomena. For example, the Mishnah's measure for an amount of liquid that, if drunk on Yom Kippur, will make the transgressor liable is "his cheek-full" (M. Yoma 8:2). But in the gemara, "real life" often becomes abstract principle and measures often strive toward standardization. This is not to say that the variation and subjectivity of the Mishnah disappears (as it does, mostly, in later Judaism). It is simply to note that the gemara tends toward systemization and principle. The insistence on a 60 to 1 measure is a step in that direction.

More important, in the present context, is the recognition that (as the gemara claims at Hullin 98b) the narrowing of nullification possibilities until a threshold of 60 to 1 is achieved is, indeed, a stringency. If taste is the operative factor, then the relative measure of foods in a mixture will change depending upon how strong the flavor of each food. A piece of bland food will be considerably easier to nullify than a food with a stronger taste. And, undeniably, the taste of many foods will be undetectable before we arrive at a quantity of 60 to 1. So the introduction of the measure raises the bar, making nullification—in many cases, at least—more difficult.

But we must also remark on what the new measure does *not* do. First, while requiring sixty-to-one does make certain nullifications more difficult, it does not do so in all cases. In fact, in certain instances it actually makes nullification possible. For example, if we are speaking of the same kind of food, relying on taste will do nothing, but application of the principal of relative quantity (whatever the quantity) will. Second, while the new measure may often be more stringent than the taste method, it does not eliminate the possibility of nullifying the prohibited substance. As any observant Jew knows, this makes an immense difference. It means that, if a drop of milk falls into a stew-pot of meat, one need not discard the contents of the pot. To appreciate this difference, imagine the contrary—a situation in which such nullification is not possible, and pots (or at least their contents), therefore, must be discarded with some regularity. Even the "stringent" measure is more lenient than no measure.

Third, and possibly most crucial, the so-called standard measure of 60 to 1 is, in fact, not standard at all. In many circumstances, the judgment of "nullified or not nullified?" will be made after the prohibited substance is mixed in. Even if the prohibited substance is still visible and has, to the extent possible, been removed, the question of relative measure remains very difficult. We are not, after all, speaking of laboratory conditions. No scales or standard measuring devices are likely to be available. The judgment will be left to the individual who may or may not consume the dish, and it will therefore be approximate, at best. In effect, the demand of 60 measures to 1 is a declaration that "a small amount of prohibited matter is acceptable, more than that is not." It does not eliminate totally the variation inherent in the "taste" standard and it does not remove the private individual from the position of judging. This latter point, in particular, demands our notice, for reasons we shall consider below.

To repeat, the move toward "standardized" measures does not change the reality of rabbinic laws of mixture entirely. It is still possible to nullify prohibited foods, at least in small quantities. Hence, the Jew must be careful in the presence of the gentile and his food, but he need not avoid his company completely. The food to be avoided, and the gentile it represents, remain "forbidden" in certain respects; they may not be "ingested" whole. But they are not taboo in the more mysterious sense. They have no miasmic quality. It is fine to be in their presence, and their small influences need not be feared. Only in quantity does their danger become great.

The law also remains imprecise, and the judge remains the individual whose food is in question. Crucially, there is no other expert here. We find no demand that a rabbi or other specialist be consulted. Rather, it is the common person who is assumed to know the law and the common person who is deemed qualified to make a judgment. We might surmise that, practically speaking, it could only be this way. We are speaking, after all, of the everyday business of food preparation, an event so common, so mundane, and so domestic, that it would be absurd to demand regular expert intervention. To require that a householder consult a rabbi every time meat gravy fell in her soured milk would make rabbinic law onerous if not impossible—not a good strategy for the acceptance of a "Torah" that the common Jew had not, in the second–fifth centuries, yet adopted.

But locating expertise in the hands of the common person has more than pragmatic significance. Whatever the practical considerations affecting the adjudication of such questions, it is not hard to imagine a class of "experts" who demand that they alone have the authority to decide. In fact, this is exactly what the rabbis did in the case of slaughtering knives or the evaluation of intestinal blemishes (both questions restricted to the activities of a smaller class of persons). And they did not stop there. Even in such private matters as the judging of the status of vaginal blood with respect to its purity or impurity, the rabbis insisted that they, alone, are the experts.[3] So when matters such as the evaluation of the permissibility of mixtures are left in the hands of common Jews, this is a decision of considerable significance. The question is, simply, what is its significance?

As we have seen before, meat eating was, in the ancient world, associated primarily with religious occasions. Furthermore, all slaughter was, in significant respects, "sacred slaughter."[4] This had surely been so centuries before in Israel. It did not cease to be so in these centuries. For this reason, laws concerning the preparation of animals for food are found in the Mishnaic tractate whose full name—*sheḥitat ḥullin*—translates as "the slaughter of common things" (associated with, but not identical to, "the slaughter of holy things"), and the tractate is in turn located in the Mishnaic order of "Holy Things." (Of course, this tractate is the very one that includes the laws we have been discussing.) Furthermore, as we will see in the next chapter, the laws of food preparation are supplemented by directions for a series of ritual blessings, to be recited prior to eating, which mark the food as sacred property rendered profane. Hence, when a person acts as arbiter of what is fit for the table—what animals are permitted or not?, what mixtures may be retained and which must be discarded?—he or she is serving in the function of priest. As the priest serves in the domain of the sacred table (the altar), the common Jew serves—the rabbis affirm—in the domain of the common table/altar. Rather than restricting authority, they disperse authority. All Israel is a nation of priests.

The democratization of this "priestly" function finds an instructive parallel in the central activity of rabbinic religion and piety, Torah study.[5] According to the rabbinic ideal, all of Israel would be students, and ultimately masters, of Torah. Just as the adjudication of questions of mixed foods marked all of Israel as "priests," so too this rabbinic ideal identified all of Israel as potential masters of the *sanctum sanctorum* of rabbinic Judaism. But consideration of this parallel engenders two important insights. First, while the rabbinic ideal might imagine all of Israel as scholars, the reality allows for only partial realization of this ideal; obviously, not all of Israel could become scholars. By the same token, neither could all of Israel become masters of the regulations concerning mixed foods. The laws that apply here are relatively technical. One would have to submit to rabbinic instruction—or be long socialized in a rabbinic kitchen—in order to have sufficient command of the details of the system. For this reason, in reality many common problems were likely to be handled by the private person, but more difficult and technical questions would have had to be brought to the rabbinic master (for those who submitted to their system in the first place, of course). The practice of mixture laws would point in the direction of a "priestified" Israel, but certain prerogatives would undoubtedly remain in the hands of the "high priests" of the rabbinic system, the rabbis themselves.

The second insight emerges from our realization that, whereas the idealized democratization of Torah study excluded women, both the image and the reality of expertise in the rabbinic eating and food preparation systems included women and men—in all likelihood, more the former than the latter.[6] Women were, with respect to the sorts of questions at issue here, no less expert than men, and they were the ones who, given the social reality, were likely to be the resident experts in "the kitchen." To be sure, women were excluded from being final arbiters in matters where the greatest technical expertise was required. But this still left a considerable range of questions where women were more "priests" of the system than men. Moreover, this was not merely an accommodation to the reality of a woman's important place in the preparation of food, for it is possible to imagine a system where those who prepare food—and therefore must judge what to do when problems arise—will be allowed no discretion whatsoever. Declare all doubtful situations "prohibited" and you have eliminated the "priestly" role. Therefore, the rabbis' yielding of everyday judgments to the everyday experts is an important declaration that, in realms appropriate for their participation (as defined by the rabbis themselves), women were entrusted and empowered masters.

In analyzing the rabbinic laws of mixtures, I have suggested that, both pragmatically and symbolically, they bespeak a relatively permeable social membrane between a (rabbinic) Jew and his or her gentile neighbor. This permeability finds full expression in the real communities of the Roman controlled Jewish Galilee in the second century and beyond. It is also a true description, as far as we know, of relations between Jews and their neighbors in the territories of Babylon.[7] But the openings intimated in the laws of mixtures stand at odds with another series of eating laws—those relating to gentile foods. In this second category of "mixture" laws there seems to be an enormous urgency to maintain impermeable boundaries. The apparently contradictory consequences of these two sets of regulations will command our attentions below.

The Mishnah which lays the foundations of these laws is found in the second chapter of tractate Avodah Zarah ("strange worship"). The tractate generally defines idolatrous worship and the distance a Jew must maintain from it. The second chapter of the tractate elaborates practical regulations whose purpose is to establish such a distance. Among these laws, not surprisingly, are several prohibiting or limiting the consumption of gentile food.

The laws regulating eating are these:

2:3. These things belonging to gentiles are prohibited, and their prohibition extends to deriving any benefit: Wine, and vinegar of gentiles that was originally wine, and Hadrianic pottery, and hides through which the heart has been removed [in the service of foreign deities]....

   Meat on its way in to idolatrous worship is permitted, but that which comes out [from idolatrous worship] is prohibited...these are the words of R. Aqiba.

2:4. [A case where there are] wine-skins belonging to gentiles, or their bottles, and the wine of a Jew is stored in them, the wine is prohibited...

The skins and grape seeds [left after pressing] belonging to gentiles are prohibited, and their prohibition extends to deriving any benefit—these are the words of R. Meir...

   Fish-hash [into which wine has been mixed] and cheese...belonging to gentiles, are prohibited....

2:5. R. Judah said: R. Ishmael asked R. Joshua [a question] when they were walking on the road. He said to him: For what reason have they prohibited the cheeses of gentiles? He said to him: because they curdle it using rennet taken from an animal that was not properly slaughtered....

2:6. These things belonging to gentiles are prohibited, but their prohibition
does not extend to deriving benefit: milk milked by a gentile without a
Jew overseeing him, and bread, and their oil (Rabbi [Judah the Patri-
arch] and his court permitted oil), [8] and boiled foods, and crushed
foods into which they put wine or vinegar, and hashed fish...these
are prohibited, but their prohibition does not extend to deriving any
benefit. (A.Z. 2:3–6)[9]

The prohibition of gentile foods is, of course, an ancient one. In fact, as we
saw in chapter three, some Jews during the Second Temple period extended
this prohibition to *any* gentile food, of any sort whatsoever. The present
list, while extensive, allows for limited exceptions.

The list is divided into two levels of prohibition. In Mishnahs 3–5 the
concern pertains to bona fide idolatry, so the prohibition extends not only
to eating but to "deriving benefit" as well. Practically, what this means is
that such foods may not be sold in order to enjoy the proceeds. In the last
of the quoted Mishnahs (6) the concern is not idolatry as such and so the
listed substances may be sold. The latter list, only part of which is quoted,
includes foods into which prohibited substance may have been mixed (such
as hashed fish or milk which has not been overseen), but it includes other
foods as well. It is these other foods that are of particular interest here.

It is hard to imagine what prohibited substance might be mixed unde-
tected into olive oil.[10] The same is substantially true of bread. Yet these
foods, apparently in their simple forms, are singled out. The question is
why? In the Mishnah's late second century Roman context, it is surely significant that, among other foods, the well-known "Mediterranean triad"—
bread, wine, and olive oil—is subject to the present prohibitions. The most
common and respected foods in the Roman world are prohibited to the Jew
if they have belonged to the gentile. The consequences of this prohibition,
again both pragmatically and symbolically, are staggering.

To fully appreciate this phenomenon, we must first emphasize that these
foods were of as great importance to Jews residing in the eastern Mediterranean as they were to Roman citizens here and elsewhere. The evidence for
this is not only their frequent mention in contemporary rabbinic literature,
but also the fact that bread and wine, at least, attract special blessings in
the blessing system (m. Berakhot 6:1). Bread is not just one food in a larger
category, and neither is wine. Each, when consumed, requires the recitation of a unique formula. This is true of bread, the rabbis explain, because
it is over bread that a person "fixes a meal" (b. Berakhot 35b, 38a). And
wine, it is hardly necessary to observe, has a role not only as a common
drink (mixed with water, in the conventional Roman fashion) but also as
a drink marking special occasions. Of course, it also has "magical" qualities that contribute to its special role in human commensality—it loosens
inhibitions and thus greases the wheels of social intercourse. Both bread
and wine were singled out for ritually significant roles in the variety of

Judaisms of this period, including early Christian circles (Matt. 26:26–29, Mark 14:22–25, Luke 22:14–19) and the Qumran sect ("The Community Rule" [IQS] vi, 3–6). Finally, olive oil had an abundant role in the ancient Mediterranean life, serving as food, fuel and an agent in personal hygiene (for anointing). But its symbolic power, while notable, was less than that of the other two legs in this triad.

So when the rabbis prohibit these gentile foods, they are fully aware of the immensity of the prohibition. How are we to understand its significance?

The obvious result of this prohibition is to make enjoying a meal with a gentile, even in the home of a Jew (because of the consequences of gentile touch with respect to wine), very difficult—and to do so in the home of a gentile would be nearly impossible. To be sure, the gentile could in theory accept the Jew's invitation to join him at his table, an uncomplicated arrangement as long as wine is not served. But what kind of host refuses to offer wine? Moreover, an invitation is an act of hospitality normally to be reciprocated, yet it would be very difficult for the Jew to accept the gentile's reciprocal invitation. The Jew could, in theory, bring his food to the table of the gentile. But the failure to share food, particularly when offered kindly by a host, is on some level an act of rejection. These slights (the failure to offer wine or share food) will communicate a clear message. If meals are central to the establishing and maintaining of social connections, then neighborly relations will be constrained. The rabbinic prohibition, if scrupulously observed, will erect a high fence between Jewish and gentile societies.

The rabbis of the gemara, at least, were fully aware of this. The most pointed evidence of their recognition is a statement explaining the various prohibitions as a causal chain: "Their bread and oil [were forbidden] on account of their wine, and their wine [was forbidden] *on account of their daughters*, and their daughters [were forbidden] on account of 'another thing'" (b. Avodah Zarah 36b, emphasis added). That is to say, if a Jew shares bread and oil with a gentile, he is likely also to share wine. And if he shares wine, he will become an intimate of the gentile and thus come to know his daughter. Under such circumstances, he might be attracted to her and even seek her hand in marriage; at the very least, he may sleep with her. And if he is smitten with her, he may be tempted to cooperate in her idolatrous rites. In consideration of this fear, better not to eat together at all.

The length of this chain of consequences suggests that idolatry is not the *only* thing the rabbis were concerned about. In fact, elsewhere in this same talmudic deliberation, they admit as much. "What did the sages see [that impelled them to prohibit gentile bread]? They were worried about marriage" (ibid. 35b). The same concern motivated them to extend the prohibition of wine (which might actually be used in idolatrous worship) to any strong drink (which is not so used) (ibid. 31b). Jews must be vigilant about maintaining their separation from gentile neighbors. The consequences of not doing so, in the judgment of the sages behind these regulations, are disastrous.

Beyond the obvious pragmatic effects of these laws were powerful symbolic resonances. To begin with, to mark these foods as forbidden was to equate them, if only analogically, with the forbidden foods of the Torah—to say that these foods, like those prohibited in Leviticus and Deuteronomy, are *impure*. But the source of their "impurity" is not biblical, it is "rabbinic" (explicitly so according to rabbinic teachings, even if we know of pre-rabbinic sources and parallels).[11] And, rabbinically speaking, the immediate source of the "impurity" of specific foods is the gentile who prepares or handles them. So, by extension, these regulations mark the gentile as impure. Admittedly, this is not a technical impurity. It is what I would call a "rhetorical" impurity. That is to say, to identify a class of people (gentiles) as "impure" is to mark them off as taboo, at least on some level. It makes no difference, in the heart of the Jew avoiding the impure gentile, whether such impurity is technical or metaphorical (particularly after the destruction of the Jerusalem Temple).[12] As part of a broad rabbinic project to create fear of the gentile—to mark him or her as "other"—these eating laws have a significant symbolic impact. We will return to this below.

Second, in their historical-cultural context, these foods constitute a vocabulary, a language. According to the Roman culinary language, it was the civilized person—the citizen—whose diet was characterized by these foods. Someone who did not share these foods, who failed to uphold the dictates of the cultural code, was "other" (Dupont, p. 114). Ironically, therefore, a Jew who ate these same foods while refusing to share them with his neighbor was essentially declaring, "as far as I am concerned, you are not civilized." It didn't matter that the gentile was, in fact, eating these foods just as was the Jew. What mattered was that the Jew (or the rabbinic legislator) judged that he was not civilized enough to share the food at the same table. In fact, according to the legislation reviewed above, virtually the only food a Jew could freely share with his gentile neighbor was uncooked vegetables. Crucially, this is a natural food, untransformed by the hand of culture (this is explicitly recognized in the Talmud Yerushalmi, Avodah Zarah 2:8, 41d). So what remains in its natural state, the Jew may share with the gentile. What has been culturally transformed, he may not. Why not? Because, in the judgment of these legislators, Jewish culture is fundamentally opposed to gentile culture. Hence, what has been shaped by that culture must be kept at a distance.

The gemara, in its law and commentary, goes even beyond this, hinting that what is at issue here is not just two human cultures—one approved and one condemned—but a human culture and an animal-like poison. Permit me to elaborate. The gemara's discussion of "poured wine" (*yayn nesekh* = wine poured out in the course of idolatrous worship) leads immediately to a discussion of "uncovered wine," that is, wine that has been left uncovered and into which, therefore, a snake may have expressed poisonous venom (see Avodah Zarah 29b–30a). The question addressed in the deliberation is this: if wine has been either mixed with water or boiled, is there still a concern for "pouring" (= idolatry) and "uncovering"? The two go hand-in-hand; when one discusses the former, it is natural to discuss the latter. In fact, as the deliberation proceeds, some authorities indicate that they would even refuse to drink *water* belonging to a gentile, lest it have been left uncovered and thus be dangerous. Those who drink their water assume its safety because, while the gentile might not be afraid of snake venom, he would certainly be concerned to keep dirt out of his water and would thus cover it in any case.

On the surface, the avoidance of gentile wine and (in some opinions) water seems to be justified on "rational" grounds. But rationality is hardly the point. We are not directed to examine the gentile's practice concerning "covering" any more than we are directed to inquire whether particular wine has or has not been used in worship. Their wine—when not first boiled—is prohibited as though it had been poisoned by a snake. The wine—and even the water—of the gentile is deemed venomous. If the wine is venomous, then the gentile must be the source of the venom. The gentile is, by association, the snake.

This symbolic association, as outrageous as it may sound, is supported by an explicit talmudic teaching, found earlier in the very same chapter of Avodah Zarah. In the course of a discussion concerning the Mishnah's law prohibiting entrusting one's animal to an idolater, the gemara quotes a teaching which declares, "the animals of Jews are more desired by them [for sex] than their wives." Why is this so? Because "when the snake came upon Eve [and had sex with her] he left his filth [= venom?] in her [and this filth infected all of her offspring for generations to come]. Israel, who stood at Mount Sinai, their filth was removed. But idolaters [=gentiles; all those] who did not stand at Mount Sinai, their filth was not removed" (22b). The statement could hardly be more explicit. Gentiles are "snake-like" in that they are permanently infected with the filth of the original snake. Their wine, and even their water, must thus be avoided as though a snake had drunk from it. The culture of Israel must remain forever separated from the culture of the snake.

To describe the gentile as venomous or snake-like is to reiterate, in only slightly different terms, that he is impure—or, at least, that he is the source of impurity. Again, this claim is supported not only by structural analogy (snake – venom // gentile – impurity) but by an explicit rabbinic teaching. In the midst of a lengthy deliberation praising the brilliance of a sage who can, in effect, prove that a pig is kosher, the Talmud describes the snake as the creature who "kills and [therefore] increases impurity" in the world. The gentile who is like the snake—who brings the death of idolatry and violence into the world—also increases impurity. Such a hateful quality is to be avoided by the God-fearing Jew.[13]

But matters are more complex than they might, at first, appear. The Tosefta already provides evidence of disagreement with respect to the status of olive oil. If "Rabbi [Judah Nesiah] and his court permitted oil," it is reasonable to conclude that, after his time (the mid-third century, shortly after the promulgation of the Mishnah) the prohibition was no longer in force. The Palestinian and Babylonian gemaras both preserve record of early compromises pertaining to bread and wine. Both record third-century opinions resisting the prohibition of gentile bread, and both conclude that, while such bread may be prohibited, this is so only if Jewish bread is available. If the only local baker is a gentile baker, his bread may be consumed without hesitation (see p. A.Z. 2:8, 41d, and b. A.Z. 35b).[14] And even the prohibition concerning wine contacted by gentiles was quickly qualified, at least by some. Prominent sages of the same period suggest that Jewish wine, if mixed with water (as was customary), could not be contaminated, and all agree that "cooking" would protect Jewish wine from the consequences of gentile contact (p. A.Z. 2:3, 41a–b, and b. A.Z. 29b–30a). As a consequence, there would be little obstacle, in practice, to a gentile serving at a Jewish banquet. And, as anyone who has tried such wine will attest, the powers of "cooked" wine are in no way diminished. If wine is dangerous because it might lead to overly intimate relations with drinking partners, cooked wine is every bit as dangerous, as the talmudic sages must surely have known.

Needless to say, the spirit of these various compromises is in tension with that of the "snake" and "sex" deliberations, found in the same gemara. And the attitudes conveyed in those deliberations conflict with those hinted at in the more permissive regulations examined earlier in this chapter—at least if our interpretation of the laws of prohibited mixtures is correct. How are we to make sense of these apparent contradictions?

It is possible, of course, that my claims concerning the significance of the mixing laws are mistaken. Perhaps, in fact, the permissions granted by the rabbis with relation to prohibited mixtures are meant to have only limited application—and should not be construed to represent porous boundaries between Jews and their neighbors, as proposed earlier. But, even if this is so (and I am not willing to admit that it is), we would still have to explain the tension between the texts which speak of gentiles as snakes and perverts and those that express a willingness to compromise earlier restrictions. There is a genuine ambivalence in these texts, one that will not be eliminated by insisting on artificial reconciliations.

The best explanation of the identified textual tension, I believe, will be found in the rhetorical strategies of the different texts, strategies which seek to balance a complex historical reality. As indicated earlier, the Mishnah earlier in the same chapter of Avodah Zarah forbids contact with idolaters because of fear of what they might do. It forbids leaving your animal with them lest they commit bestiality. A Jewish woman must not be alone with them because they might rape her. A Jewish man must not be alone with them because they might murder him. Building upon the concerns expressed in the Mishnah, the gemara sounds its alarm in an even more extreme way, culminating in statements like the one quoted above, declaring that they would rather have sex with our animals than with their wives. Of course, if the Jew believed that they were apt to commit such heinous crimes, he would avoid their company as much as possible—and that may be precisely the point.

Curiously, late in the deliberation of "idolaters and their sex-habits," the gemara takes a turn and suggests that the alarmist position, prohibiting their animals because of fear they had sex with them, is merely the opinion of an individual, R. Eliezer, while the sages reject this view. In the talmudic system, if an individual disputes a collective (as in this case), the individual is rejected and the law follows the view of the majority. So the alarmist position, expressed first in the Mishnah and then exaggerated in the gemara, has no practical consequence. The question is this: if the gemara was going to conclude with leniency, why did it spend so much time demonizing (or, should I say, "serpentizing") the gentile "other"? The answer, I believe, is simple: the rabbis behind these texts are engaged in a balancing act. On the one hand, they live in a world in which regular neighborly contact with gentiles is unavoidable. In fact, archaeological discoveries and documentary evidence alike have suggested that neighborly relations would often quite good. Jewish culture was certainly part of the mainstream culture, and Jews were profoundly influenced by their neighbors and their ways. Thus, the law had to find a way for its subjects to at least coexist with their neighbors, and perhaps more. On the other hand, such regular and even intimate contact was, from another perspective, a threat. The more Jews participated in the ambient culture, the more they were likely to be influenced by it. And foreign ways, including prohibited worship, were always only next-door. So the very same rabbis who permitted contact sought to make their followers wary of such contact. They could approach the neighbor, but they should not get too close. How to do this without actually prohibiting contact? By constructing an image of the "other" that was frightening and even dangerous. Did this image conform to reality? In most cases, probably not. But the image would nevertheless nag and restrain. This would serve as an effective counterbalance to the more permissive strain contained in the law as decided.

I see the same balancing act at work in the eating laws. The several sets of laws stand in a relationship of leniency and alarm. The laws of mixtures permit mixing, the laws of gentile foods respond by counseling separation, and compromises in those same laws yield, if only partially, to a reality characterized more by mixing than by separation. In reality, Jews of this period mixed constantly with their neighbors, for reasons both commercial and social. In response, the rabbis sought to erect boundaries of attitude that permitted intercourse of one kind (social and commercial) but would assure that there be no intercourse of the other kind. In doing so, they symbolized an identity that was, at the same time, accepting but anxious— accepting of the humanity of the other, but suspicious of his impieties.[15]

6   The rabbinic period
Blessing food

Jewish eating practices, as ordained by the rabbis, are defined, as much as by anything else, by the ritual recitation of blessings before and after the partaking of food. The details of this ritual, constituted of prescribed words and modest deeds, are a significant part of what distinguished rabbinic Jewish eating from other eating, Jewish or gentile. In fact, if we assume that the common ancient meal was comprised of bread, oil, a vegetable, and wine, then the blessing ritual will be the only thing that regularly distinguished the eating of one group from the eating of the other. It is essential, therefore, to examine this rabbinic ritual in detail, for it contains and communicates essential elements of rabbinic Jewish identity.

Of course, the association of blessings and eating did not commence with the rabbis. The Torah already requires that "you shall eat, and be sated, and *bless* the Lord, your God, for the good earth which He gave you" (Dt. 8:10). The so-called Community Rule of the Dead Sea Scrolls mandates of its community that "together they shall eat and together they shall take council. And any place that there be ten men of the communal council...and they set the table to eat or the wine to drink, the priest should first put forth his hand to bless the bread or the wine..." (IQS vi, 3–6). And Josephus reports of the Essenes that a priest would recite grace before and after their meals (Wars II, 8.5). However, in none of these cases do we preserve words for such blessings, nor do we know whether precise formulae were prescribed. It is possible (again, there is no way to know) that the blessings prescribed in these texts were meant to be spontaneous, emerging from the heart of the one called upon to bless. In any case, the rabbinic ritual, the themes and even words of which are defined with considerable precision, stands without apparent precedent. We may thus analyze it as a unique and innovative rabbinic formation.

Before we can interpret the rabbinic blessing ritual, it is necessary to say something about what rituals are, how they work and how, in consequence of our answers to these questions, they are best interpreted.

Rituals are practices the intention of which is to distinguish the common from the now-less-than-common. In Catherine Bell's carefully considered definition, ritualization is a way of acting that is designed and orchestrated to distinguish and privilege what is being done in comparison to other, usually more quotidian activities. As such, ritualization is a matter of various culturally specific strategies for setting some activities off from others, for creating and privileging a qualitative distinction between the 'sacred' and the 'profane,' and for ascribing such distinctions to realities thought to transcend the powers of the human actors.[1] (Bell 1992, 74)

In other words, wine might "just" be wine and bread "just" bread, but when consumed at certain times, according to certain rules, accompanied by certain words and with the participation of certain persons, it could be the wine and bread of communion. With slight modifications in time and practice, it could be the wine of *kiddush* and the bread of *hamotzi* at the beginning of a Sabbath or festival meal.

An excellent example of such a strategy of difference, intended to transform the mundane into the distinguished, is the lighting of Hannukah lights according to rabbinic custom. In the rabbinic age, there was no such thing as a special Hannukah lamp. Hannukah lights were simply common oil lamps used in a slightly different way. For a common oil lamp to become a Hannukah lamp, a Jew would have to take such a lamp on one of the days of Hannukah, place it outside the entrance to his courtyard on the side of the entry opposite the mezuzah, recite the appropriate blessing and then light the lamp. If he performed all of these acts on a day that was not Hannukah, then the lamp was not a Hannukah lamp. If he failed to place it outside, or placed it too low or too high or on the wrong side of the door, there would be no way to distinguish it as a Hannukah lamp. If he performed all of the requisite acts but failed to recite the proper words, it would remain a common lamp. Only through the execution of a carefully orchestrated set of distinguishing acts could the lamp be recognized as—and therefore *be*—a Hannukah lamp. In the absence of the requisite strategic performances, it would remain a mundane lamp. Of course, all of these acts of difference were intended to create difference and comment that this activity, and thus this day, was different from other days. Furthermore, the number of lamps lit on any day of Hannukah could also serve to communicate which day of Hannukah is was, what degree of piety the participant wished to display, and the rabbinic school to whose direction he adhered. The ritual both announced and created distinctions—as would all rituals, rabbinic or otherwise.[2]

The rabbinic food-blessings ritual is, we shall see, all about making distinctions. In addition to distinguishing those who observe the ritual from those who do not, the ritual distinguishes between one kind of food and another, between one way of eating and another. By demanding that the person about to consume food be fully aware of the type of food she is about to eat, the way it was prepared, and the setting of its consumption, the ritual creates contours of preference and privilege that cannot help but impress the person performing the ritual. He or she will now recognize that food is not merely food, but that different foods have distinct places in the "divine" scheme. Eating will no more be a quotidian act but an act that notices the Creator and His design.

Before examining the precise details of the blessing system, we must consider the meaning of the broad ritual—a ritual which demands that, before enjoying the fruit of God's creation (so the rabbis would say), a Jew must recite a blessing that takes notice of the fruit's origin. In multiple places and ways, the rabbis comment on the meaning of their blessing system.

The Tosefta begins its discussion of blessings with the following teaching:

> A person should taste nothing until he blesses, for it says "The earth is the Lord's and the fullness thereof" (Ps. 24:1). One who derives any benefit from this world without [first reciting] a blessing has stolen sacred property, until the [performance of the] commandments [relating to blessings] permits it to him. (Tos. 4:1)

The tradition of the Yerushalmi, which attributes this teaching to R. Aqiba, is otherwise identical to the Tosefta. And the Bavli's record is virtually the same, adding only that one who derives benefit without first reciting a blessing has as though benefited "from the Holy things of Heaven" (Ber. 35a).

What is the meaning of all of this? Lawrence Hoffman, in his *Covenant of Blood* (1996), captures the rabbis' understanding exactly:

> ...for the Rabbis of the classical period...The universe is holy in its essence, belonging to God who made it. It presents itself to us as sacred, so it must actually be *de*sacralized before we can use it....Blessings are thus a desacralizing vehicle, for they function to render sacred food "profane," removing it from the earth's inherent delivery system and making it fit for everyday human consumption.[3]

Hoffman then adds a very important observation: "Some things cannot be so desacralized: the first fruits of one's produce, for example, or the first three years of a fruit tree's harvest, or the portion of any given produce that must be tithed. All of these are foodstuffs that must be offered back to God; only what is left over after the offering can be eaten" (160).

The sense that permitted food is sacred substance rendered profane is supported by the rabbis' location of their laws of kashrut in the section of the Mishnah devoted to *sacred* things (as discussed briefly in the prior chapter). In the larger division of the Mishnah which discusses laws pertaining to the Temple and the sacrificial system, the rabbis elaborate how animals intended for everyday consumption (*ḥullin*) should be chosen, slaughtered, etc. This very location suggests that such animals and their meat are actually holy things rendered profane. The same is suggested by the terminology the rabbis employ to describe their categories. The terms *kodashim* and *hullin*—holy things and everyday things—are effectively cognates of the Arabic terms *haram* and *hallal*, used by Muslims to describe their meats before and after they have been properly slaughtered (for the equivalence of *kodesh* and *haram*, see Leviticus 27:28). The cognate terminology is evidence of a cognate system of ideation. Before proper steps are taken, the stuff of God's created world is *kodesh* or *haram*, off-limits because it belongs to its creator. But God has given us permission to derive pleasure—to consume—some parts of God's creation if we take the required steps to recognize its origin. If we partake before taking these steps, then we steal what belongs to God. If, however, the proper steps are taken—with foods God has given us permission to consume—then what was previously God's is now ours, and we may consume such foods with pleasure.

This same conceptual structure explains the perpetual "mystery" of why the Mishnaic tractate Berakhot ("blessings") is located at the beginning of the division of "Seeds." The tractates of this division outline regulations pertaining to steps that must be taken with the produce of the field ("seeds") before they may be eaten. A variety of "priestly gifts" must generally be taken—tithes, heave-offerings, first fruits, and so forth. The corner of the field and gleanings must be left behind, the produce of certain years is altogether prohibited. As Hoffman explains, these steps remove the portions of the produce which remain the property of God or God's earthly ministers, and some produce will never be available for regular consumption. But if the defined steps are first taken, then most of the produce of the field can be made available for the human table. Of course, as explained above, this is precisely the purpose of the blessings. So the tractate on blessings finds its obvious home in the company of other tractates that describe how to desacralize the produce that God creates. It is the first of tractates that view and define the world as a holy creation which, to begin with, is not the property of its human inhabitants.

The language of the rabbinic blessings highlights and emphasizes this implicit system of meanings. Without yet going into detail, it is sufficient to observe the general formula which characterizes many of the rabbis' food blessings. As listed in the sixth chapter of Mishnah Berakhot, the blessings praise God who "creates the fruit of the tree" or "creates the fruit of the vine" or "creates the fruit of the earth." Blessings that break this precise formula bless God "who brings forth bread from the ground" or "by whose word all things are" (or "come into being"). What is notable about these several blessings is that they speak of God as creator of the food to be consumed and *they all do so in the present tense*. The language of the blessings does not mean to refer to a historical past—the creation of the world when God set the cycles of nature in motion. It refers to a God who creates these things everyday and continually, a God who, in the language of another rabbinic blessing (one not for food), "renews, in His goodness, everyday the act of creation." God is actively and continually the creator of the earth and its fruits, and what God creates belongs, naturally, to God. What God demands is that, before His creation be enjoyed by humans (or at least by Jews), they recognize its source and owner.

The rhetorical force of the food blessings, in their combination, is extremely powerful. If the rabbis declare that nothing may be consumed before reciting such a blessing, and if eating is an everyday act, then they are asking the Jew to recite these formulae many times, each and every day. Through regular recitation, the reciter will constantly be reminded of God's works in the here and now. He will be forced to notice God's presence and prerogative, as well as God's generosity and grace. Acts such as eating a meal or taking a snack, which might otherwise be mundane and worthy of little note, become occasions for heeding God's presence in creation—God's mundane miracles, if you will. Significantly, of all of the rabbis' eating practices, this would have been the most common in their own age, for while meat was consumed only on special occasions, and mixtures would have been an issue only from time to time, this is a practice which, if observed, would frame any act of eating. And the framing is, in its words and deed, a profound interpretation of the common world. The Jew who observes this ritual is one who, in contrast to her less sensitive neighbor, will be constantly aware of the active presence of God in her or his life.

Beyond their general rhetorical force, the eating blessings, in their specificity, draw a map of creation that is equally as significant for understanding matters of rabbinic identity. The Mishnah's teachings concerning blessings before eating are these:

1. For fruit of the tree, one says "who creates the fruit of the tree," with the exception of wine, for upon wine one says "who creates the fruit of the vine." For fruit of the earth one says "who creates the fruit of the earth," with the exception of the loaf, for upon the loaf he says "who brings forth bread from the earth." And for vegetables one says "who creates the fruit of the earth;" R. Judah says [no, one should rather say] "who creates species of grasses."

2. If, for fruits of the tree, he blessed "who creates the fruit of the earth," he has fulfilled his obligation. But [if he recited] for the fruit of the earth "who creates the fruit of the tree," he has not fulfilled his obligation. And for all of them, if he said "by whose word all things are" he has fulfilled his obligation.

3. For something that does not grow from the earth, one says "by whose word..." For vinegar and for unripe fruit that has fallen from the tree, and for locusts, one says "by whose word..." R. Judah says: Anything that is a curse [such as fallen fruit] one does not bless for. (Berakhot ch. 6)

What is first evident from the Mishnah's preliminary list is that there are blessings of greater or lesser specificity. The most general, and most inclusive, of the blessings is "by whose word all things are [= exist]." Fruits of the tree are included in the fruits of the earth, but not vice versa. And wine and bread are clearly subcategories of fruits of the tree and fruits of the earth respectively. However, though the most general of the blessings would subsume everything in its words, the system outlined here clearly prefers greater specificity. It also, obviously, privileges certain specific kinds of food.

Particularly notable, in the list quoted above, are the special blessings for wine and "the loaf" (= bread). Each is naturally and rightly contained in a larger category; wine is produced from grapes, the fruit of a tree (vines), and bread is produced from wheat or some other grain, the fruit of the earth. Yet each is marked by its own unique blessing. What is the significance of the rabbis' singling out of these particular foods? Both, of course, are culturally transformed from their natural states, both in significant ways. Grapes, untransformed, would be mere "fruit of the tree" (not the vine), and wheat mere "fruit of the earth." Only when the grapes are pressed and their juice fermented does it become "fruit of the vine." And only when the wheat is ground into flour and then baked into loafs does it become "bread from the earth." So something in the processing, the work of human hands (or feet), contributes to changing (and elevating?) the status of the natural materials.

But this is not a sufficient explanation. There are many foods that, before being consumed, are transformed from their natural states. The Mishnah explicitly lists vinegar, for example. Yet neither this, nor, by implication, other foods attract special blessings. So there must be some other quality in wine and bread that requires singular notice in distinct words. That quality, it seems to me, is their status as two legs of the Mediterranean triad (why the third leg, olive oil, does not require a special blessing will be discussed later in this chapter). As we discussed in earlier chapters, bread and wine (along with olive oil) constituted the exemplary—one would not err in saying "ideal"—Mediterranean diet. They bore a cultural and even religious significance that was unparalleled. The diet of the civilized Roman, as opposed to that of the barbarian, was centered on these foods. In the cultural world the rabbis inhabited, it would have been near impossible to view wine and bread as neutral, unmarked foods.

Nor was the Roman, nor the Greek before him, unique or original in privileging them. The Bible frequently mentions "grain, choice wine and refined oil" in combination (see, e.g., Deut. 11:14 and Hosea 2:10), and when Deuteronomy remarks that "man shall not live by bread alone, but upon everything that comes from God's mouth will man live," (8:3) the intent is clearly to say that humans need more than food, but, as far as food itself is concerned, bread is nearly sufficient. That these are the foods that require specialized blessings, therefore, is surely more than coincidence.

In fact, the special blessings mark their long-standing special status in the ancient diet.

The distinctive blessings for bread and wine suggest a system of hierarchical priorities, as the rabbis behind the Mishnah are quite aware. In fact, the rules of the Mishnah engage the question of priority quite explicitly:

4. If he had before him multiple types [of food], R. Judah says: If there is among them one of the seven species [mentioned in the Bible as the produce of the Land of Israel], he blesses upon it. But the sages say: He may bless upon whichever of them he desires.
5. If he blessed upon wine before the meal, he has exempted [from blessing] wine [drunk] after the meal. If he blessed upon the appetizer before the meal, he has exempted relishes served after the meal. If he blessed upon the loaf, he has exempted minor dishes, but if he blessed upon minor dishes, he has not exempted the loaf. The School of Shammai say: Nor even food prepared in a pot.
7. If they first brought before him a salted dish, and a loaf with it, he blesses upon the salted dish and exempts the loaf, because the loaf is secondary to it. This is the general rule: Whenever there is a main food and something secondary along with it, he blesses for the main food and exempts the secondary food.

The dispute in Mishnah 4 makes the fundamental issue at hand resoundingly clear. Recognizing that meals might regularly be constituted of many foods from several categories, and appreciating that requiring a blessing upon each and every food would be unwieldy and ultimately inoperable, the rabbis allow that a blessing should be recited over the preferred food at a meal. The question, however, is how is "preference" determined? R. Judah suggests that Jewish preference should be defined by the ancient Biblical tradition, and the Jew's love and attention should be turned toward the special foods of the Land of Israel. The sages who dispute R. Judah, by contrast, respect a purely subjective definition of preference, recognizing that different individuals will prefer, and therefore give priority to, different foods. Should the blessing system give voice to individual preference or cultural-historical values?—that is the subject of the dispute here, a dispute in which both sides merit consideration and therefore official record in the Mishnah.

But other factors must also be considered, as Mishnahs 5 and 7 testify. Once blessed before a meal, it is unnecessary to bless again for the same food, even if the body of the meal is finished. Some foods exempt other foods from blessings—bread exempts minor dishes, salted dishes exempt bread. Unusually, the Mishnah goes so far as to express a general rule: main foods exempt secondary foods but not vice versa. The Mishnah offers several illustrations of the application of this principle, and it is not difficult to imagine others. For example, it may be that olive oil does not demand a special blessing (like wine and bread) because it is always secondary. It was used, in the age in which the Mishnah was composed, mostly to dip bread into (i.e., when it was being used for food). It would thus have been exempted by the blessing recited over bread. But, even while the rule allows for easy illustration, it raises as many questions as it answers: How are "main" and "secondary" to be determined? Are the cases spelled out in the Mishnah meant to be hard and fast rules, or are they mere illustrations? Are they recognized as being culturally determined or are they assumed to be immovable? The Mishnah is asking for finer and finer distinctions, but it is not always transparent in indicating how these distinctions are to be made.

Another important distinction demanded by the blessing ritual concerns the nature of the eating: is it formal or informal, a meal or a mere snack, a collective engagement or the taking of nourishment by an individual? Mishnah 6 of this same chapter begins to articulate the difference: "If they were sitting to eat, then everyone blesses for him- [or her-] self; if they 'reclined,' one blesses for them all." The word translated as "recline" is the rabbinic Hebrew word for partaking a formal meal in the fashion of a Greco-Roman symposium (it is the same word that appears in the "Four Questions" of Passover when the child asks "Why on this night do we all recline?"). The distinction being drawn here is thus between a formal and an informal meal, between a *real* meal and the casual taking of food. In the one case, even several individuals eating at the same time are assumed to be eating alone. In the other case, they have formed a collective, a fellowship. And a fellowship merits notice in the rituals therein enacted.

The distinctions dramatized in the before-meal blessings are similarly expressed in the after-meal blessings. So, if one ate a food that is a "main food" or constitutes a meal, one recites the extended after-meal blessing comprised of three blessings; if not, one recites a shorter blessing (Mishnah 8). If one ate a formal meal, in fellowship, the blessings are introduced with a ceremony of "invitation" ("let us bless together") (see 7:1), and, according to one opinion, the greater the number of people who dine together, the more elaborate the wording of the invitation (7:3). But, since this ceremony of invitation marks a formal, "public" meal, women, slaves and minors are excluded from the counting of participants (see 7:2); such individuals do not, in the rabbis' opinion, participate in public society.

So the rabbis, in the Mishnah, outline a system of food blessings that demands that one who participates in the system constantly make multiple, significant distinctions: what type of food is being eaten, how and by whom? Food, in this system (as in all other systems) is a social and cultural reality, and this reality is, in light of the blessing ritual, impossible to ignore. The one who blesses will regularly notice—and construct or reinforce—historical-cultural preferences, social inclusions or exclusions, and commensality or isolation. Though the Mishnah leaves many details unnoticed, the questions that must be asked when one eats, and must therefore choose a blessing, are already perfectly evident.

The Mishnah's successor documents give evidence of the fact that the rabbis did not cease to ask these questions. The Tosefta (redacted mid- to late-third century), for example, pays particular attention to the ways the cultural state of a food will affect its blessing. It begins with wine. In its discussion of formal and informal eating, the Mishnah (Ber. 7:5) recorded the opinion, attributed to R. Eliezer, that "they should not bless upon wine until they put water into it." The accepted Greco-Roman way of drinking wine, at least at formal meals, was to "mix it" (dilute it) with water. Such mixed or diluted wine was the mark of a symposium-like meal, and the mixing itself was an important component of the formal ritual of the meal. What R. Eliezer seems to be saying, therefore, it that wine should not be blessed unless it is wine taken in a formal setting with all of the attendant rituals (the sages disagree, opining that wine should always be blessed).

The Tosefta refines this dispute. In its record (Ber. 4:3), the dispute concerns whether one should recite the *special* blessing for wine. R. Eliezer rules that unmixed wine should be blessed as "the fruit of the tree" while mixed wine should be blessed as "the fruit of the vine." (The sages require "fruit of the vine" in either case.) In R. Eliezer's opinion, the special quality of wine is expressed only in a formal setting, and in such a setting wine will be mixed. In effect, outside of the more formal context, wine is not *wine*—it is merely the fermented juice of the "fruit of the tree"—and hence it should attract no special notice in the blessing ritual. Whether or not other sages agree with R. Eliezer in this particular case, the principle he is expressing finds support elsewhere.

The following rulings express the principle most clearly:

6. If one chews wheat-grains, he blesses over them "who creates species of seeds." If he baked them or cooked them, when the pieces of bread are extant, he blesses over them "who brings forth bread from the earth" and he recites after them the three blessings [of the extended after-meal blessing]; If the pieces are not extant, he blesses "who creates various kinds of sustenance" and afterward blesses the single blessing.
7. If one chews rice, he blesses over it "who creates the fruit of the earth." If he baked it or cooked it, even though the pieces [of rice-loaf] are extant, he blesses "who creates various kinds of sustenance" and says no blessing afterward. (Tos. Ber. ch. 4)

Wheat is a species of seed. But when it has been ground into flour, prepared as dough and then baked, it is no longer seed but bread. And even this is not completely true, for it is bread only when it is recognizable as bread. If it has been cut and ripped and otherwise reduced to its more basic material, it is no longer bread but "sustenance." The same is true, with appropriate modifications, of rice. To begin with, rice is "the fruit of the earth." But, having been culturally produced, it becomes sustenance. It can never, like wheat, become bread. And the rice-cake clearly does not have the same preferred status as bread. Yet, in its transformed state it is not the same rice it was before. It therefore requires a different blessing.

When the question comes to priority in blessing, distinctions in cultural state and preference become even more important. So a whole loaf of fine bread takes priority over a whole loaf of home-made bread. But a whole loaf of home-made bread takes priority over a fine loaf that has already been broken. A wheat loaf takes priority over a barley loaf, even if the wheat loaf has been broken and the barley loaf is still whole. But barley takes priority over spelt. The latter ruling is notable because, the Tosefta remarks, "spelt is better than barley." So why does barley come before spelt? "Because barley is one of the seven species [mentioned in the Torah as produce of the Land of Israel] and spelt is not one of the seven species." Wheat in particular, and the seven species in general, always take precedence (4:11; Lieberman 4:15).

So while the question remains the one already articulated in the Mishnah, the Tosefta pushes to make finer and finer distinctions. Some species are preferred over others; their preference is, in part, a consequence of their biblical association with the Land of Israel. Fine products are preferred over inferior products, whole—perfect—is preferred over broken. Once again, the one who must bless is called upon to consider the culinary landscape and make fine distinctions. This is not, if he does the job, a flat landscape. The earth that brings forth food is rich and varied, producing high and low, better and worse. The blessings that "notice" these differences create and reinforce them in the experience of the performer of the ritual at the very same time.

The noted preferences, though they will be elaborated further in subsequent rabbinic documents, already reveal much concerning rabbinic values and identities. For the early rabbis, eating was an expression of both Jewish and Roman identities, that is to say, through the observance of these rituals, the Jew would express his or her values as a Jew in particular and as a Roman citizen more generally. The Jewish self was expressed, first, in the ritual itself, which was a uniquely Jewish, rabbinic ritual. The language of the blessings, some of their formulae and many of their associations were biblical and thus traditionally Jewish. Furthermore, the foods privileged in this blessing system were foods already marked as special in the biblical text—either the staples whose abundance is evidence of divine goodness, or the species with which the Land of Israel is praised and blessed. And, of course, the God praised as perpetual creator in these blessings was the "Jewish" God (= the God with whom Jews were in a covenantal relationship). He (in their conceptualization) was this one God, King of the world, whose works were evidenced in the fruits everyday consumed.

At the same time, the one who practiced these rituals gave expression to his identity as a civilized Roman citizen, one who respected Roman preferences and values. Thus, only mixed wine was truly wine, at least on a formal occasion. And such formal occasions, following Roman custom, were the only true settings for genuine fellowship. Only observing the rituals of these occasions could a good Roman citizen, including the Jew, partake of a meal in the full and proper sense of the term. In that setting, the company would together enjoy mixed wine, proper appetizers and full loaves baked of fine flour. In this way was the good Jew also the good Roman.

The Yerushalmi (or "Jerusalem Talmud"), finished in Palestine a couple of centuries after the Tosefta, carries forward both of these agendas. With respect to the "seven species," for example, it directs (Ber. 6:4, 10c) that, whenever a person is faced with several of these species at the same time, "what comes first in the verse comes first for blessing, and what is adjacent to [the word] 'land' comes before all else." Of course, to observe this ruling properly, a person must know the verse (Deut. 8:8) by heart. The participant in the ritual will thus become the person of the living text.

In the matter of proper etiquette at a Roman meal, the Yerushalmi (6:6) quotes a Tosefta (ch. 4) which spells out in detail the order and rituals of such a meal. Following the Tosefta, it also rules that the person who at a formal meal recites the blessing must be the first one to partake, unless he wants to give someone honor by giving him priority, in which case, the rabbis say, he may follow the rule of honor. To make the rule intimated here absolutely clear, R. Abba adds in the name of Rav: "those who are reclining are forbidden to taste anything until the one who blessed first tastes" (6:1, 10a). Rules of priority are carefully enacted and they must be scrupulously observed. Otherwise, a person would reveal himself to be a boor.

Beyond merely carrying forth and strengthening the inherited tradition and its concerns, the Yerushalmi (7:5; 11d) adds a regulation and an insight that allows us to appreciate more fully the rabbis' understanding of the blessing ritual. Speaking of the blessing after the meal, R. Ba the son of R. Hiyya b. Abba teaches: "If he ate while walking, he must stand and bless. If he ate standing, he must sit and bless. If he ate sitting, he must recline [formally] and bless. If he ate reclining, he must enwrap himself and bless. And if he did this, he is like the angels who serve God...." The actions or body positions here described clearly progress from more casual to more formal. The person who eats while walking is eating the ancient equivalent of fast food. On the other extreme, we have seen that the person who "reclines" while eating is participating in a fully formal meal. Thus, when R. Ba directs that the walker must stand, the stander must sit, etc., he is insisting that the person reciting the blessing after the meal take a position one grade more formal than the one he had assumed while eating. In his view and in the Yerushalmi's, the reciting of a blessing following eating is a formal act (or one requiring greater formality), and formality must be enacted. Notably, the formality is enacted through fine acts of physical difference—the walker stands, the stander sits, the sitter reclines. We could imagine that, in the absence of broader cultural codes associating sitting or reclining with greater formality, other acts of difference could have functioned equally as effectively to mark the "blessing time." For if the time of reciting a blessing is more formal, formality itself is a matter of acting differently, less commonly. So, on a basic level, these body rituals "merely" reveal that blessing time is *different*, and that is the crucial point. In fact, if enacted properly, the person who, like an animal, eats to gain sustenance will, though the transformation brought about by the ritual enactment, spend a few moments like an angel.

The later and better known Talmud, the Bavli, repeats much of the tradition it has inherited concerning the food-blessing rituals. It also elaborates details that were nowhere before it elaborated. But its most important contributions to our conversation are its insightful commentaries concerning rituals and disputes we have already seen. The Bavli, for example, has its own opinion why wine has a special blessing. Typically, as important as its final answer are the possibilities explored along the way. So, upon asking (Ber. 35b) "why is wine different?," the Bavli first answers "because it is changed for the better." This is rejected, though, because olive oil is also "changed for the better" yet it does not have a special blessing. The second possibility then: "wine provides sustenance, but oil does not provide sustenance." This is rejected as untrue, but is followed by the suggestion that "wine satisfies while oil doesn't satisfy." This assertion is accepted: wine, like bread, does satisfy, and furthermore, the Talmud adds, it makes one happy. For these reasons wine is special and requires a special blessing. But why then, the Talmud asks, does one not recite the full three-fold blessing after meals following the drinking of wine, as one does subsequent to eating bread? Because "people do not make a meal over it."

In this discussion we learn which differences are, in the opinion of the talmudic authors, the differences that matter. In their estimation, it might be worth noticing in ritual something that is, through the work of human hands, changed for the better. The same is true of something that provides sustenance, and it is certainly true of a food that leads to one's satisfaction. A food that serves as the anchor of a meal obviously demands a special blessing, in this case the full blessing following the meal. Finally, a food that makes for joy and happiness should surely be remarked upon in words that distinguish it from other foods. These, variously, are qualities that merit—or might merit—*special* notice, for as the Bavli says repeatedly, "since he has benefit [or pleasure] from it, he must bless." Anything that provides some benefit or pleasure requires a blessing. Some foods simply invite a more unique blessing.

The Bavli similarly adds important words of clarification in connection to disputes regarding the priority of foods and their blessings. Its first discussion (Ber. 39a) begins with a story. The Talmud tells of two students who were sitting before Bar Kappara. They were served a variety of foods, including cabbage, cooked greens and young poultry. One of the students was given permission to bless by Bar Kappara, and he recited the blessing over the poultry. The other student sneered at him, believing that he had chosen the wrong food over which to bless. After concluding that both students agree that the actual blessing to be recited over all of the foods in question is the same ("by whose word everything is"), the Talmud interprets their dispute in this way: the student who blessed over the poultry is of the opinion that preferred food should have priority whereas the one who sneered at him is of the opinion that food which provides sustenance should have priority (apparently assuming that this is true of cabbage but not of poultry!). The dispute, in other words, is over whether the subjective preference of the one reciting the blessing should control or the "objective" quality of the foods involved.

The next case (39b) begins with the following dispute: If a person had in front of him a whole loaf and broken pieces, R. Huna says he may bless over the broken pieces if he chooses and thereby exempt the full loaf, whereas R. Yohanan insists that blessing over the whole loaf is "a mitzvah of the highest order." R. Yohanan goes on to add, though, that if the whole loaf is made of barley and the broken piece made of wheat, everyone would agree that one should bless over the wheat bread. In this latter case, the accepted ruling negotiates two possibly contradictory judgments, that is, whether a whole loaf is preferable or a loaf of a more "important" substance. Both are admitted to be worthy of preference. The only question is what to do if the two factors would lead to a different decision. R. Yohanan's answer is that "importance" is more important, but a more perfect physical condition might also cause one food to attract the blessing before another.

The third commentary of this kind refers directly to the Mishnah which explicitly introduces the question of priority. In the Mishnah, you will recall, there was a dispute: "If he had before him multiple types [of food], R. Judah says: If there is among them one of the seven species, he blesses upon it. But the sages say: He may bless upon whichever of them he desires." Commenting on and building upon this Mishnah, Ulla declares (41a): "The dispute is when their blessings [= of the foods in question] are the same, in which case R. Judah is of the opinion that the seven species are preferred and the sages are of the opinion that the more desired kind is preferred, but when their blessings are not the same, everyone agrees that one must bless one and then bless the other." Ulla's commentary merely makes explicit what we understood to be intimated earlier in the chapter, that is, that R. Judah values the biblical connection and the sages value subjective preference. He merely adds that these factors are in play only when the question is which food attracts the blessing, not which blessing is to be recited. In the latter case—assuming that neither is the "main food" and neither "secondary"—the appropriate blessings for each food must be recited.

What is important in these talmudic commentaries is that they notice and make explicit what we assumed all along, that is, that the blessing system is about preference and priority. Because this is so, multiple and often contradictory factors will come into play in the operation of the system. There will be questions of subjective preference, cultural preference, traditional privilege and nutritional value. When decisions are made—say, that the seven species should always have priority—these will be declarations that some values are more important than others. But several disputes are recorded in the Mishnah and many more find a place in the gemara (the talmudic commentary on the Mishnah). And, though many questions are decided, others remain open even as the talmudic deliberations come to an end. What this means, of course, is that questions of collective identity and preference, indirectly expressed in questions pertaining to the recitation of blessings, do, in the end, remain open. Some elements of the identity of the Jew who would recite these blessings the rabbis insist on deciding. But others they admit they ought not decide.

Still, in the end, there are qualities of identity that the blessing rituals undoubtedly give expression to. The Jew, in the rabbis' eyes, is a person who recognizes God's ongoing creative presence in the "mundane" world. His is the God of the Hebrew Bible, the God who, despite the claims of other nations, is the true King of the world. The Jew is uniquely connected to the Land of Israel, and she will, whenever possible, prefer the produce thereof. At same time, the Jew is a civilized person, a full citizen of the Roman world. Hence, she prefers the food that the Roman prefers, particularly since the biblical tradition, of the more ancient Mediterranean, shares the same preference. He (now strictly so) will ideally enjoy his meals—at least those which mark occasions—in the fashion of a civilized Roman, taking dips, wine, bread, and other foods in the order enjoined by accepted Roman ritual.

These values will be expressed not only by the Jews mouth and words, but also by his body. So, at the formal meal, he will recline in the fashion of the comfortable Roman citizen. And when she recites her blessing(s) after a meal, she will assume a position that marks the importance of the occasion, however brief it might be. Practically, this means that she will slow down, come to a stop, assume a more formal posture, all to express her esteem for the ritual itself. For, in the rabbis' opinion, the Jew is also the person who values the body and the rituals it performs.[4] Given this latter nexus of preference, it is not surprising that one of the most elaborated rabbinic rituals is the one that celebrates the consumption of food, the substance that sustains body and soul.

7 Waiting for the next meal

As we saw in chapter four, once the rabbis instituted the prohibition of mixing meat and dairy foods, the question immediately arose of how, practically speaking, this mixing was to be avoided. What, in other words, counts as "mixing" and what steps are necessary to avoid it? The gemara in tractate Hullin proposed two sorts of methods for avoiding mixing: (1) washing one's hands and either wiping or rinsing one's mouth, and (2) waiting some period of time ("until tomorrow at the same time" or "until another meal") after eating meat before one eats dairy. The former steps seem to define "mixing" as the contact of the two categories of food, for they facilitate the physical removal of the actual food substance from one's hands or mouth. The assumptions of the latter method are less clear, for, on the one hand, it could be directed at avoiding the mixing of residual tastes which might remain long after the actual food substance is removed. On the other hand, it could be directed at accomplishing a "symbolic" separation of the foods, seeking to avoid mixing literally at the same meal. The gemara, while offering these different methods, was utterly unclear concerning how they might relate, and it would be left to centuries of rabbinic commentators to work out the details. As we will discover in the present chapter, the solutions they would propose would be as diverse as in any area of rabbinic practice. Ultimately, where a Jew was found on the map of these possibilities would define his community affiliation as much as any halakhic choice. If you knew how long a Jew waits between meat and dairy, you could more-or-less tell where she came from and the community with which she identifies.

Notably, the waiting period that subsequent generations of Jews would take for granted as being required is barely mentioned by the generations of rabbinic authorities (the geonim) who led the Babylonian academies after the gemara's completion. This inattention seems to have a simple explanation: following the gemara, these authorities seem to assume that washing and wiping one's hands and mouth are the easier and therefore more likely methods of avoiding mixing. Why would one wait when one could clean away the potentially offending substance and be done with one's concerns? Hence, the Halakhot Gedolot (ninth century; Laws of Blessings, ch. 6) simply says "the fact that our sages permit cheese after meat derives from the statement of R. Nachman [in the gemara, who said that washing one's hands between meat and cheese is obligatory];" once one has washed—or, according to a second recorded opinion, wiped one's mouth—further steps are judged unnecessary.

Following the approach of Halakhot Gedolot was the French sage, Rabbenu Tam (R. Jacob b. R. Meir, 1100–1171), who insisted that the prohibition of eating dairy after meat applies only when one fails to wash one's hands and wipe one's mouth. If, however, one physically removes the meat, no waiting at all is necessary.[1] Yet, remarkably, even if one is unable to wash and wipe—that is, if one is forced to wait until "another meal"—actual waiting is still apparently barely necessary. In an unattributed comment on the Talmud's next page, apparently following the same overall approach as that of Rabbenu Tam, "another meal" is interpreted to mean: "not a meal we are accustomed to make, one morning and one evening, but even immediately, if he cleared the table and blessed, it is permitted...." According to this line of interpretation, waiting, as such, is neither essential nor desired. What is necessary is separation, and this might be accomplished either by removing the food substance or by creating a symbolic barrier (that is, a ritualized boundary between one meal and another). By taking the steps to mark one meal off from another, one avoids creating the prohibited mixture, thus fulfilling one's obligation according to rabbinic ordinance.

But while Rabbenu Tam, following Halakhot Gedolot and other geonic authors, was relegating waiting to a secondary, back-up position, other prominent authorities were seeking to tip the scales of the law in another direction. The first figure to advance the approach privileging waiting as the preferred method of separation was R. Isaac Alfasi (R. Isaac "of Fez," 1013–1103). Commenting on the relevant gemara, Alfasi writes: "and we learn from this which R. Hisda said—"If one ate meat, he is forbidden to eat cheese"—that it is not permissible to eat cheese after meat unless one waits the measure [of time] that is necessary for another meal, for we do not find one who permits the eating of cheese after meat in less than this period." To be sure, it is possible to construe this to mean something like the comment of Tosafot quoted above; Alfasi offers no specific period of time for his required waiting, and it is not impossible that he understands "another meal" to mean just that, regardless of how much later it might be eaten. Still, his rhetoric suggests that he has something else in mind, and it seems more reasonable to ask, therefore, what he understands the normal passage of time between one meal and another to be.

Whatever Alfasi's intent, Maimonides (1135–1204), his heir in the tradition, decided the law with characteristic clarity. The gemara's requirements of washing and wiping he understands to apply only when one has first eaten dairy and intends then to eat meat (*Mishneh Torah*, "Forbidden Foods," 9:26). When one first eats meat, on the other hand, "he should not eat dairy after it until there is between them the measure of time to another meal, that is, *approximately six hours*, because of the meat between the teeth that is not removed with wiping" (9:28, emphasis added). Maimonides here offers three opinions that are essentially without precedent: (1) Washing and wiping are not, in his view, alternatives to waiting; they are methods of separation that apply only when dairy is consumed first. (2) Following meat, one cannot consume dairy until one has waited until a normal "next meal," that is, in his opinion, approximately six hours. In other words, "next meal" is not meant to define a symbolic next stage. It is merely an easier way to describe a conventional period of time. And (3) the reason one must wait after first eating meat is that meat stubbornly remains between one's teeth. As a consequence of this reality, wiping one's mouth is insufficient and waiting six hours is an uncompromisable minimum.

Substantially following Maimonides approach, but with a notable difference in his definition of the time period required for waiting, is R. Menachem ha-Meiri (Provence, 1249–1306). In his work entitled *Magen Avot*, Meiri defends a variety of Provencal practices in the face of different Sephardic customs. One of these differences pertains to separating the meat of fowl—as opposed to other meats—from dairy. Recognizing the fact that, according to one dominant talmudic opinion, fowl did not count as "meat" (because fowl do not produce milk), Sephardic custom required no wait following the consumption of fowl before eating dairy. Meiri insists that, despite this difference, the authorities who declared fowl to be "meat" meant this to be so in all respects. While defending this position, he shares his views concerning what is required before eating dairy after meat *in general*. He writes: "the general rule is that all meat foods, whether of cattle or fowl, one cannot eat cheese after them until *six or five hours* pass, for that is the measure [of time] between one meal and another" (Magen Avot, "the ninth matter;" emphasis added). He elaborates that this is necessary because if one does not wait this long, the meat stuck between his teeth will not have dissolved. He adds that active removal of such meat will be to no avail, for small scraps will remain stubbornly present. Only the waiting period will assure that such scraps will effectively be eliminated.

Notable in Meiri's approach is, first, that he estimates the period between "one meal and the next" in rough and approximate terms; in his system, Maimonides' definitive six hours becomes "six or five hours." Still, it is crucial to recognize that Meiri's approximation is not an infinitely yielding one. "Six or five hours" obviously would exclude "two or one." Therefore, in Meiri's approach, in contrast to that of Tosafot, "the next meal" is not a mere symbolic construct. The express purpose of waiting until the next meal is to provide time for meat stuck between the teeth to "dissolve." So his immediate concern is not time as such, but to provide assurance that the substance of meat and dairy will not be mixed. The time one waits guarantees that there will be no mixing, so the wait cannot be compromised.

The interpretive tradition whose path we are following here, unlike the Franco-German tradition represented by the Tosafot, has taken the fear of mixing a significant step beyond its origins, absolutizing the demand for separation and abandoning recognition of its symbolic quality. Let us not forget: in the rabbis' understanding, the "Torah's" prohibition of mixing meat and dairy pertains only to cases where they are cooked together. Any further requirement—say, insisting that cold meat and cheese be kept apart—is a rabbinic enhancement of the Torah's law (again, as the rabbis interpret it). Thus, when one eats dairy after meat at "the next meal," whether fifteen minutes or six hours later, one runs no risk whatsoever of transgressing the Torah's prohibition. By choosing to valorize the talmudic teachings that require extreme separation, by defining their purpose to be the avoidance of any possible mixture of the offending food substances, and by seeing these as unyielding minimums, the approach of these authorities effectively obscures our recognition of the fact that none of this is actually necessary according to the rabbis' understanding of the Torah. Perhaps this is—wittingly or unwittingly—their point: rabbinic law, like Torah law, is Torah. Its prohibitions must be protected by the same powerful fences as the Torah's prohibitions. As Jewish society has finally become, powerfully and unambiguously, *rabbinic* society, rabbinic interpretation has come to define mechanisms that will symbolize the full gravity of rabbinic power. The boundaries, even when rabbinically defined, must be absolute. Dairy substance must be kept separate from meat substance, and this absolutely.

Following this same tradition is R. Jacob b. Asher (1270–1343), who begins his comments (*Arba'ah Turim,* Y.D. 89) by accepting and expanding upon the opinions of Maimonides.[2] He repeats Maimonides requirement of waiting six hours, but adds that after six hours one must still remove any meat scraps that might be stuck in his teeth before eating dairy. He admits that this is more than Maimonides would require (he believes that, for Maimonides, after six hours the residual meat substance is no longer "meat" for purposes of this law), but he insists that it is better to be stringent where possible. Then, later on in his comment, he quotes his father, R. Asher, as approving of the generally accepted custom of never eating cheese after meat, even if it be the meat of fowl. But he adds that this applies only if the substance of the meat or cheese is present (= visible) in the cooked dish. If, however, one has eaten from a dish with either meat or dairy ingredients—which are not, however, visible in the final product—one may eat of the other sort of dish without taking any steps at all. In fact, following a dish made with meat ingredients, one may eat actual cheese (or other dairy) immediately so long as one washes one's hands in between.

The law, as formulated here, is once again concerned with the *substantive* mixing of meat and dairy. The reason one must wait at least six hours after eating meat before eating dairy is that, whether one can detect it or not, meat remains between the teeth for at least this long. This also explains why, if meat scraps are detectable even after six hours, one must remove them; meat is meat, whether or not its taste remains. But this emphasis has apparently ironic consequences: the focus on *substance* goes hand-in-hand with a lack of concern for *taste* as such. This explains why a "dish" (*tavshil*) prepared with either meat or dairy ingredients—*the detectable substance of which is not present*—creates no categorical prohibition. If taste is present but substance is not, then one may follow the other with little or no act of separation.

This approach is not inconsistent with talmudic precedents, and it makes perfect sense within the defined interpretive paradigm. But this should not lead us to ignore the emphases and preferences expressed in this tradition. Defining the system in terms of actual food substances, and therefore requiring maximal separations, has social and other consequences. Jews who respect the authority of these masters—most of them Sephardic (using the term loosely)—will effectively be barred from eating dairy after meat on the same day (assuming meat is consumed at the evening and not the morning meal). But the Franco-German tradition, represented by Tosafot, has not disappeared during these centuries, and the more minimal waiting requirement defined by that tradition has been accepted, in practice, in much of Germany, Poland and adjacent lands. So, in the centuries under discussion (twelfth through fourteenth), these differences in eating practice will effectively distinguish Sephardic and Ashkenazic Jews. Each will be recognized by the period he does or does not wait.

But the situation is—or will become—considerably more complex. For the full elaboration of this complexity, we must turn to the record of the next couple of centuries.

As would be expected, the great Sephardic sage, R. Joseph Caro,[3] in his sixteen-century codification, repeats Maimonides' ruling: one should wait six hours after eating meat before eating dairy. But the simplicity of Caro's ruling is deceptive, for it represents the culmination of only one tradition. The alternative tradition is, as we said, alive and well. But it is also subject to challenge from within, a challenge that reflects other sorts of divisions within the community. This development is worthy of lengthy consideration.

In his comment responding to Caro's ruling, R. Moses Isserles writes, "the common custom in these lands [= Poland, Ashkenaz] is to wait one hour after eating meat...and there are those who are punctilious and wait six hours...and it is proper to do this" (Y.D. 89, 1). Isserles recognizes the more stringent standard and states his preference for it. But he also reports on what is apparently a more widespread custom of waiting just one hour and, despite his stated preference, he appears to accept the legitimacy of the more popular practice. At the very least, he does not inveigh against it. By contrast, his contemporary, R. Solomon Luria, defends the more stringent standard by means of a more polemical rhetoric, suggesting that the stakes are higher than Isserles' report would reveal. Luria writes:

> The law for anyone who has within him a whiff of Torah [is this]: if he ate meat...he will not eat cheese after it until he waits...six hours...And our master, R. Israel Isserlein wrote in his *She'arim*: "Many have made

it their custom to be lenient, and on their own they make a compromise to wait [just] one hour after a meat meal...even though we find no reason or hint for this measure [of time in the sources], in any case, who will condemn them since Tosafot...permit [waiting less]? Still, those who are modest withdraw their hands from the morning meal until the evening meal..." up to here [are his comments]....And it is impossible to condemn those who are not sons of Torah, but with respect to sons of Torah, it is proper to condemn them and to castigate them in order that they not be lenient [by allowing themselves to wait] less than six hours.... (*Yam shel shelomo*, ch. 8 ["Any meat"], #9)

Clearly, what we witness here is more than merely divergent customs. The different practices are said, by both Luria, writing in sixteenth-century Poland, and Isserlein, writing a century earlier in Germany, to divide Jews between those who are pious and those who are not. Isserlein, quoted with approval by Luria, insists that the custom of waiting one hour has no source. In his estimation, it is an ignorant compromise, invented by common folk with no supporting authority. By virtue of this (non-) source, the lenient practice marks off those who follow it from those who follow the "proper" practice. "Sons of Torah" wait six hours, those who are not "sons of Torah" wait only one. The former are imbued with Torah, they are modest, pious, Jews. The latter, by contrast, lack even a "whiff of Torah;" they are so far gone that reproving them would do no good.

Yet, even in the midst of his obvious frustration, Isserlein admits that Tosafot and other authorities would have no objection to the more lenient requirement. In fact, as we saw earlier, for those who follow the reasoning of the Halakhot Gedolot or Rabbenu Tam, even an hour's wait would be unnecessary. It would clearly be absurd to label these authorities as not being "sons of Torah." Indeed, it is indisputable that, at least up to the development of these new polemics in the fifteen century or so, perfectly pious Jews could separate their dairy from their meat without waiting multiple hours—and without fear they would be called ignorant commoners or worse. So why has the matter of waiting become the kind of "marker" issue we see here, and what is the meaning of this divisive new development?

Perhaps this development is partially a result of an increase in the consumption of meat in Europe in the late Middle Ages. Even before this time, the aristocracy prized the eating of meat.[4] And there are reports that common folk in service to the upper class enjoyed small amounts of meat in their regular diet (Flandrin and Montanari, 264). But it is clear that, for most of the Middle Ages, peasants in Europe subsisted mostly on cereals and vegetables.[5] This changed only in the late fourteenth and fifteenth centuries when, following the Black Death, a variety of factors combined to lead to an enormous increase in meat production and consumption. The sharp drop in European population during the plague opened up abundant pasturelands that had earlier been used for raising cereals. On these lands, large quantities of livestock were reared, primarily for their meat. As a consequence, for the first time, butcher shops, inns, and eating houses could offer varieties of meat in quantity, including beef, mutton, pork, poultry, pigeons, goats, and lamb (Mennell, 44–45). In fact, the evidence shows that, during this period, the quantity of meat consumed by even average people could be considerable, amounting to perhaps several pounds a day.[6]

What this all means is that, until the late fourteenth and fifteenth centuries, most Jews (as others) would have consumed little meat on a regular basis. With little meat in their diets—except, presumably, on the Sabbath and festivals—the question of how to separate dairy from meat in one's diet would have been a relatively insignificant concern. But, precisely during Isserlein's lifetime (c. 1390–1460) the European diet changed, and meat became a regular item on the table of the common person, including Jews. If the taste of meat was now regularly in the Jew's mouth, we can understand why he or she might have been tempted to "compromise" with the demands of a longer waiting period. Earlier, this stringency would have made little everyday practical difference. But now it would be a significant concern, potentially onerous. "When can I eat dairy?" would now have become a regular question, and halakhic answers that permitted a quicker transition would certainly have been preferred. Can it be mere coincidence that it was at this very time that meat, and its dietary separation from dairy, came to be the focus of rabbinic polemics? This appears to me most unlikely. Rather, as meat became a central food in the everyday diet, its symbolic power became potentially far more significant. It seems that the polemic we have seen took advantage of this potential to make other arguments.

I say that the rabbinic arguments here must go beyond their overt concern with separating dairy from meat because, even if we recognize the new culinary reality, this still fails to explain the direction of the rhetorical development we have seen. Indeed, the argument is less about what is required to separate dairy from meat than it is about what separates the pious from the problematic. Our question must therefore be, why is this the time that eating practices are deployed to separate one kind of Jew from another?

A hint at other influences may be found in Isserles' remarks pertaining to the next couple of rulings in the same chapter. In his next comment, Isserles reports that "there are those who are stringent even with meat after cheese"—that is, they wait before eating meat after cheese just as they wait before eating cheese after meat—"and thus we practice, that we do not eat even the meat of fowl after hard cheese. And there are those who are lenient [in this], and we should not condemn them…however it is better to be stringent." Next, responding to Caro's ruling permitting one to eat a "dairy dish" (= prepared with dairy ingredients, now invisible) after a "meat dish," Isserles reports: "and they have now accepted the practice to be stringent and not to eat cheese after a meat dish, just as after meat itself, and *one should not be different [in this] and 'break the fence'*…." (emphasis added). We see here two critical developments. First, Isserles obviously lives in the midst of a trend—a trend that he supports—towards stringencies in these matters. In these specific cases, accepted custom, as he views it, now ignores the traditional difference between actual meat or dairy and dishes prepared with their ingredients, as it ignores the difference between eating meat first and eating dairy first—at least in the case of hard cheese. Each of these developments is quite remarkable, because neither has a talmudic source and both significantly transform the way kashrut will have to be observed. Second, these new, more stringent practices are recognized as identifying religious allegiances and differences within the Jewish community. Isserles is explicit in this regard in the latter quoted comment, and Luria makes it clear that even Isserles' former ruling (waiting after hard cheese) effects differences within the community, for he protests this stringency and labels it an act of "sectarianism." This, of course, is all in addition to the multiple, explicit comments that associate the preferred, more stringent practices with the pious, and recognize that these customs will separate those who adhere to them from the less pious. The phenomenon that is given specific form here is one of "unnecessary" stringencies that either give rise to or support divisions within the community.

Crucially, the already noted examples do not stand alone. The testimony of authorities writing on the eating laws leaves no doubt that, for some Jews, at least, eating regulations in general were becoming steadily more restrictive in the sixteenth century. This is precisely the period, for example, during which Jews began to maintain separate meat and dairy dishes in a comprehensive, systematic way, as we will see in the next chapter. Notably, Isserles does not yet report this general development, but he does observe new stringencies in keeping separate pitchers (95, 6) and salt dishes (95, 7). Isserles provides other examples, as well. He writes:

1. "The law pertaining to the cover of a pot is like the law pertaining to the pot itself, and there are those who are *stringent* with respect to the cover, saying that even though it was not used on the same day, it is dealt with as though it were used on the same day, and this is the practice is some places, and this is my practice because of the [local] custom, *but it is a stringency without reason*." (Y.D. 93, 3)
2. "And we are accustomed to be *stringent* to eat food according to the category of the vessel [in which it had been prepared that had previously been] used on the same day [for milk or meat]...*and it is merely a stringency*...." (94, 5)
3. "And there are those who are *stringent* with roasting and boiling, prohibiting the secondary transmission of a taste [which had earlier been permitted]...and the custom is to prohibit it before the fact, but after the fact it is permitted." (95, 2)
4. "And we are not now accustomed to rely on a non-Jew [to taste a dish to determine whether a prohibited taste has been imparted to it, as the earlier sources recommend] and we estimate everything [to

determine whether there is a measure of] sixty [to one of permitted to prohibited food, and only then would the mixture be permitted]." (98, 1) (all emphases added)

The source and frequency of these comments leaves no doubt that the phenomenon of increasingly greater stringencies characterizes the experience of certain segments of East European Jewry, particularly within Poland. But why here, and why now?

The community about which Isserles and Luria testify was living under conditions with rare precedent in Jewish history—conditions that were, in significant aspects, new and unique. Beginning already in the early sixteenth century, and more powerfully in the mid-century and beyond, Poland and its Jewish community experienced an extended period of economic prosperity and relative religious toleration. The testimony of contemporaries suggests that, despite occasional exclusionary decrees, Jews now flourished in Polish society. They owned land, engaged in a wide variety of occupations and business ventures, and even entered partnerships with their non-Jewish neighbors. Some were quite well off, building large homes and passing on considerable fortunes to their children. They viewed Poland as a comfortable and even privileged place for a Jew to settle.[7]

This was a period during which Polish culture thrived. During the reign of Sigismund Augustus (1548–72), in particular, economic growth and political and religious tolerance lead to unprecedented creativity in Polish letters and learning (Baron, 52–61). Sigismund himself was an "enlightened patron of Renaissance humanism."[8] Members of the Polish aristocracy traveled to Italy to study science and philosophy, bringing back enlightened attitudes upon their return. As a consequence, Polish cultural life flourished impressively[9], and elite trends had their effect on popular attitudes as well (Baron, 59). Crucially, Jews were not excluded from these phenomena.[10]

As Jews participated and gained respect in Polish society, they developed relationships with their non-Jewish neighbors. As already mentioned, Jews and their neighbors created business partnerships. Christian clergy investigating relations between Jews and Christians in Plock noted, in 1551, that "nobles and burghers lived in close harmony with the Jews, though without keeping common feasts."[11] Jews often dressed like their neighbors, worked with them, and even socialized with them. Not unexpectedly, this sometimes led to activities that were, from the perspective of the rabbinate, highly problematic. Common Jews were known to share beer and wine with their Christian neighbors. They sometimes ate in their homes and their establishments. And they even became intimate with one another; Meir ben Gedaliah of Lublin writes, perhaps with some hyperbole, that "many" Jewish men transgress and have sex with non-Jewish women.[12]

In other words, the confluence of factors in Poland in the sixteenth century contributed to creating a culture in which, on the one hand, the yeshivas with their many students and scholars grew and flourished (a product of the relative peace and prosperity that Polish Jewry enjoyed), while, on the other hand, many Jews lived as much as Poles as "sons of Torah." From the perspective of the pious, this latter phenomenon must have been viewed as a real danger, as some contemporary rabbinic warnings suggest. So, over the course of this century, different segments of Polish Jewry came to develop two inclinations: the one, to participate as fully as possible in a flourishing Polish culture while minimizing (and sometimes transgressing) traditional restrictions upon this participation, and the other, to strengthen the traditional practices that would, both pragmatically and symbolically, separate the "Torah-true Jew" (to borrow a more modern phrase) from his non-Torah neighbors, Jewish and non-Jewish alike. Furthermore, it seems reasonable to assume that the latter segment was motivated, at least in part, by a reaction to the former.

My interpretation here merely takes Luria and like-minded authorities at their word. If they view the more lenient practice of waiting only one hour as representing the custom of the common Jew—the one who is not a "son of Torah"—then I see no reason to doubt their claim. If they seek to persuade those who will be most influenced by their authority, the "sons of Torah," to wait six hours, then I assume the distinction they wish to construct is meaningful. The evidence would suggest that Polish Jewry was, during their lifetimes, divided along the very lines they report. It was necessary, therefore, to protect the pious from the less pious.

Notably, the distinction drawn by these sages was not restricted to Poland (Isserles, Luria) and Germany (Isserlein). J. Buxtorf, a Christian Hebraist writing in Basel in the early seventeenth century, is familiar with precisely the same division between the practice of the common Jew and the "very pious." He writes: "A person who partakes of meat or meat broth should not eat any cheese or anything else made from milk for a whole hour; those who are very pious wait six hours." He then adds: "A person who cannot wait that long should remove the meat cleanly from between his teeth...and with a piece of dry bread, dry out and remove the taste of meat."[13] Buxtorf's testimony is crucial for evaluating the meaning of the rabbinic record. He echoes precisely the earlier statements that view the different practices as distinguishing those who are pious from those who are not. But his manner of recording this makes it clear that most Jews wait only one hour, while it is the unusual and particularly pious few who wait six. Moreover, he adds that the more ancient, ultimately talmudic method of dividing meat from dairy by completely cleaning one's mouth is still available for those "who cannot wait." So while some period of waiting seems to be preferred, the alternative methods of separation known to earlier generations are still available at least to common Jews. The uncompromising insistence on waiting, and on waiting a relatively long period, seems, in these lands, to be the mark of the pious.

So from at least Poland (and, given their sixteenth-century alliance, Lithuania) in the east to Switzerland (along with the Savoie region of

France, then under Swiss control) in the west, Jews experienced a divide between those who were "common" and those who were "pious," and the latter sought to distinguish themselves from the former. What better way to accomplish this than by insisting on stringencies in laws regulating how, when and where one may eat? Wait longer, the authorities recommend, and keep a greater distance between substances that should not be mixed. If you wait six hours, you will genuinely live your piety, and you will be readily distinguishable from others who do not. Notably, the social separation the authorities support is itself supported and signified by a practice of *more extreme separation*. If the separation of dairy from meat represented from its very beginnings *the separation of Jew from Jew* (even if later Jews were unaware of this meaning), then we should not be surprised to discover, once again, separation practices pertaining to the same foods representing a parallel inner-Jewish separation.

The function of the waiting period as a community marker continues into later centuries as well, though many distinctions, in fact, fade away. So while the custom of common Polish and other Ashkenazic Jews might once have distinguished them from Sephardim who, following Maimonides, insisted on a six-hour wait, in reality the pietists in Ashkenaz triumphed and the standard custom among the masses also came to be six hours. But this did not erase all distinctions. Dutch Jews continued to follow the more lenient practice and wait only one hour. And Jews of German origin waited three hours, though there is no source for this practice in the traditional literature.[14]

In view of the widespread dissemination of opinions such as those of Isserles in modern centuries, and the consequent standardization of practices—particularly "pious" practices—throughout the Jewish world, we should not be surprised to discover that the view of the "*maḥmirin*"—the "stringent ones"—came to dominate. The printing press had revolutionary implications for societies everywhere, not least for Jewish societies. What is noteworthy is that, despite such standardization, differences in the waiting period continue to serve select Jewish communities in asserting their particular identities. For example, many Conservative Jews who observe kashrut (as most, however, do not) now wait three hours. This sets them apart from Orthodox Jews, who insist on six hours, and from Reform Jews who, as a matter of principle, eschew these restrictions entirely (though some, particularly in the rabbinate, have returned to these practices, selecting the custom that seems to them best). Interestingly, it also sets them apart from the tradition of their ancestors, most of whom would have waited six hours. But three hours is, and has probably always been, a compromise, and it is precisely such a compromise that will best symbolize the position of Conservative Jews, who seek consciously and in principle to wed tradition and modernity. The symbol of the eating practice serves perfectly to communicate this position—as eating practices have thus served from antiquity.

8   Separating the dishes

One of the most prominent characteristics of kashrut as practiced by modern observant Jews is the systematic separation of all things "dairy" from all things "meat"—at the very least, separate dishes, cutlery, pots and pans, utensils and cabinets. In some cases, this separation extends to sinks, counter-tops and even refrigerators. But nowhere in our conversation of the history of Jewish eating practices to this point have we encountered such a practice. This is not due to neglect or selective reading. In fact, when one examines the literature of the rabbis who, as we saw, instituted the meat-dairy prohibition, one finds little evidence of such a practice. Nowhere in all of talmudic literature is there a hint that the rabbis demanded a systematic separation of dairy and meat utensils. Nor do we find such a requirement in the vast medieval literature that interprets and codifies talmudic precedents. In fact, not until modernity does a rabbinic authority explicitly require such a comprehensive separation. This is not to say that no separation was demanded. Authorities clearly required that certain utensils, having been used in certain ways, must be kept apart. But the comprehensive, systematic separation we take for granted is a relatively late development. When and why this practice arose is the subject of this chapter.

THE RABBINIC FOUNDATION

As we saw in an earlier chapter, the Mishnah institutes a variety of requirements pertaining to the separation of meat and dairy: they could not be cooked together, nor could they be consumed side by side on the same table, nor could they be carried in such a way that they might come into contact with one another (all m. Hullin 8:1–2). But, crucially, the Mishnah makes no mention of cooking or serving utensils in this connection. "Dairy" or "meat" are qualities of foods, not of utensils, and it is the foods that must be kept apart. In the Mishnah's view, this will be accomplished by assuring physical separation of the foods.

The earliest rabbinic document to suggest that a utensil might take on the quality of the food for which it has been used is the Tosefta. In its language, quoted several times in the Talmud, "A pot in which he cooked meat, he should not [then] cook milk in it, [if he cooked] milk, he should not cook meat in it...and if he did cook, [it is prohibited] when it gives taste" (t. Terumot 8:16, with parallels at b. Hullin 96a and 111b, b. Zeb. 96b). This teaching stands essentially alone in recording such a regulation, so it is difficult to know precisely what it means. Considering only its language, it is possible to read this as a statement that once a pot has been used for either meat or dairy, it takes on the quality of that food and must be reserved for use with that category of food and not the other. But, in light of its isolation in the corpus (if this were its meaning, we would expect many other similar regulations), other readings are more likely. The concern of the legislator here seems to be for the transmission of the taste of one category of food to the other. Having used a pot—generally, in that period, made of clay[1]—for one category, a person should not immediately use it for the other category, thus mixing tastes that should not be mixed. What must be done before the pot is used for the other category of food? Perhaps a certain period of time should elapse (the Talmud assumes that the passing of the day will eliminate the taste). Perhaps only a proper washing is required. In the absence of more information from the author of this teaching, we cannot know.

In one talmudic discussion, this Tosefta is quoted in the company of other teachings that may help illuminate its meaning (at least in the eyes of the Talmud). At Hullin 111b, we find the following teachings in relatively close sequence:

A. R. Nahman said [that] Samuel said: A knife that he used to slaughter, it is forbidden to cut hot food with it....

B. R. Judah[2] said [that] Samuel said: A bowl in which he salted meat [to remove its blood], it is forbidden to eat hot food in it....

C....Is it not taught: A pot in which he cooked meat, he should not [then] cook in it milk, and if he cooked [milk in it, it is prohibited] when it gives taste....

D. It has been said: Fish which were put in a bowl [that was used for meat], Rav said—it is forbidden to eat it in milk pudding, and Samuel said—it is permitted to eat it in milk pudding.

The first two teachings (A.–B.) are concerned with blood (the consumption of which is prohibited by the Torah) that might have been absorbed into a utensil, either during slaughtering or salting (to remove residual blood). If the utensils are then used with hot food, the absorbed blood might be re-emitted and consumed. Absorption, therefore, is a factor in the law, and it may be of concern with relation to other prohibited foodstuffs as well. This concern will help us make sense of the latter two teachings, both of which are similarly worried that (the taste of) absorbed substance might be re-emitted.

The last teaching (D.) is particularly interesting in the present context, because it extends the concern to dishes. Moreover, the Talmud's elaboration of this rabbinic dispute has profound implications for our topic. Consider the following explanations:

> "Rav said—it is forbidden" for it is a case where taste is imparted, "and Samuel said—it is permitted" for it is a case of the secondary transmission of taste (literally: "it is giving of taste the son of giving of taste").

Shortly following these explanations, the Talmud adds: "The law is—fish that were put in a bowl [that was used for meat], it is permitted to eat it in milk pudding."

So the Talmud decides in favor of the permissive opinion, based upon the notion that "the giving of taste the son of giving of taste" yields a permitted condition. The question, of course, is what this notion might be. To answer this, we have as direct evidence only the case before us.

The question being debated by Rav and Samuel pertains to fish—presumably hot—placed on a dish or bowl that had been used for meat[3]—presumably hot and presumably on the same day (otherwise other principles would render this a non-problem); may it then be eaten with a milk pudding? In such a case, the taste of the meat would first have been transmitted to the dish and then, when hot fish was placed on it, this same meat taste would have been transmitted to the fish. This, then, must be what is meant by "the giving of taste the son of giving of taste" = secondary transmission of taste. Crucially, the example speaks of a neutral food (fish) placed in a dish that had been used for meat, asking whether it may then be eaten with dairy. It does not speak of an actual dairy food placed in the same dish. So, there are clearly some restrictions or hesitations in place. But they are still limited according to the accepted talmudic practice.

To be specific: There is evidently no concern whatsoever if dishes or other utensils had not been used on the same day. There is also no concern if, at some point in the transmission chain, the food and utensil/dish were not hot (= less than a temperature that might scald the hand). And even if they had been used on the same day, and even if the food or vessel was hot, there is no concern for the status of a neutral food placed in the dish or vessel. In other words, in a world in which meat was eaten with relative rarity, primarily on festivals or special occasions, there would have been reason for concern only rarely. In practice, all one would need to bear in mind would be recent *unusual* meals. Neither this teaching nor any other in the Talmud would require one to maintain separate dishes.

MEDIEVAL DEVELOPMENTS

Rabbinic authorities in the period following the completion of the Talmud—the Geonim—have relatively little to say about matters of separation. The center of their focus, when it comes to Jewish eating practices, is the status of gentile wine. The great library of documentary materials that testifies to everyday Jewish practices in North Africa and Palestine primarily in the tenth through thirteenth centuries—the Cairo Geniza—similarly reveals little about this practice. Goitein, in his general observation, declares "the dichotomy of the kitchen into a meat and a milk section...is unknown in Jerba and never mentioned in the Geniza."[4] It is never mentioned, it seems clear, because such a practice was unknown. The silence of the sources is reflective of an absence in reality.

But when we come to the High Middle Ages and beyond, both in Ashkenaz and Sepharad, the matters we are now exploring attract more substantial comment. From the circle of the great talmudic commentator, Rashi (1040–1105), emerges the following brief instruction: "it is forbidden to eat milk with spoons with which one ate hot meat foods, unless he immerses them in boiling water" (*Sefer Ha'oreh* 110). This is an important extension of the brief talmudic teachings seen above, though it shares with them a lack of clarity concerning its precise meaning. Does this authority mean to suggest that spoons, once used for hot meat, should forever be kept separate unless and until they are immersed in boiling water ("kashered")? Or is his intent to prohibit such use in relatively close succession, say, on the same day, unless the utensil is first immersed in boiling water? If the former, then—for those following this ruling—this would represent a significant step in the direction of modern practice. But the ruling is not clear, and from other testimony, both contemporary with this teaching and later, it seems to me unlikely that such a stringency developed so early.

The rulings of R. Baruch b. Isaac of Worms, in his *Sefer Ha-Terumah* (completed shortly before 1202; quoted as an addition in the Mahzor Vitry), similarly leave room for question. The relevant passages are these:

> (54) The law concerning "milking" dishes which he washed in a pan of meat, or the opposite: if both of them were used on the same day, it is all prohibited. But if one was not used on the same day and the other was, it is all permitted...and the same is the law with respect to dishes of meat, used on the same day, that were washed in boiling water, in the boiling vessel, with "milking" dishes that were not used the same day.

> (44)...if a spoon is "milking" and he inserted it in a pot filled with a meat stew, or the opposite, when the spoon has not been used the same day, the spoon is prohibited and the stew is permitted....

(65) The law regarding a knife with which he cut meat and he wants to cut cheese with it, or the opposite, the knife must be inserted into the ground ten times [in order to eliminate the taste of what it cut first]....

R. Baruch's formulations might be taken to suggest that utensils or cooking vessels take on the quality of the category of food with which they are used, at least until active steps are taken to remove that quality. If this were correct, then we could translate "milking" as "dairy" or (to use the Yiddish) "*milkhig*" and "of meat" as "meat" or "*fleishig.*" But this is not obviously what the pertinent Hebrew terms mean. I have intentionally translated the Hebrew "*ḥolevet*" as "milking" in order to preserve the strangeness of this term and prevent us from too quickly assuming its meaning. Crucially, the word is nowhere used in classical rabbinic literature. It is a medieval term, a neologism in this context. Moreover, it is an active verb—a participle—and it would be literally translated, as I have, as "milking" or "giving milk." In fact, its more natural use is demonstrated by Rashi in his comment at Hullin 69a (to provide just one example), where it means "lactating" (s.v. "*et ḥelbo*"). In our context, the term suggests that the vessel or utensil has recently been in contact with dairy and has absorbed at least its taste, and perhaps even its substance.

Still, R. Baruch uses the term even for a utensil that has not been used on the same day, so the terminology—and hence the category—seems to "stick." But without going into the technical details of the present rulings, it is still evident that the status of a utensil is closely connected to its recent use. Thus, if one category of utensil was not used on the same day, then, when samples from the two categories are washed together, *even in boiling water*, all are permitted. So, while there is a hint of categorization here, it is only a hint. The rabbinic author is, in the end, concerned with individual knifes, spoons and dishes (= bowls). We do not have here evidence of a requirement of systematic separation.

Maimonides, in his monumental codification of the law, adds almost nothing to earlier precedents. In a stunningly ambiguous ruling, he merely repeats—word for word—the language of the earliest pertinent talmudic teaching and writes, "A pot in which he cooked meat, he should not [then] cook in it milk, and if he cooked [milk in it, it is prohibited] when it gives taste" (*Mishneh Torah*, Prohibited Foods, 9:11). He says nothing about a time limit, nor does he use language suggesting that the pot becomes a "meat pot." Nowhere else in his codification does he use such a label either. Crucially, Joseph Caro, in his later commentary, assumes that the prohibition, as understood by Maimonides, applies only on the self-same day. Whether or not this is an accurate reading, it is clear that Maimonides neither imagines nor requires a permanent categorization of cooking pots (let alone other utensils or vessels).

The question of the status of the pot "in which he cooked meat" is a point of major contention among authorities of this period, however, and attention to their opinions is essential. For obvious reasons, the question of the ongoing status of the pot—and of the food cooked in it—will be crucial in determining the contours of the observant Jewish kitchen and what may be done in it. If a pot may be used for foods of the opposite category in relatively short order, then there will be no need to designate pots as "meat" or "dairy." But if a pot retains its status, then, for all practical purposes, it will be a meat or dairy pot. We shall carefully examine discussions of this question below, as we begin to witness the formation of bona fide categories, at least for cooking pots. This will be one of the first steps in the creation of the kosher kitchen as we know it.

The great Spanish talmudist, R. Shlomo Ibn Aderet (the "Rashba," 1235–1310), addresses at length several practical questions of separation. In an opinion quoted by his younger contemporary, R. Jacob b. Asher,[5] Aderet expands and clarifies the talmudic ruling concerning cooking pots: "if one cooked vegetables in a pot of meat [= a pot that had been used for meat], one is permitted to cook cheese in it afterward because the power of the absorbed meat had been diminished and weakened to the point that it is not appropriate to apply to it the prohibition of meat and milk" (Tur, Yoreh Deah, 93). According to Aderet, if a pot was first used for meat and then for a "neutral" substance such as vegetables, one would be permitted to use it for dairy without taking any further steps. Aderet may well be assuming here that, if such an intervening step were not taken, the pot would retain the quality of what had been cooked in it. But, in practical terms, the present scenario creates the opportunity for enormous flexibility. Of course, according Aderet's ruling, one must be aware of what one has most recently used a pot for. But, at the same time, one need not have separate pots for meat and dairy. In fact, given contemporary conditions, even a single pot could have sufficed. Of course, common people were unlikely to have had the means or the space to accumulate more than a few pots. Furthermore, though meat consumption in Europe would increase considerably after the Black Death, at this stage, common people would still have eaten little meat on a regular basis. So, in Aderet's day, it would not have been difficult to keep track of those occasions when meat had been cooked in a pot or of the sequence of other foods for which it might have been used. It would have created little hardship to insist upon cooked vegetables (the most common of foods) after the occasional meat and before dairy. Thus, we do not exaggerate when we suggest that a single pot would have sufficed. Multiple pots, differently assigned, were certainly unnecessary and therefore not imagined.

In another, more lengthy comment, Aderet does demand several steps of separation. In one of his responsa,[6] Aderet forbids the eating of cheese on a cloth on which one has eaten meat (or vice versa) because there might be small pieces or drippings from the meat, or because a knife used for cutting the meat might have been wiped on the cloth. He further forbids the use of a knife "with which one regularly cuts meat" for cutting cheese, because "most of the knives, the fat of the meat is congealed on it...." His concern, clearly and rather explicitly, is the actual contact of the particular food items. He assumes a reality in which food is placed directly on the cloth—there are no personal plates—and the danger of contact and combination is immediate. He therefore requires that the cloth be washed before it may be used for food items in the other category. In the same world, knifes are not well washed, so knifes, typically covered with the remains of meat, may not be used for dairy. But having demanded these real steps of separation—and even requiring what we might call a meat knife—Aderet (like those before him) knows nothing of a systematic division between meat and dairy utensils.

R. Jacob b. Asher (1275–1340), in his ground-breaking halakhic composition, the *Arba'ah Turim*, returns to the question of the status of the pot. He is one of the first explicitly to formulate the ancient talmudic ruling with reference to the factor of time: "A pot in which he cooked meat, he should not [then] cook in it milk, and if he cooked [milk] in it within a twenty-four hour period, it is prohibited. But if he waited twenty-four hours before he cooked in it, it gives an undesirable taste and is [therefore] permitted" (Y.D. 93).[7] At this point in his comments, it appears that the status of the pot becomes irrelevant after twenty-four hours. But R. Jacob goes on to quote several recent authorities who debate the ongoing status of the pot. According to one, even within twenty-four hours, if a sufficient quantity of one category of food was cooked after the other, he may continue to use the pot for the second category of food. According to another, if the pot was made of pottery, he may never use it again. According to a third—the "Ba'al Ha-Ittur" (1122–1193)—he may use it for either category. According to R. Peretz (d. 1295), if he used it for the other category after twenty-four hours, the pot should not be used again (though food cooked in it would be permitted) unless, in the case of a metal pot, it was first "kashered." If the pot was pottery, it would have to be broken and thus not used again.

Jacob ben Moses Moellin (the "Maharil," c. 1360–1427), writing roughly a century later, continues the path of his recent predecessors when speaking of the separation of dairy and meat—his comments (found in *Sefer Maharil*, "All of the Laws of Meat and Milk") are brief and his rulings tend to be quite lenient relative to what will come to be accepted in later centuries. But there is one change in his language that demands our notice. Commenting upon a vessel used for one type of food (meat or dairy) found among vessels used for the other, he speaks of the "type" (or "category" or even "species;" in Hebrew, *min*) of vessel as opposed to the type of food that had been cooked in it; others before him had used this term to refer to the foods themselves. His language suggests, of course, that he thinks of his food vessels as separated into categories—a significant step in this history.

Moellin's language may be influenced by recent pietistic developments in his circles. Moellin was a student of R. Shalom of Neustadt (c. 1350– c. 1413). In his writings, Neustadt recalls "that there was, in his days, a householder...who practiced great piety in his house, and when he would eat meat there was a special house [= room?] for meat and also a special house [= room?] in which to eat dairy." The report highlights the exceptional nature of this case. But it is nevertheless recorded approvingly, and perhaps even with admiration. Such steps would clearly be unnecessary according to the letter of the law. But law may require one thing and piety quite another, and this is clearly offered as a meritorious model of piety. So Neustadt's approval may well influence Moellin's formulation, and though the law as Moellin records it would not yet demand a comprehensive separation, his linguistic and conceptual categories may.

Nor is Neustadt's the first record of such a pietistic move. The Sefer Hasidim, attributed to R. Judah ben Samuel the Pious (1150–1217), reports of "one fellow who would write on his bowl 'milk' and inscribe the letters and on another bowl he wrote 'meat' and likewise inscribed, in order that they be recognized and he not come to eat meat with milk" (#708). This is clearly, one way or another, important testimony. But before making sense of this report, we must say a word about its probable date.

Sefer Hasidim is a composite text, and it is difficult to date precise sections of the whole. The manuscript in which this report is recorded has been dated to c. 1300,[8] though some have simply described it as "14th century."[9] On the other hand, there is a relatively clear reference in the text to the year 1254 (par. #1527). All things considered, we would probably not be mistaken in saying that the tradition quoted above derives from the second half of the thirteenth century.

What is the meaning of the report? Sefer Hasidim is the product of German pietists of the twelfth through thirteenth centuries. Many of its reports and recommendations reflect local customs motivated by pietistic concerns. The present report would seem to be one such example. The report is clear, moreover, in indicating that this is the practice of one individual. The question, however, is this: what, precisely, is this individual's unique practice? Is it the fact that he inscribes his bowls with indications of "milk" and "meat," or is it the fact that he maintains separate bowls at all? The emphasis of the writer is on the former fact (the markings), but the latter may also be a relatively idiosyncratic practice.

The writer goes on to report that "his friend said to him that it is better not to write...," but the reason given in the text makes no sense at all, so it is impossible to recover the source of the objection—or even its precise object. There is little we can learn with confidence, therefore, from this isolated testimony. The most we can say with prudence is that perhaps as much as a century before Shalom of Neustadt, one Jew in the Rhineland, influenced by the broader pietistic currents that moved German Jews at the time, separated his dishes (two of them, one of each). As we have seen, contemporary halakhic authorities would not have required this. But the acts of individuals matter as well.

What emerges from this combination of opinions and reports is the recognition that there are ongoing and significant differences of opinion in law and practice. According to some, there would be no need to assign cooking pots to permanent separate categories. According to others, there clearly would be. For these latter figures, a pot in twelfth or fourteenth century France or Spain would be meat or dairy, if not in name then surely in practice. But even for these figures, such a separation applies primarily to pots, not to "kitchens" as a whole. Given their use, it is easy to understand why pots might be subject to different, more stringent concerns or regulations.

At the same time, certain individuals in certain communities—to be precise, German Jews influenced by local pietism—have accepted "mainstream" stringencies and extended them still further. In the homes of these individuals, pots and knives *and even bowls* have been separated into "milk" and "meat." There is no evidence, yet, that this step has spread beyond these limited circles. But this early practice will grow in influence. We shall return to this development below.

INTO MODERNITY

When we turn to the early Modern period, we are confronted with confusing and even conflicting evidence. On the one hand, some rabbinic compositions suggest that little has changed. But other rabbinic testimonies indicate that community practice, if not the actual letter of the law, has developed significant stringencies. And the voices of lay Jews—or former Jews—describe a popular reality that, at least in certain locales, prefigures the common stringent practices of later centuries. Let us consider these various bodies of evidence carefully.

R. Joseph Caro, a renowned Sephardic authority living in Safed, codified Jewish practice in its multitudinous detail. In his Shulhan Arukh (the relevant section was published in 1564), Caro recorded a series of opinions that either repeat those of his predecessors or modestly extend them to newly specified scenarios. So, for example, like Aderet, Caro forbids cutting cheese with a knife that is customarily used to cut meat (Y.D., 89, 4). He also forbids eating cheese on a cloth that has already been used for meat (ibid.). But he explicitly permits one to keep jugs used for milk and meat together in the same cabinet (95, 6). And he even rules that "plates used for meat that were washed in a kettle used for milk, in water hot enough to scald one's hand, even if they had both been used [for meat and dairy] on the same day, it is permitted..." (95, 3). So, on the one hand, the law continues to express an active fear for the actual combination of meat and dairy food products. And it is true that at least some utensils take on the name of the category of food for which they have been used. But, on the other hand, Caro explicitly does not require (or imagine) the division of a kitchen into meat and dairy territories, and he permits sorts of mixing that will later be forbidden. All things considered, Caro reflects relatively minor developments in the law, but nothing truly significant.

At the same time, R. Moses Isserles' (1530–1572) glosses on Caro's rulings suggest that Jewish practices in Poland and Germany, at least, have begun to shift in notable ways. In response to ruling after ruling, Isserles dissents that practice as he knows it is more restrictive. Commenting on Caro's restrictions regarding knifes, Isserles adds "all of Israel [= all Jews] have already made it their custom to have two knifes, and to mark one of them so that it will have a sign, and they are accustomed to marking the one used for dairy, and one should not change the custom of Israel" (89, 4). Concerning Caro's permission to keep different categories of vessels together in the same cabinet, he avers that "there are those who are more stringent in this, and it is better to be more cautious in a place where it is unnecessary [to mix them]." The same impulse is reflected in an adjacent comment, where Isserles praises those who keep separate salt dishes for dairy and meat (95, 7), and, in the same connection, R. Shlomo Luria (1510–1574, quoted in *Turei Zahav*) proclaims that it is the established custom of Jews in Germanic lands to have such separate dishes for salt.

In another connection, Isserles reports that "there are those who are stringent with the cover [of a pot], saying that, even if it was not used on the same day it is treated as though it were used on the same day"—as we have seen, a vessel not used on the same day was traditionally treated far more leniently—"and this is the accepted practice in certain places, *and this is my practice because of established custom, though it is a stringency without reason*" (93, 3, emphasis added). Of course, if pot-covers retain the quality of what was cooked in the pot even for days after the cooking, it will be necessary to maintain a separation between "meat" and "dairy" covers in a more permanent and scrupulous way. And even with regard to the question of washing vessels, where Caro permits vessels used for either meat or dairy to be washed together promiscuously, Isserles supports the custom of permitting this only if one category of vessel was not actually used on the same day (95, 3). If used on the same day, one would have to wash them separately.

Collectively, these reports of increasing stringency in mid-sixteenth century Ashkenazic practice can be understood as pointing toward an outcome that will be realized in the complete separation of meat and dairy dishes, utensils, etc. Surely, several of the quoted testimonies indicate that, in the awareness of these authorities, separation is already practiced in many details. But, despite its testimony to significant developments in customs relating to separation, this material still does not provide evidence of a comprehensive, systematic separation. In fact, in his comment insisting upon stricter cautions in washing dishes, Isserles makes it clear that practice, as he would regulate it, is still relatively lax, at least when compared with the customs of later centuries. His comment continues:

> [what I have said] refers specifically to [washing dishes together in] a boiling kettle [= a kettle that was placed directly on the fire to boil the water], but if they were washed one after the other, or even together in a vessel that had not been on the fire, it is all permitted...and if he poured boiling water, which is neither of meat nor of milk [= it had not been boiled in pots used the same day for meat or milk], upon utensils of meat and milk together—and even if fat/grease is on them—it is permitted. (95, 3)

Each of these rulings has its technical reason, based upon principals articulated in earlier sources. But it suffices for us to notice that, even in this more stringent environment, vessels used for meat and those used for milk may be thrown together with relative ease. And it is not even clear whether Isserles' category associations are meant as permanent designations (that is, whether vessels or utensils, in general, belong to the category of meat or that of dairy) or whether they simply refer to recent usage. In light of the recorded regulations, it would still be relatively easy to use the same pot or utensil one day for meat and several days later for dairy. In fact, the only items that have explicitly been permanently assigned to milk and meat categories are knifes and salt dishes.

But, of course, the halakhic codes are not the only evidence we have. We saw already above that thirteenth- through fourteenth-century pietistic treatises from German lands provide evidence of more comprehensive separation of dishes, at least in limited pietistic circles. There is another body of evidence, written in German, suggesting that, already by the early sixteenth century, Jewish practice in German lands was far more stringent than rabbinic authorities would insist, or even than they report.

The earliest evidence of this development is found in the work of a Jewish convert to Christianity, Antonius Margaritha. Margaritha, son of the chief rabbi of Regensburg, converted to Christianity, in the small Bavarian town of Wasserburg, in 1522. In 1530, he published a book entitled *Der gantz Jüdisch Glaub* ("The Entire Jewish Faith"), with the aim of exposing the purported anti-Christian content of Jewish law and practice.[10] This work is a remarkable record of contemporary Jewish practice, sometimes distorted and polemical but often quite matter-of-fact. It provides, in its details, witness to customs unmentioned in the record of rabbinic authorities of the same period. In his chapter on "their food and vessels, and also how they slaughter and de-vein their livestock," Margaritha reports that "The Jews use two kinds of vessels, one for meat and the other for milk. Therefore, they have two kinds of pots, bowls, spoons, platters and knives...." Margaritha's list is a comprehensive list of the sorts of cooking, serving and eating vessels likely to be found in the home of his day—pots for cooking, bowls and spoons for soups and stews, platters for serving and knives for multiple purposes (see later in this chapter). As importantly, his list represents a specification of his general rule, that is, that Jews use different vessels for meat and milk.

It is difficult to read this report as saying anything other than that Jews separate their kitchens, whatever they may look like, into dairy and meat categories. Of which Jews is he speaking? He seems to be making a universal statement: Jews, as far as he knows them, separate dishes. But there is room to be skeptical. As noted, Margaritha's presentation is sometimes distorted and polemical. It is possible that Margaritha chooses to describe what he deems the "weird" practice of the few and represent it as though it were the common practice of the many. It is also possible that his prejudice leads him to notice only the "odd" or "unusual," ignoring the practices of other Jews. Still, there is no explicit evidence of a polemical bent in his present description; indeed, his language seems quite neutral and straightforward. In light of these contrary considerations, it would be best that we evaluate his report cautiously. At the very least, there can be no doubt that what he says is accurate for some Jews of his time and place, and this, by itself, is undeniably significant, for this is the first time we hear of the comprehensive mapping of the Jewish kitchen into "meat" and "dairy." What we witness here, in other words, the birth of the "modern" Jewish kitchen.

By the eighteenth century, evidence shows unambiguously that the practice of separating completely everything pertaining to meat or dairy foods has become widespread. So, for example, one M. Marcus, writing in London about *The Ceremonies of the Present Jews* (1728, 1729), reports that Jews have one "set of Dishes, Plates, Knives, and forks for meat, and another for Butter, Milk, and Cheese" (p. 4). A quarter of a century later in Germany, Carl Antons, who converted to Christianity in 1748, writes about these same matters, leaving no room for doubt concerning the practice of separation in the Jewish home. In the eleventh chapter of his *Kurzer Entwurf*, Antons writes that "every Jew must have double plates, from the least to the greatest." He adds that, "in order to be really careful, they mark either the meat dishes with the word Basar, meat, or the milk plates with the word chalebh, milk." Finally, he reports that some wealthy Jews, to avoid problems that might be caused by their cooks, build two separate kitchens, one for meat and the other for dairy.[11]

Notably, the material evidence reinforces the literary record in at least one crucial respect. The Jewish Museum in New York has in its collection twenty plates, mostly of pewter, that have the Hebrew words for milk or meat on them. Of these, only one has a distinct inscription date: 1777/8. But the style of the lettering helps date some of the others, and eight were apparently produced in the eighteenth century.

So the separation of dishes is already practiced in Germany, in limited pietistic circles, as early as the thirteenth century. And it seems that it has come to be practiced more commonly in German-Jewish homes of the early-to-mid-sixteenth century. It is well established among European Jewry as a whole by at least the middle of the eighteenth century.

Ironically, though, if one examines the "official" rabbinic documentation alone, one finds little evidence of such comprehensive separation. In fact, reading the rabbinic rulings, one is left with the impression that, in general, little has changed for centuries, and stringencies are pious extensions of the law controlled by local custom. As we saw, this is true not only of Caro's delineation of the requirements of the halakha, but even of Isserles' reports, which include practices that go beyond the basic demands of the system. It is also true of later rabbinic compositions. As far as I have been able to find, it is only when we turn to latter-day codifications that the permanent, systematic separation of dishes—or something like it—finds explicit mention.

R. Abraham Danzig, in his *Ḥokhmat Adam* (first published Vilna, 1814), comments that "one must, in any case, fix a usage [= either meat or dairy] for a pot" (48, 4). To be sure, his ruling is restricted to pots, but at least he is clear about the need to assign pots to a category. A more comprehensive statement is found, finally, in the *Arukh HaShulḥan* of R. Yehiel Halevi Epstein (the relevant sections of this work were first published in Warsaw in 1894–8). Epstein writes:

> ...and the custom has already spread that in all houses where there is cooking [= kitchens?] there is a plank set aside for placing [upon it] meat pots and a plank set aside for placing [upon it] dairy pots, and for all things of dairy and meat there are special utensils, *and Jews are holy and they are very stringent with themselves in this*. (Y.D., 88:11, emphasis added)

Further on, he adds:

> Small and big dishes in the house, of meat alone and of dairy alone, should be made of two [different] kinds, for recognition, that they not be confused. And the same [should be true] for spoons and forks and the same for all utensils—or they should make markings on those of dairy—and thus have all of Israel made their custom. (Y.D., 89:16)

I am not confident that a statement such as these will not be found in a more obscure halakhic source of a slightly earlier period. But this would do little to change the phenomenon we have already observed: Rabbinic codifications pertaining to the separation of Jewish kitchens into "meat" and "dairy" lag well behind popular practice. But why is this the case? We might surmise that the popular stringencies reported in the writings of Margaritha, Marcus, and Antons (as well as others, not reviewed here) were as yet unknown to the rabbinic writers. Perhaps they were not yet practiced in the communities in which these authorities lived? This is highly unlikely, however, first because the record documents the practice of separation in at least Germany, Switzerland, and England during these centuries—a significant geographical range—and, second, because the Jewish culture of Poland was related to and influenced by that of Germany. It is nearly impossible to imagine, therefore, that notable numbers of Jews separated their dishes, in a comprehensive way, in Germany but not in Isserles' Poland.

It is far more likely that the noted "lag" is a product of the conservatism of rabbinic writings, a conservatism that has ironic consequences when it comes to popular stringencies such as these. Broadly speaking, rabbinic codifiers tend to repeat, in identical or similar words, the formulations of the sources from which they draw. The best example of this, in the present case, is Maimonides' codification, which is virtually identical to its talmudic source and gives little hint that the law has been elaborated and extended. The same is true, though in different measure, of each subsequent "generation" of halakhic writings, which articulates its claim to traditional authority by incorporating the formulations of its predecessors. So if prior codes spoke of separating knives or pots, rather than all kitchenware, then subsequent codes will tend to employ the same language, even if, in practice, all kitchenware is being separated in a permanent and comprehensive manner. Indeed, this conservatism has what are apparently lenient consequences because, if these writings "err" in any direction, it is in the direction of what *was* rather than what has come to be, that is, in the direction of what halakha actually requires rather than what common custom has come to expect.

Even Epstein, whose formulation reports and praises the most stringent developments, does not hesitate to admit the difference between the two. He is unambiguous in describing the practice of comprehensive separation as a "custom" (*minhag*). By employing this term, he admits that it is not demanded by the halakha (the letter of the law). He further speaks of at least the first custom (separate "counters") as a relatively recent one, and in both cases his language suggests that separation is a popular development, one assumed by "Israel," for he offers no literary source for the practices he reports. Finally, the rhetoric of the statement I have emphasized—*"Jews are holy and they are very stringent with themselves in this"*—shows that, despite Epstein's obvious support of the practice, he is aware that it goes beyond what the halakha would require. Why, after all, employ such hyperbole if the practice being praised can be taken for granted? If the practice were well-grounded in the sources, a simple, declarative sentence, in the normal style of such halakhic writing, would have sufficed. Epstein applauds the fact that Jews, as he knows them, are stringent with themselves in these matters. Evidently other Jews, in earlier generations and places, saw no need for such stringencies.

THE TECHNOLOGIES OF EATING: A BRIEF HISTORY

So the practice of separating meat and dairy dishes has developed significantly from its Talmudic roots. From simple directives demanding caution with recently used pots or dishes, the law has developed to a point that it literally determines the map of the observant Jewish kitchen, requiring at least separate cabinets for the abundance of meat or dairy cookware, serving and eating utensils, and in the case of the "wealthy," separate sinks or even separate kitchens. Having traced the path of this development, the challenge remains for us to explain, as far as we can, *why?*—why did a few, simple regulations, laid down in the Talmud to keep the tastes of meat and dairy separate, develop into a comprehensive system that, in its fullest formulation, has come to represent the kitchen of the observant Jew, and even Jewish observance itself?

Part of the answer to these questions will be found in the history of what we might call the technologies of eating. People in earlier centuries ate in very different ways, employing different utensils than we or, as often, no utensils at all. In the early Middle Ages, eating forks had yet to be invented, and hands were often used for transporting solid foods to the mouth. According to Islamic norms, food was taken from a common tray, placed on a low table, with one's fingers.[12] In Provence, knifes were kept for personal use, and they would be used both for cutting and spearing foods. Collective dishes—typically wood or bronze trays or deep platters—were used to serve all present at a meal, and only bowls might be used by individual diners.[13] Since soups were the common food for the masses in medieval Europe, spoons and ladles were also essential utensils.

Forks were unknown before the eleventh century, and there is rare evidence of them for centuries thereafter. To perform the function now served by forks, people would use either their hands or, as commonly, knifes, whose points were handy for impaling foods and bringing them to one's mouth. As late as the early seventeenth century, in Italy, forks were used for carving, not eating. But evidence suggests that their use did spread during this century, and by the late eighteenth century, French etiquette manuals require full settings of silverware, including forks. Still, as late as the beginning of the twentieth century, bourgeois people in Vienna were still carrying cakes to their mouths with knifes, showing that old habits die hard and relatively more recent practices must struggle to win complete acceptance.[14]

As far as plates are concerned, a similar trajectory of development may be sketched. As described above, in earlier centuries in North Africa, the only "plates" were platters or trays, intended to serve the assembled diners collectively. Trenchers of wood or bread were more common, the former used, again, for common service. Metal flatplates are found in Italy in the early sixteenth century, but hard plates for individual use do not become more common until the seventeenth century. In the seventeenth through eighteenth centuries, the bourgeoisie employed silver plates, while the aristocracy preferred ceramic plates. Still, such plates were not generally accepted, in France at least, until the nineteenth century. The Jewish Museum plates, mentioned above, reflect this history almost exactly. The earliest plates in that collection, all of pewter, are from the eighteenth century, and the ceramic plates are all from the nineteenth or twentieth century. Crucially, the telling of this history indicates how important the question of class is in considering these developments. If the wealthier classes were using plates, common folk were still forced to rely on old "technologies," at least until the mass production of inexpensive plates. As is the case with forks, common use of plates is a genuinely modern phenomenon (Visser, 191–92).

These realities have an obvious impact on the eating regulations of Jews in the Middle Ages. As we have seen, in their writings, rabbinic authorities of these centuries focus time and again on the same utensils: knifes, pots, bowls, and spoons. Not once is there a mention of a fork, and plates (used for serving, not individual eating) are rarely discussed. Of course, the subjects of rabbinic deliberation reflect exactly the realities we have described. Knifes were the most important utensil, used for cooking, serving, and eating. Pots were the central and essential means by which foods were prepared. Bowls were used for both serving and eating, as soups and stews formed one of the foundations of the common diet, and spoons, therefore, were essential eating utensils. In any given household, all of these would have been present in relatively small numbers (a couple of pots would serve for a family, individuals kept their own knifes), so the sorts of "sets" that typify modern kitchens would have been unavailable. Simply put, sets of dishes were not separated during these centuries, at least in part, because there were no sets of dishes to separate.

In fact, rabbinic authorities were aware of changes in the technologies of eating and commented on how such changes would affect Jewish eating regulations. Responding to a questioner who asks about the need to change tablecloths between meat and dairy meals, R. David b. Solomon ibn Abi Zimra (1479–1573, the "Radbaz") refers to an opinion of Ibn Adret (the "Rashba") that supports such a requirement. But he then adds: "the words of the master applied only when they placed the meat and the cheese [directly] on the cloth, for there is then a concern that they might get stuck on one another, but it is our practice to bring all foods to the table in bowls, so even if there are meat droppings on the cloth, they [= the different foods] will never touch one another." So Radbaz recognizes that eating customs have changed, and understands that such changes will demand different precautions in practice. He recalls a reality in which food was placed directly on the table, and when individuals used the same tablecloth to clean their hands between foods. But in his day, food is kept in bowls—not placed directly on the table—and small cloths (napkins) are distributed to diners to wipe their hands (he adds this observation below in the same comment). In his opinion, this change should lead to greater leniency with respect to the separation of cloths. But as we look forward to the centuries in which flat plates and full sets of cutlery become more and more common, the same sensibility might well demand more systematic separations of the vessels that actually contain and manipulate food. When dishes become common, they will be separated. When forks join knifes and spoons at each setting, they, too, will be separated. "Separate dishes" is—at least in part—the halakhic Jewish response to a new reality.

But while it is true that such separation is not surprising, neither is it "natural" or necessary. There is more to this story than the history of how foods were brought from the pot to the mouth.

There is not a single, linear history of how foods were consumed, and the ancient reality in Palestine, viewed in juxtaposition with the leniency of the earliest rabbinic laws, shows that later separations were not inevitable. Excavations at Qumran, providing evidence of the practice of at least one community in the late second Temple period, uncovered a large storage room filled with hundreds of serving and eating vessels. Crucially, vessels for serving and those for eating were stored separately, and there was a far larger quantity of the latter than of the former. Moreover, these eating vessels were simple pottery, manufactured, clearly, for common use. Together, the quantity and simplicity of these vessels suggest that they were intended for use by individuals during their meals. Included in this large stash were cups, bowls and flat plates with raised rims. So personal dishes—not only those for communal serving—and plates—not only bowls—characterized the eating technologies of the community at Qumran.[15] Because this reality does not "follow the usual [Roman] custom of eating out of common dishes," Jodi Magness argues that the community's practice must stem "from their belief that impurity could be transmitted through food and drink."[16] In other words, the practice of eating from personal plates, like other practices of the Qumran community, was, in her opinion, sectarian. But other evidence suggests that these Qumran utensils may not be as unusual as Magness believes.

The discoveries at the Bar-Kokhba caves, reflecting early second-century practice, similarly reveal that personal plates were at least sometimes employed for eating in ancient Palestine. Though the number of dishes found at the site is small, their purpose is relatively unambiguous. Four complete dishes were found in a basket belonging to a woman named Babatha, indicating that they were for personal use. Two are shallow plates, and the other two are bowls. All are of a size appropriate for use by an individual, and all are made of unfinished wood, an inexpensive material. Other plates of a similar nature (either whole or in fragments) were discovered in the same caves, and all likewise suggest that Jews (and perhaps others) in Roman Palestine occasionally used individual dishes for taking their meals (see Yadin, pp. 132–35 and plates 39–40).[17]

Moreover, even if Magness is correct in suggesting that the use of individual plates was motivated by a concern for the transmission of ritual impurity, she goes too far in suggesting that this consideration was restricted to the Qumran sectarians. In fact, the rabbis themselves, in the Mishnah, exhibit abundantly their similar concern, devoting parts of one tractate (*Toharot*) to the matter of impurity transmitted by foods, and the bulk of a second, extremely lengthy tractate (*Kelim*) to the potential impurity of utensils and vessels. If fears of impurity led to the use of individual plates, then the rabbis (or, at least, those of their number who dedicated themselves to eating common foods in a state of purity) can be expected to have done the same. At the very least, they surely knew that some Jews in Palestine—not only sectarians—employed individual flat-plates to eat, and they knew, therefore, that their law had to treat this reality.

Yet the rabbis, in the Mishnah, never once mention the need to keep personal plates separate if they have been used for milk or meat. Nor is such a reference, in their name, found anywhere in the talmudic literature. That they did not enunciate such a requirement is not, however, due to the absence of a reality to which it might apply. They did not demand the separation of dishes not because they did not know of dishes, but merely because they did not imagine such separation to be necessary.

Even in the context of later centuries, the expansions we have seen cannot be considered necessary outcomes of developing principles. To recognize that these practices might have developed in other directions, consider, again, the following rulings by Caro and Isserles pertaining to the washing of dishes:

> (Caro) Dishes of meat that were washed in a dairy kettle, in water hot enough to scald the hand, even if both of them had been used on the same day, it is permitted, for it is [a case of] the secondary transmission of a permitted taste....

> (Isserles) And there are those who prohibit...unless one of the vessels had not been used on the same day...and this is our practice, and one should not differ. But this is specifically when they were washed together in a vessel in which the water had been boiled, but *if they were washed one after the other, or even together in a vessel in which the water had not been boiled, it is all permitted*...[and] *if he poured boiling water which is neither of meat nor of milk* [= it had not been boiled is a vessel used for one of those substances on the same day] *upon vessels of meat and milk together, even when grease is on them, it is all permitted*....(Y.D. 95, 3, emphasis added)

These regulations describe the realities of dishwashing long before the invention of the modern dishwasher, when dishes and utensils were washed in large kettles or basins of hot water. But even at a remove from this reality, it is easy to appreciate how relatively lenient these rulings are. They depend upon a simple principal, that is, that "the secondary transmission of a permitted taste" is permitted. The prohibition of mixing meat and dairy begins when one substance "gives taste" to the other. When food is cooked in a pot, it gives taste to that pot. When another food is cooked in the same pot, the pot transmits the earlier taste to the second food, but at a much-diminished level. The rabbinic rule holds that such a secondary transmission of a taste which itself is permitted—such as milk or kosher meat but not pork—will not lead to prohibition. Thus, if meat dishes are first washed in a basin so that the basin absorbs the taste of the meat, and then dairy dishes are washed in the same basin, absorbing some of the meat taste earlier absorbed by the basin, the rule holds that it will all be permitted. This is the principle that is at the foundation of the regulations quoted above.

Following them to their most natural conclusion, these rulings would permit the separate washing of both meat and dairy dishes in a single dishwasher. Yet few observant contemporary Jews would even consider such a practice. Now, there are real concerns that might lead to a more restrictive practice.[18] But it is clear that the major authorities of the sixteenth century did not deem such concerns to be prohibitive. The insistence that we account for *all* potential problems is itself a phenomenon worthy of attention and interpretation. If the system developed in more stringent directions, separating the dishes rather than letting them be, we must seek to understand why.

THE STRINGENCIES OF THE PIOUS

The practice of maintaining separate dishes may be seen as a part of a more prevalent tendency in post-Medieval Jewish practice to choose the more stringent route—in regulations pertaining to eating and in many other matters as well. That there was a surge in eating related pieties in the late medieval and early modern worlds is clearly illustrated in the record we have recounted above. As we saw, the earliest example, describing a Jew who would mark his bowls with the words "milk" and "meat," is found in a late thirteenth century report in Sefer Hasidim, the "Book of the Pious." Another early report, attributed to R. Shalom of Neustadt, describes a pietist who went so far as to have one "house" for dairy and another for meat. Together, these examples suggest that the phenomenon has its origins in the homes of the self-styled pious, a small number at the earliest stages of this development.

But by the sixteenth century, stringencies pertaining to the separation of meat and dairy dishes and utensils have spread to broader circles in Germany and adjacent lands. The question is, why? The forces behind these developments, we suggested in the prior chapter, emerge from the realities of these communities in the early modern period. The key to understanding the relevant historical dynamics is found in the comment of R. Shlomo Luria, who, while speaking of the amount of time one must wait after eating meat before eating dairy, distinguished between the practices of "those who are not *children of Torah*" and those who are (see *Yam shel shlomo* to Hullin, ch. 8, #9). What is the meaning of this distinction?

Luria and Isserles lived in early modern Poland, a land that was, in their day, a mostly hospitable place for Jews. Having ample opportunity to take advantage of the spirit of openness that prevailed at that time, Jews there flourished both economically and culturally. They often enjoyed close relationships—economic and social—with their non-Jewish neighbors, and the practice of many was surely forced to bend before the demands of these relationships. The evidence of such "bending" is widespread and unambiguous (see pp. 136–7).[19] So, from the perspective of the rabbinic authorities, at least, contemporary Jewry was divided between the pious and the less-than-pious. Means of distinguishing the latter from the former were crucial, and developments in eating practice—such as the amount of time one waited between meat and dairy—served this purpose well.

Separating the dishes, like separating one's consumption of meat and dairy, could serve the same purpose, creating a profound symbolic and pragmatic boundary between more and less pious Jews. Significantly, in his condemnation of another stringency, Luria reveals his keen understanding that such customs will inevitably serve to divide between one group and another. Speaking of the eating of meat after cheese (ibid., #6), a practice permitted by the Talmud, Luria condemns the custom of those who refuse to do so as "sectarian" (*minut*). By refusing to do what is permitted, they "separate themselves" from the community, creating divisions between Jew and Jew. This is undeniably true. But we must not fail to recognize that such stringencies and differential practices do more than merely divide; they at the same time *reflect* and *reinforce* such divisions. There is a dynamic relationship between the practice and the social grouping, according to which divisions lead to different customs and different customs strengthen and multiply social divisions. This is as true, of course, of keeping separate dishes as it is of the other stringencies that took root during this period.

The development of the practice of separating dishes transformed the kitchen of the pious Jew into a comprehensive symbol of his or her piety. Separating the dishes into meat and dairy sets, she at the same time separated herself, the more pious Jew, from another, less pious one. By marking her plates, some for meat and some for milk, she marked herself off from her neighbor who did not (yet) observe this custom. As had been true centuries before—at least if my explanation of the origins of the milk-meat prohibition is correct—once again the eating regulations were enlisted to distinguish one sort of Jew from the other. Both symbolizing and effectuating the separation of the more observant from the less observant, this practice would constitute a powerful bulwark against an encroaching modernity.

But, having recognized the symbolic and pragmatic similarities of this practice and that of waiting between meat and dairy meals, we must still ask why the practice of separating dishes seems to have been more widespread, at least in the sixteenth century. The answer, it seems to me, lies, at least in part, in the different stages on which these practices are enacted. The obligation to wait between meals is potentially as much a public as it is a private performance. It restricts what a person may eat, and therefore with whom she or he may eat, for hours after the consumption of meat. Of course, this restriction pertains both in one's private domain and abroad (that is, "*fleishig*" is a status that you carry with you), and so it has both private and public consequences. But the point is that it *does* have public repercussions, because it might lead one to say "no" when asked to share a dairy meal or snack, whether with a friend, a neighbor or a business acquaintance in the marketplace. Observing these strictures, a Jew will advertise himself as pious before the world, particularly since the pressures of that world invite "compromise" (lenient is easier). At the same time, the Jew who fails to observe these strictures will mark himself, in public, as not belonging to the circle of the pious. Accommodating business and even social relationships with gentiles by accepting the less demanding practice (waiting one hour as opposed to six), he will show where his priorities truly lie.

By contrast, keeping separate dishes is a more private affair. The precise arrangement of one's kitchen, the number and types of one's dishes, how they were used and kept, and how they were marked, would be known immediately only to a person in her or his home, or in the home to which she or he had been invited. This means that this practice constituted a relatively intimate communication, one by which members of a household expressed the message of piety to themselves and to their close friends. Being kept "behind closed doors," the kitchen was subject to more private, domestic influences and less subject to the pressures of social and other forces on the outside. This latter point is crucial, and requires expansion.

The kitchen was (and is), from the perspective of the developing "normative" tradition, a rather odd, because hybrid, realm. It was, of course, the primary arena for the acting out of many complex rabbinic food regulations. However, the rabbis were not actually the authorities in the kitchen—at least not on a regular basis. Rather, the kitchen was a place for the exercise of popular authority and local expertise. With the rarest exception, the authority in most Jewish (as non-Jewish) kitchens was the woman of the household.[20] It was she who prepared the foods and it was she, therefore, who negotiated and adjudicated questions and problems relating to kashrut. This fact had significant ramifications for Jewish practice.

It meant, first of all, that the kitchen was a place where women would display their own, domestic piety, often to other women. Its dynamics, therefore, would differ radically from those that characterized the marketplace or public realm, where the piety of men would be more on display.

As we said above, the public domain was one in which Jews and gentiles—mostly men—mixed. It was a place where the pressure to compromise was palpable and the expression of resistance—through, say, refusing to eat with one's acquaintance or client—symbolically bold. Needless to say, the dynamics inside the household were different, more the product of the qualities of women's lives in this same time and place.

Jewish women during these centuries in Europe were mostly not learned, and they were surely unschooled in the technical details of the laws of separating dairy and meat. What they knew, they knew mostly from experience: from watching their mothers conduct in their kitchens when they were girls. From the model of the prior generation, they knew, more or less, what must be done in any given circumstance. But while they mostly knew the "what," they often did not know the "why," at least not as a rabbi would. And this ignorance had its consequences. What would a woman do when things were mixed in her kitchen in ways she did not know how to fix? The safe choice, for a pious woman, would always be to take the more stringent path. And to avoid such problems, the same woman would take precautions, establishing more restrictive standards to assure that difficulties would not arise. Not being able to rely upon the technical rabbinic principles that would allow more lenient solutions, she would build in protections that would help her avoid what, in her kitchen, run according to her standards, would lead to unacceptable loss—loss of time, of food (which had to be discarded) and of resources (plates that would have to be replaced, etc.).

A reliable source has shared the following story: When this person, the son of a famous rabbi, was young, his mother took a trip away from home, leaving him and his father in charge of the home and the kitchen for the first time. When his mother returned a couple of weeks later, she was horrified by what she saw in *her* kitchen; she immediately accused her husband, the rabbi, of "treifing up" (= rendering unkosher) the kitchen. Of course, he had done nothing of the sort. He had merely conducted himself in the kitchen according to what rabbinic sources would require. But this was not good enough for her. She, the ultimate authority in her kitchen, had established her own standards, and these standards required steps that were unheard of in the literary record. When popular folk, doing their best to protect the kashrut of their kitchens, make the rules, these rules will inevitably be more stringent.

For these reasons, we should not be surprised that keeping separate dishes seems to have been, already in the sixteenth and certainly by the eighteenth century, quite a popular Jewish practice; by contrast, the practice of waiting six hours was far more restricted in the sixteenth century, and continued to be less widespread even in later centuries. The former was engendered by the influence of women in the domestic realm, the latter by men negotiating the public realm. Each expressed his or her identity in her or his respective realm. And since a statement of "more pious" or "less pious," more alike or more apart, is meaningful only by comparison to the alternative, the stage on which these identities were enacted influenced fundamentally the precise form they took.

Looking forward, we should also not be surprised then that when pious Jewish women had to decide what to do with their modern kitchens in the modern world, they decided in favor of a complete and systematic separation. As the story recounted above suggests, these women, who knew what their mothers did but not what the law actually required, had little choice but to choose the direction of stringency. Through their self-imposed separations, they constantly reminded themselves, their families and their neighbors *who* they were and *to what community* they belonged.

9 Crossing boundaries

We have seen numerous times in prior chapters how Jewish eating practices have served to separate Jews from their neighbors. Biblical laws differentiating pure and impure animals, post-biblical and rabbinic enactments outlawing certain gentile foods, talmudic, medieval, and early modern developments pertaining to the separation of meat and dairy, would all, under certain circumstances, have made it difficult if not impossible for Jews to have joined their neighbors at a common table. Yet it has not always been evident to all Jews that such an outcome, intended or not, was desirable. In some settings, Jews enjoyed comfortable relationships with their gentile neighbors and might have desired to cement those relationships through shared drinks or meals. In other settings, Jews were dependent upon their neighbors for their protection, livelihoods, and such, and would have found it difficult, socially and pragmatically, to maintain the sorts of separations that Jewish eating regulations demanded. Boundaries, though having their purpose, are not always desirable. Jews recognized this, of course, from the very beginning.

It is not mere coincidence, therefore, that shortly after Paul is called to serve as apostle to the gentiles, the narrative of the Book of Acts addresses the question of Jewish food restrictions and the divisions they create. According to the story recorded in Acts chapter 10, a certain Simon, called Peter, when lodging in Jaffa, experiences a vision in which heaven opens up and a large sheet containing a variety of impure creatures descends to the ground (vss. 11–12). A voice directs Peter to kill and eat the animals (vs. 13), but Peter refuses, declaring that "I have never eaten anything that is profane or unclean" (vs. 14). The voice responds: "What God has made clean, you must not call profane" (vs. 15). This exchange is repeated three times, we are told (vs. 16), whereupon the vision ascends again to heaven. After this vision, Peter accompanies a mission that had been sent to retrieve him by Cornelius, a Roman centurion, back to their master in Caesaria. Upon meeting Cornelius, Peter declares: "You yourselves know that it is unlawful for a Jew to associate with or to visit a Gentile; but God has shown me that I should not call anyone profane or unclean" (vs. 28). Later, he continues: "I truly understand that God shows no partiality" (vs.

34), showing that he appreciates the normative implications of the food vision. And still later, defending himself to "circumcised" believers who challenge his willingness to eat with the uncircumcised, he reiterates the parallel (11:1–12), explaining that God had directed him to consider clean, and therefore to eat, what had earlier been thought profane, and that he was similarly directed to cease making distinctions between "them"—the uncircumcised—and "us"—the circumcised. In other words, the distinctions demanded by the law with respect to foods require that parallel distinctions be made between peoples. The moment the Jew (Peter) wants to overcome the boundaries that divide "us" from "them," the eating restrictions must be compromised or eliminated.

Through the centuries, as Jews lived with non-Jewish neighbors, negotiating constantly the precise nature of their relationship with those neighbors, they repeatedly had to ask the same question as the one intimated by Peter in Acts: When and under what circumstances will the boundaries constituted by the eating regulations stand, and when—and to what extent—will they yield or even fall? What makes this question so interesting is that, contrary to the impression left in the story of Acts, the possible answers need not be conceived dichotomously. An infinite number of permutations is available to the Jew who might want to, more or less, eat like a Jew while joining his or her gentile neighbor in food or drink. She might, for example, compromise the restriction on gentile bread—the substance of which is kosher—while observing restrictions on prohibited substances and mixtures. He might use the law to negotiate more lenient boundaries between "permitted" and "prohibited," eating cold vegetables with his gentile business partner while failing to symbolize his extreme piety. It is the range of possible negotiations and compromises that we will explore in this chapter, examining how shifts and choices in manners of Jewish eating reflect and represent related shifts or choices in the Jewish identities of given communities.

It is necessary to emphasize that, while we may employ terms like "negotiations" or "compromises" to describe the shifting boundaries between the "inside" or "permitted" and the "outside" or "prohibited" territories defined by the eating regulations, no single term will describe with full precision the phenomenon we seek to explore. In some cases, Jews who ate certain foods in certain ways recognized that their eating choices represented bona fide transgressions. They knew that what they were doing was, on some level, prohibited, and they chose to do so anyway. They compromised the law so that they could eat with—or in the manner of—their gentile neighbor. But in other cases, Jews might have eaten prohibited foods, or in a prohibited manner, out of "ignorance." They might have been so "assimilated" that they did not even know that they were following a proscribed path. Were such Jews "compromising" the limits imposed by Jewish law? Could their eating be described as "transgressive eating?" And what if they knew they did not know the law, at least as delineated by the rabbis? Is ignorance an excuse in such cases, or would we interpret such ignorance as itself a kind of compromise?

And what of Jews who chose to follow interpretations that allowed for certain leniencies? These leniencies might have facilitated eating combinations that would be condemned by some authorities, but not by all. For some, these choices will be characterized as transgressions, for others they will at worst be "stretches," and for others they will simply be different customs. But what if lenient interpretations or customs are found to be present in more open societies, societies in which Jews and gentiles live in peace, with greater acceptance each of the other? Here, the internal Jewish negotiation might be subsumed in the rabbinic interpretation, "justified" on the basis of authoritative sources. Yet we might still recognize what motivates the leniency and understand that here, too, the separatist Jewish identity struggles with the one that reaches out.

The cases we will consider cover the range of possibilities outlined here, though it will not always be possible to determine where, precisely, along the spectrum a particular case belongs. Still, we will always ask whether and how the "liberal" or "transgressive" eating phenomenon we identify expresses the Jew's desire to live with his neighbor, to renegotiate the boundary between "inside" and "outside" in the interest of identifying with the cultural environment in which he finds himself. Much of what we suggest will remain speculative, for we are interpreting coincidence, not uncovering explicit or direct cause. The abundance of such coincidences, though, suggests that many compromises or reinterpretations of Jewish eating restrictions are, in fact, attempts at re-imagining what it means to live and identify as a Jew in a gentile world.

Writing in the late eighth century in Babylonia (Iraq), Pirqoi ben Baboi reports that the Jews of the Land of Israel do not abstain from eating animals whose lungs are affected by adhesions—thus rendering them technically unkosher—because "they do not have in their hands even one law from the Talmud's laws of slaughter...."[1] He explains their failure as the product of ignorance, and indeed it may have been, for the Mishnah—which they surely knew—does not list this blemish as one of the causes of disqualification (see m. Hullin 3:1). This disqualifying blemish is identified first in the Babylonian Talmud—there is no Palestinian Talmud on this Mishnaic tractate—and Palestinian Jews may have been unaware of it. Or they may have known it but not accepted the authority of the Babylonian authorities who made this extension.

But, shortly before Ben Baboi's comment quoted earlier, the failure of Palestinian Jews to observe this and other laws is characterized as being "*like* the custom of [those subject to foreign] persecution" (Ginzberg, 559, emphasis added). Is it possible, then, that the purported "ignorance" of the Palestinian Jewish population is a consequence of the political-social conditions in which they lived? Palestine in the late eighth century was, like Babylonia, under Abbasid Muslim rule. These Muslim authorities did not actively persecute Jews, though they did restrict them as *dhimmi*—as non-Muslim "people of the book."[2] There is no reason to believe, however, that the ability of Jews to study their sacred books would have been restricted. Indeed, no such persecution is even claimed, as the author describes their practices as being merely "like" the ones of those subject to persecution, not the actual product of persecution. But Muslim society in this period was a powerful, highly regulated one, and Jews would have been subject to the pressures and influences of that society. Given the fact that it was controlled by a religious law originating in a revealed scripture and given by a single God, Jews even felt, or aspired to feel, somewhat at home in this society.[3] Significantly, Muslim law, beginning with the Quran, prohibited the eating of "carrion and blood and the flesh of the swine" (2:173), just as had Jewish law before it. And the Muslim procedure for slaughtering animals was virtually identical with that prescribed by halakha. But Islam had no parallel regulations pertaining to the lungs and other internal organs. We may wonder, therefore, whether the practice of Palestinian Jews ignoring such concerns may be a partial "Muslimization" on their part—whether out of their own desire or because of powerful cultural influences. The fact that at least one Babylonian Jew, also living in a Muslim society, condemned the leniency of his Palestinian brethren would not militate against this possibility; different people or groups negotiate the same challenges in different ways. This can only be speculation, however, for we have very little evidence in this case.

At the same time, the present interpretation is perhaps challenged by the fact that, in several other questions pertaining to eating restrictions, the Babylonian community is more lenient than the Jewish community in Palestine. This phenomenon is found in three matters: the oils and butter of gentiles, the bread of gentiles, and boiled legumes of gentiles (= prepared by gentiles). In all three cases, Palestinian rabbinic authorities prohibit the listed foods and Babylonian authorities permit them, either outright or, in the case of bread, by requiring the Jew to "participate" in the baking by throwing a small twig into the oven to help supply fuel for the flame. In all of these cases, the local custom begins in an opinion expressed in the Talmud of that community, either the Yerushalmi or the Bavli. But the division between the practices of the communities does not end there. Notably, the talmudic division persists into later periods, so that the law of the Geonim continues to divide Palestinian and Babylonian Jewry in their practices relating to these foods.

Mordechai Margulies proposes several explanations in his exposition of these differences. He accepts the talmudic testimony regarding the antiquity of the Palestinian prohibitions, and regards the Jewish community's concern for maintaining its ritual purity in the Land of Israel as the first motivation for their insistence upon a greater distance from their gentile neighbors. After the destruction of the Temple, Jewish resentment of foreign rule and its hardships contributed to their distancing. He further suggests that the concentration of Jews in Palestine would have allowed them to refrain from using gentile foods, relying, as they could, on their own production. In this same connection, prohibiting the consumption of gentile foods would have encouraged Jewish self-reliance. By contrast, the Jewish community in Babylonia was presumably less densely concentrated, and they thus would have had to depend on their gentile neighbors for certain day-to-day provisions.[4]

The problem with Margulies' explanations is that the differences in practice of which he is speaking persisted for centuries, when some of his claims would have been more or less true, depending upon the precise period on which we focus. In the talmudic period, Jews in Galilee (where most Palestinian Jews resided during these centuries) lived in the midst of a diverse population, one that included many gentiles.[5] It is not clear that, during this period, Palestinian Jews would have lived together in larger numbers or in greater concentration than those in the cities of Babylonia. There were significant Jewish communities in the cities of Iraq (Babylonia) in the late talmudic and Geonic periods, and there is no obvious reason why they should not have wanted to maintain their distinct identities through similar stringencies. Consideration of Orthodox communities in twentieth-century Brooklyn shows that Jewish communities in larger, more diverse settings can create their own industries to produce their own foods, and there is no reason why Babylonian Jewry cannot have done the same. Thus, certain of Margulies' explanations must be challenged, despite their initial "common sense" quality.

Others of his suggested explanations are more reasonable, particularly when restricted to the talmudic period itself. The Palestinian Jewish community did resent foreign rule on its soil, and they continued to pray for the restoration of Jewish sovereignty.[6] As Rome yielded to Byzantium (in the latter part of the fourth century, before the composition of the Yerushalmi), their resentment must have increased, for now they were dominated by pretenders to the title of "Israel."[7] New legal restrictions surely reinforced their hatred.[8] We will have no trouble understanding why, in such a setting, some Jews might have prohibited mixing with gentiles through any means possible—not least through relevant food restrictions. To be sure, as centuries passed, and Byzantium gave way to Islam (with a brief Persian interlude), these motivations will have lessened. But we may imagine that, once such restrictive practices were established, they would have been difficult to jettison. In this way we may understand the persistence of restrictive practices in Palestine even into the Muslim period.

In Babylonia, by contrast, the Jewish diaspora, beginning in the talmudic period, had many reasons to be lenient with regard to such matters, but not precisely those identified by Margulies. As observed earlier, even smaller communities *could* have separated themselves further from their neighbors by insisting on their own butter, bread, and cooked vegetables. Convenience or other pragmatic considerations do not always determine the outcome of such religious-cultural questions. If "pragmatic" considerations are to triumph, they must be supported by other factors. In this case, the most powerful factor would have been the Jews' desire—recognized or unrecognized, explicit or not—to live peaceably with their Babylonian neighbors and hosts. By permitting the sharing of foods that were not technically "unkosher," and by finding ways, through interpretation of the law and its principals, to dismiss earlier (= Mishnaic) restrictions or concerns, the rabbis and their followers will have made a significant contribution to the possibility of harmonious relations between Jew and non-Jew. By lowering the fence that would have separated the two populations, the rabbis declared that Jews in this period and place were *Babylonian* Jews. Indeed, the pride of place experienced by the Babylonian diaspora is amply in evidence in talmudic (see Bavli Ketubot 110b and following) and later teachings.[9] In these leniencies in their eating practices we witness another expression of the same pride.

We noted earlier that the stringency-leniency distribution in these regulations (Babylonia = lenient), and the interpretation we have offered to explain this distribution, seems to conflict with what we suggested in connection with Palestinian leniencies regarding the kashrut of internally blemished animals. In light of our latter interpretations, in might seem preferable to explain the earlier difference simply on the basis of Palestinian ignorance of Babylonian elaborations of the law. It is not obvious to me, however, that this is so. The cases of "gentile" oils, bread, and legumes are different, in significant ways, from the case of lung blemishes. The question of lung blemishes is an internal Jewish question, having nothing directly to do with the foods of non-Jews. These latter cases, by contrast, relate to gentile foods directly; the very question is whether the boundary between Jew and non-Jew can be breached for purposes of consuming these foods, all of them central to the everyday diet. The former case, if our interpretation is correct, is merely an instance of cultural influence, one that does not involve explicit crossing of recognized community boundaries. The latter, of course, represents just such a crossing. So we need not view the contrary leniency-stringency distributions or the interpretations we have proposed as logically contradictory. After all, we are merely saying that even those who insist on stricter boundaries are inevitably influenced by the environment in which they live. There is nothing new or surprising about such an observation.

Besides, it is not clear that the Palestinian practice was as stringent as the preserved rabbinic record would have us believe. In an admittedly polemical epistle, the Karaite, Sahl ben Masliah (second half of the tenth century), writes that the rabbis permitted Jews in Jerusalem to eat "forbidden kinds of food... such as foods prepared by Gentiles... They said that it was permissible to take and use oil from vessels owned by Gentiles and made out of camels' hides, or beverages and sweetmeats made by Gentile confectioners, or to use flour milled by Gentiles who do not first cleanse the grain from impurities and mice droppings."[10] One of these claims (the one pertaining to oil) directly contradicts the rabbinic record as it relates to Palestinian practice. But this does not mean that the author's present claim is incorrect, only that each respective record does not preserve the whole picture. It is difficult to ascertain the accuracy of the other claims, though some appear unlikely (would the rabbis have permitted oil kept in the hides of an unkosher animal?). But the details matter less than the general claim, that is, that the rabbis assumed a relatively lenient stance concerning Jewish use and consumption of gentile food products. Even if, in light of their polemical context, the specifics of ben Masliah's argument must be viewed with some skepticism, we may probably grant the general point of his argument. Why so? Because, to the outsider (the Karaite, who did not accept rabbinic methods), rabbinic arguments and loopholes, which found reasons to grant permission in cases the earlier law had prohibited, surely must have appeared extremely yielding. This would certainly be so if the author knew the positions of Babylonian rabbinic authorities. If local Palestinian Jewish populations followed the Babylonian approach, then the claim of ben Masliah would be unimpeachable (in general if not in all details). Perhaps, then, what we see here is a divergence within rabbinic communities of Palestine. If their practice was not monolithic, then we can accept both the rabbinic and the Karaite testimonies. In any case, it is worth our noticing that lenient rabbinic positions make them appear to condone social intercourse with the "enemy." Indeed, there is some truth to this assertion.

One area where the leniency of Babylonian Jewry with respect to foods and gentiles is particularly evident is in the matter of wine. We may recall that the prohibition concerning gentile wines is rather ancient. It is first mentioned, as we saw (chapter 3) in the first chapter of Daniel, and is repeated multiple times in Jewish writings of the late Second Temple period. The prohibition is appropriated by the rabbis, who understand it actually to constitute two distinct prohibitions: one against wine used in foreign worship (*yayn nesekh*—the assumed idolatrous intent of the gentile renders prohibited even Israelite wine that the gentile merely touches) and one against gentile wine which, though not used in ritual, might lead to overly intimate relations between Jews and gentiles (*stam yaynam*). Whatever the reason, the talmudic rabbis agree that all gentile wine—or even Jewish wine handled by gentiles—is prohibited to the Jew.

A few references will suffice to demonstrate that Babylonian Jews during the Geonic period—that is, Jews living in the Islamic world, under the religious hegemony of the heads of the great yeshivas (= the Geonim), during Islam's first several centuries—were frequently willing to compromise these prohibitions, with or without rabbinic approval. In an early example, an unnamed Gaon is asked whether wine touched by a Muslim who intends to render it prohibited upon the Jew in fact makes it prohibited. In elaborating his question, the questioner reports that there are "those in our place" who permit such wine, not only for sale but even for drinking. The Gaon responds that such wine should be prohibited because "the Arab today does serve idolatry;" eliminating any possibility of an immediate grant of leniency.[11] But his proffered reason opens the window on later, more lenient possibilities, as a later responsum of R. Hai (939–1038) makes clear.

R. Hai, asked a complicated question regarding Jewish wine sent together with gentile wine on a ship, begins his response by offering some ground-rules. "First of all," he begins, "it is fitting to know that if these gentiles you are concerned with are of the religion of these Arabs whose religion [= Islam] prohibits wine...and curses those who drink it," then there is no reason to be concerned if they touch our wine. He goes on to explain that R. Yehudai who, in the mid-eighth century, expressed some ambivalence on this matter, lived during a time when converts to Islam were not yet "cleansed" of their earlier idolatrous ways. But in later times, Muslims could rightly claim to be pure monotheists, and there was no fear, therefore, that they might touch wine with idolatrous intent. The story is different, R. Hai adds, with respect to Christians, who do indeed offer what must be considered idolatrous libations (Assaf, 79).

Following the Geonic precedent, some later authorities also allowed more lenient rulings—compromises, if you will—with respect to wine handled by non-Jewish monotheists. The Italian Rabbi, R. Isaiah of Trani (the "Rid," 1180–1260), offers what must be the most lenient of positions articulated by a medieval halakhic authority. In his comments on the Talmud (Avodah Zarah 57a), Trani begins by recording an opinion offered earlier by R. Zemach Gaon to the effect that the touch of a Muslim does not render Jewish wine entirely prohibited (it may be sold but not drunk) because Muslims do not worship idolatry. Trani himself goes on to disagree with this earlier opinion, suggesting that, since the Muslim will never offer idolatrous libations, his touch has no effect on Jewish wine, and it may therefore continue to be drunk by the Jew. (The same is not true, he emphasizes, with respect to actual gentile wine, which is prohibited because it might lead to intimacies.) In a noteworthy final comment, Trani adds that, in his opinion, even Christians are no longer suspected of offering idolatrous libations, and it would make sense, therefore, to be lenient with respect to wine touched by them. But Trani hesitates to offer this permission in practice. Clearly, he recognizes that the weight of rabbinic opinion would not go so far.

Intriguingly, in one of his responsa (#120), Trani remarks that there is much to be said regarding "the wines of our kingdom according to the weight of the halakha," but he refuses to record his opinion in writing. "Were I with you face-to-face," he writes to his questioner, "I would tell you, but I will not write it to you because these things should not be written, and don't inquire after them." In this remarkable statement, Trani hints that he has something to say that could evidently jeopardize him. If this comment appeared in another context, we might guess that the "something" pertains to the king or other gentile authorities and he is afraid that, should they discover his opinion, they might act against him. However, given what we saw of his opinion above, it seems more likely that he is, in fact, afraid of the condemnation of his rabbinic colleagues because his actual opinions are far more lenient than they would allow. Yet he is willing, in his novellae, to state explicitly and in writing his permission to drink Jewish wine handled by Muslims and even, in theory, Christians. Could it be that the opinion he is not willing to put in writing is even more lenient—perhaps that he might even permit bona fide "gentile" wine from the hand of an uncompromisingly monotheistic Muslim? Unfortunately, given his expressed hesitancy, we shall never know.

Whatever his actual opinion, it is clear that Trani does go farther than many others are willing to go. His elder contemporary, Maimonides, permits a Jew to benefit (= to sell) from Jewish wine handled by a Muslim, but no more (*Mishneh Torah*, Prohibited Foods, 11:7). Authorities of the Franco-German school during this period may or may not permit sale of such wine, but there is no clear source permitting its drinking. More lenient local customs may exist, but the authorities do not support such practices, and some applaud those who take upon themselves the most stringent positions (see Tosafot A.Z. 57b, s.v. *"la'afukei"*).

Whatever the limits of rabbinic leniencies, common Jews undoubtedly succumbed, on occasion, to the temptation of more "open borders" with their neighbors, as evidenced in their more casual treatment of the wine prohibitions. The author of *Sefer Ha-manhig*, R. Abraham b. R. Nathan ha-Yarchi (twelfth through thirteenth centuries), reports that some Sephardic communities have no concern whatsoever that their wine might be handled by Muslims, and they (the Jews) even sit and drink their wine with these same neighbors, showing that the original fear of wine leading to more intimate neighborly relations is a real one. He adds that "there are persons [= Jews] who purchase their wine during the harvest season in villages in the houses of gentiles, and the gentiles measure out the wine and give in to the Jews in their skins...."[12] The author unhesitatingly condemns this practice, but his testimony reveals the living reality of what he wants to condemn.

What is clear from all of these sources, and from the halakhic range they represent, is that wine has retained its capacity to serve as the symbolic territory where the battle between those who would mingle and those who would maintain strict Jewish separation is fought out. For this reason, the opinion of those who diminish or dismiss the problem of "the gentile touch" is especially significant. The question asked by the Jews of these centuries is not merely the technical one, whether construed halakhically or theologically. Yes, it is important to know whether the neighboring peoples—Muslim or Christian—are "worshipper of idols." But it seems to me that they are at the same time asking whether these people, once they have given up their idolatry, are "people" in the same sense that Jews are people, or whether they are to be shunned as "other" because they are not Jews. It is surely possible to maintain that their touch contaminates Jewish wine even when there is no suspicion of idolatry. Such an approach is quite typical of Jewish practice in the Middle Ages and beyond. So when multiple authorities, in the Muslim world in particular, insist that "they are no longer idolaters" and hence their touch does not contaminate, we must recognize this as significant. Simply put, this position declares that, in this historical-cultural context, we no longer need maintain our separation, at least not to the same degree. But why not? The obvious answer is that we and they, whatever our differences, are also substantially the same. We worship the same, single God. We shun foreign deities and observe the will of the One, true creator. While we do not observe the same covenantal commandments, our practices do overlap; notably, our most hated food, pork, is also taboo to them. For these reasons and more, it makes sense to lower the boundaries between us, whether marked by wine or by other foods and eating practices.[13]

Returning to the practice of the Babylonian Jewish community, we find another noteworthy manifestation of the "lowered boundaries" of which we have been speaking. The case in question is again mentioned in the responsa of the last of the Geonim, R. Hai. The inquiry directed to R. Hai is this: may a Jew roast his or her meat in an oven belonging to gentiles?[14] Clearly, the question assumes a reality in which some Jews are already doing what is questioned. And their doing so is, obviously, highly problematic (hence the inquiry to the rabbinic authority). An oven belonging to a gentile and used by a gentile would not be "kosher." Non-kosher meat would have been roasted in it, and the drippings of the meat might have been left in the oven or absorbed into its walls. We may presume that, all things being equal, the answer to the question would be obvious: the observant Jew should not use such an oven. So why are Jews doing so? In all probability, we must imagine a reality in which the oven the Jew wants to use is a *communal* oven. Private ovens were rare during this period (as they were throughout the Middle Ages) and most people would have had to depend upon a communal oven to roast anything at all. Hence, the compromise they make—whatever the answer given by the halakhic authority—is pragmatically "necessary," at least to some extent. But this cannot be the whole answer, because even if it is difficult for individuals to afford adequate private ovens, there is little reason that the local Jewish community cannot construct an oven for its own use. Why depend on the oven of gentiles (in this case, probably Muslims)? The unavoidable answer is that the desire to take advantage of ovens belonging to and used by gentiles is also partially a consequence of the same relatively peaceful neighborly relations of which we have already spoken. If we live together, we must cook together; when we cook together, we declare that we live together. Compromises of one's "principles" (in this case, of the halakha) are rarely as necessary as they seem. They appear necessary, in this case, because living together as cordial neighbors is a valued reality.

R. Hai's answer is an interesting and perhaps surprising one. He writes: "If the meat is put on a spit and is not touching the earthenware [wall] of the oven—*even if there is un-kosher meat with it in the oven*—since it has not touched it, the meat is permitted…this is permitted only after the fact, but not to begin with [emphasis added]." He finds a way, interpreting the law liberally, to permit the meat that has been cooked in this manner—at least after the fact. Doing so, he saves any such (expensive) meat from the need to dispose of it. But he also lowers the risk of associating with gentiles, thus making neighborly cooperation more likely. Significantly, he permits the meat by assuming that problems (such as juices dripping from the prohibited onto the kosher meat) will not occur—and while recognizing that what he is permitting after the fact really ought to be prohibited. To appreciate the leniency of even this after-the-fact permission, we need only recall any of the many Jewish communities, medieval and modern, that would never permit such meat. It is extraordinary what can be compromised when neighborly neighbors, living in a familiar and attractive culture, beckon.

Roughly a century and a half later, in France, Rabbenu Tam (1100–1171) grants permission for Jews to use mills and ovens belonging to Christian priests to prepare their own bread (Tosafot, Avodah Zarah 44b, s.v. "*nehenin*"). Admittedly, the technical questions involved in this situation are different from those confronted above. Unlike gentile meat, gentile bread is presumably technically kosher, and there is little fear of dripping or spattering in this latter case either. But we are still speaking of the preparation of Jewish foods in gentile ovens, an act which, though perhaps pragmatically desirable, will nevertheless bring Jews together with their neighbors, even for something as significant as the baking of their "daily bread." Besides, the baking of bread is arguably more significant for two reasons: first because, as we have seen all along, bread is a central, highly symbolic food (and one which was, if of gentile origin, especially prohibited, along with wine and oil, in the Mishnah), and second, because the neighbors who are here generously offering the use of their ovens are Christian priests. So, while we may say that, technically speaking, the crossing represented here is relatively insignificant (the Jew who bakes bread this way barely trespasses the territory of the prohibited), the boundary being crossed is extremely significant. To depend upon the priest for one's bread, with full approval of the rabbinic authority, is to admit a common stake in a common society—at least at the level of what matters most, that is, one's life. These gentile neighbors, willing to accept and support the Jew who lives among them, are not the demon; in some ways, they are not even the enemy. In this case, we immediately and unambiguously see that the questions that challenged Jews in the world of early Medieval Islam would continue to confront Jews in Christian Europe through the High Middle Ages.

In the European context, the question that returns over and over again is the question of the permissibility of gentile foods, and particularly gentile bread. As we have already commented, though breads baked by gentiles were assumed to be kosher in terms of their ingredients, gentile bread was, as a central and symbolic food, prohibited in early rabbinic sources. Babylonian and, following them, European Jews permitted gentile bread, but with significant conditions. First, it was preferred that the Jew participate in the preparation of the bread, at least symbolically, by, for example, contributing a twig to fuel the flame of the oven. Secondly, gentile bread was permitted only if Jewish bread was unavailable; some suggest that it would be permissible only if the Jew had nothing to eat for several days. Yet, despite these restrictions, the evidence of Jewish consumption of gentile bread is widespread.

The tosafist whose comments are recorded at Avodah Zarah 66b reports that "there are those who permit the purchase of warm bread from gentiles" on the Sabbath (s.v. *"amar rava"*). Notably, the concern of the writer is the permissibility of consuming bread baked by the gentile on the Sabbath. He expresses no reservation concerning the bread of the gentile as such. R. Abraham b. R. Nathan ha-Yarchi, writing in roughly the same time and territory, praises the piety of those who refuse to eat gentile bread when Jewish bread is available, obviously implying that there are many who ignore halakha's restrictions and eat gentile bread in any case.[15] And slightly later, in Vienna, R. Isaac b. Moses condemns those who choose gentile bread over Jewish bread, suggesting that Jewish laxity in this matter is widespread. In fact, the way he describes this reality is highly revealing: "Everyone [= Jew] has grown accustomed to purchase bread from his good friend [literally: his lover] the gentile, and they don't worry about his daughters" (*Or Zaru'a*, Avodah Zarah, 188). In other words, the Talmud's stated motivation for at least the wine part of the wine-bread-oil prohibition—that is, that eating these foods *with* gentiles or *of* gentiles would lead to overly intimate relations with them *and their daughters*—is disregarded because precisely what the Talmud was afraid of has come to pass. The nexus between compromised food restrictions and closer relations with neighboring gentiles could hardly be stated more explicitly.

Not surprisingly, the same communities of Jews compromise related food restrictions as well. An unidentified Tosafist (Avodah Zarah 35a, s.v. *"ḥada"*) reports that in many places Jews eat the cheeses of gentiles because vegetable rennet is used in the preparation. A more specific testimony to the same effect, locating this lenient practice in Narbonne, is found in the *Or Zaru'a* (Avodah Zarah, #186). And R. Jonah Gerondi (= of Gerona, d. 1263) addresses particularly caustic remarks to groups of Jews who allow themselves to eat gentile cheeses and other cooked dishes (*Sha'arei Teshuva*, 3, 8). R. Isaac b. Moses insists that the accepted practice in all territories with which he is familiar is to prohibit these foods, and he concludes his remarks emphatically by declaring: "God forbid that any fearer of Heaven should permit himself this thing [= the consumption of these foods]!" Once again, we witness the rhetorical division of Jews into the pious and (by implication) the non-pious. The pious say no to the foods of their neighbors, but others evidently do not. They, it would appear, are more interested in living with their neighbors.

The evidence we have seen here originates in various European settings, from France to the Mediterranean coast of Spain to Italy, all during the twelfth and thirteenth centuries. These were centuries during which the experience of Jews in Europe can best be described as "mixed." The violence of the First Crusade brought considerable suffering to certain European Jewish communities. Other anti-Jewish violence—originating in subsequent crusades, blood libels, or garden-variety Christian anti-Semitism—regularly threatened Jewish homes and livelihoods, and the Jewish sense of security in the lands of the European kings was often tenuous. But we should not allow these generalizations to blind us from the fact that, between attacks and disruptions, European Jews lived their lives much as did many of their neighbors, supporting themselves and their families as best they could. Some Jews, and particularly merchants and money-lenders, were relatively comfortable, even leading Pope Innocent III (1198–1216) to complain that "Jews have become so insolent that by means of their vicious usury...they appropriate ecclesiastical goods and Christian possessions...[and] they do not hesitate to have Christian servants and nurses...."[16] As even the Jewish testimony, quoted above, would indicate, when the influence of hateful ideologies abated, Jews lived with their Christian neighbors in relative peace. During these normalized periods, the question of relations and boundaries had to be addressed.

Again, the halakhic manipulations, compromises, and transgressions reviewed above represent the manifold negotiations and renegotiations of boundaries in which medieval European Jewry engaged. Some, wishing above all to assert their piety, distanced themselves from their Christian neighbors by reinforcing the food boundaries first erected by their rabbinic forebears. Others, trying to establish some common ground, found ways, within the letter of the law, to permit gentile foods, even when such permission contradicted the spirit of the original rabbinic edicts. And still others simply disregarded the inherited rabbinic restrictions, finding life in the company of Christian comrades too desirable to allow for unnecessary impediments. Crucially, in this age before the regular presence of meat on the European table (after the Black Death in the mid-fourteenth century), the common diet continued to be constituted by the very foods at issue here: bread, cheeses and cooked vegetables. By marking these foods, if gentile in origin, as taboo, Jews would declare that Jewish and Christian tables—and everything those tables represent—should occupy different territories. Jews who, on the other hand, ate these same foods, sought, in effect, to sit down at a "common table." If we are not only *what* we eat but also *with* and *like whom* we eat, then these Jews were communicating their sense that, despite the tribulations of life in Christian Europe, they understood themselves to be as much like their Christian neighbors as they were different.

It will come as no surprise that, with the onset of modernity, the same food-and-identity questions addressed by Jews of the Middle Ages emerged with even greater urgency. Rabbinic testimony suggests that, even in early modernity, Jews allowed themselves considerable "leniencies" (some would call them transgressions) with respect to the food of gentiles. In an oft-quoted responsa (#72), R. Solomon Luria complains that Ashkenazi Jews have no misgivings about drinking wines in gentile inns, nor do they hesitate to eat fish cooked in pots in these same establishments. With rhetorical flourish, he remarks that "the stringent one is the one who believes the inn-keeper that they did not cook in this pot...," suggesting that they at least bothered to ask about the pots. Others of Luria's responsa provide additional evidence for the common disregard of wine prohibitions, suggesting that Jews in many communities imbibe gentile wine, at least in private, and that "no one" tries to stop such behavior.[17]

Not long afterward, Leon of Modena reports similar transgressions. He writes that "from time immemorial, our forefathers in Italy habitually drank ordinary wine."[18] Whether what he claims was true "from time immemorial" may surely be questioned (how would he know?), but there is little reason to question that it is true of his own day (this comment was written in 1608). Ariel Toaff characterizes the situation in these words: "If necessary, ordinary must and wine would be used, without excessive scandal, and a blind eye was turned to the fact that it was produced by Christian feet" (p. 75). In a territory where wine was the most widely produced and consumed beverage, this reality is no less meaningful for its unsurprising nature. Precisely because wine was so central to the Italian diet, and because it could be produced in such abundance, the willingness of Jews to drink gentile wine takes on a particular significance.

Because wine was abundant, their willingness was obviously not a consequence of mere pragmatism. Jews could have produced wine for themselves, thereby observing the restrictions of the halakha. Clearly, the ease with which they are reported to have consumed common gentile wine is evidence of their sense of being at home in local Italian societies. To be sure, they had resided in this land from time immemorial (or, to be more precise, from at least the first century), so in a very real sense they *were* at home. Their practices, and particularly their disregard of the very prohibition that could most powerfully distinguish "us"—the servants of the true God—from "them"—worshippers of foreign gods—communicated their comfort in this place, their fundamental identification with their neighbors, and their desire to share in their common fate as residents of the same communities.

The open and relatively widespread disregard of inherited eating restrictions evidenced in these responsa already exhibits a quality that is distinctly modern. The freedom felt by these Jews to eat with or like their neighbors, in certain significant details, at least, suggests their desire to be like them—or even their belief that they *are* like them. In an earlier chapter we saw Luria distinguish between pious "sons of Torah" and other, less pious Jews in sixteenth-century Poland, demanding that the more pious distance themselves from the less pious by accepting a more rigorous ritual of waiting between meat and dairy foods. We noted, in that connection, that many Polish Jews of that period flourished, economically and otherwise, and their relations with their gentile neighbors were sometimes quite close. Some of those gentiles were quite accepting of their Jewish neighbors, having adopted the sort of enlightened humanism then supported by the Polish royalty. The life of the book, strengthened by the recent proliferation of printing houses, helped to create a larger educated class, shifting some measure of authority from guardians of the tradition to the more critically inclined intellect of the individual. These forces were far from universal at this early stage, but they were present. This means that the Jew's gentile neighbor was now more likely to be someone he or she would want to emulate, at least in the qualities just enumerated.

The same, of course, was true of the Italian Jew in the early seventeenth century. He was living, after all, in the land that had been transformed first by the Renaissance, and now by the dissemination of books from the many important Italian presses. In urban centers, enriched by a flourishing trade, he would find himself in the company of gentiles who enjoyed an astonishing art culture and a new, modern literature. One need not read far into Modena's diary (itself a modern form!) to appreciate the "modern" qualities of the society he describes. So here, too, the Jew would find himself attracted by many of the qualities of his neighbor, and easily tempted to share the wine or (nominally permitted) victuals of that same neighbor.

Indeed, as these forces would grow more and more powerful with the progress of the modern age, Jews would again and again find their aspirations frustrated by the limitations of Jewish food regulations, and they would frequently find themselves struggling against those same limitations. This struggle came to the fore in the wake of the enlightenment, and particularly following the civic enfranchisement of Jews in several European countries in the late eighteenth and early nineteenth centuries.

Already in the early decades of the legal acceptance of Jews by their Christian brethren, many Jews neglected the dietary laws in some degree. Needless to say, it is impossible to recover the proportions of this or that Jewry who allowed themselves freedoms in this regard, and there are few contemporary sources that comment on this phenomenon directly. Nevertheless, it is clear that at least private leniencies were not unusual. So Michael Creizenach, an early "Friend of Reform" in Frankfort, argues in 1842 on behalf of lenient interpretations of the dietary laws "in order to lessen rather than to increase the number of Israelites who neglect the dietary laws in their homes."[19] Creizenach obviously believes that the lack of observance of food-related restrictions that he witnesses around him is a consequence of unreasonable and oppressive stringencies in the law. He imagines, therefore, that if the law were opened up, and some of its medieval accretions removed, Jews would return to the observance of kashrut in greater numbers. The concern he expresses is clear evidence of a phenomenon that is evidently relatively widespread. I suspect, however, that his analysis of the problem is naïve, his diagnosis misguided. Even the comments of the elite leadership of the liberal Jewish community, who tend toward ideological justifications of reforms in this as in other practices, reveal that there is another dynamic at work here.

In a letter dated March 19, 1845, Abraham Geiger, a prominent leader of early Reform in Germany, expresses his shock to Leopold Zunz upon learning that the latter had "decided to keep a strictly kosher home." Geiger objects that "it is precisely these dietary laws that are so void of rationale and at the same time *such a hindrance to the development of social relationships. Truly, the ideal of the deeper sense of brotherhood among men* should have priority over the revival of that sense of separation which is both devoid of color and is of very dubious value.... "[20] Only a few years later, Samuel Holdheim writes in this way to a group of reformers in Hungary:

> ...the many dietary laws...have lost altogether their religious truth and significance for us now that these representations have become foreign to our whole mode of thought and we look upon God as the one and only Father, and *consider and love all men as his children and our brethren*.... The abrogation of the dietary laws is highly desirable, since, in addition to being *a disturbing feature in the civic and social life of the Jews, these laws are particularly prone to continue the differences between them and the other inhabitants.*[21]

What each of these writers makes clear is that the desire to relax or eliminate the dietary restrictions is motivated by the desire to remove boundaries between Jews and their Christian neighbors. But this desire is itself motivated by the opinion that all humans are God's creatures, all members of a single human race. As brothers and sisters, it is good for Jews and Christians to share their common condition and common fate. Food laws that both symbolize and enforce differences cannot, therefore, be tolerated. Like Peter those many centuries before, these Jews recognize that the first thing that must "go" when the gulf between Jew and Gentile is eliminated is the eating system that marks us as "pure" and them as "impure."

Perhaps the most important public statement of this principle is that of "The Pittsburgh Platform," formulated by a group of reforming rabbis gathering in that city in 1885. Of particular import, for our purposes, is the juxtaposition of the renunciation of the dietary laws with a statement of faith in the messianic quality of advanced modernity. The words of the Platform are these:

> We hold that all such Mosaic and rabbinical laws as regulate diet, priestly purity and dress originated in ages and under the influence of ideas altogether foreign to our present mental and spiritual state. They

fail to impress the modern Jew with a spirit of priestly holiness; their observance in our days is apt rather to obstruct than to further modern spiritual innovation.

...We recognize in the modern era of universal culture of heart and intellect the approaching of the realization of Israel's great Messianic hope for the establishment of the kingdom of truth, justice and peace among all men. We consider ourselves no longer a nation, but a religious community....[22]

Again, the dismissal of the dietary restrictions accompanies a declaration of the essential unity of all peoples, expressed here with a new twist. Not only is humanity *ideally* one, but the historical accidents that have divided humans, nation from nation, religion from religion, are nearing their end. As modern nations come to recognize the enlightened truth ascertained through the exercise of reason and moderation, the divisions that have plagued humanity are well on their way to disappearing. Modern people live, it is claimed, at the dawning of the true messianic age. If this is true, of course, then the dietary restrictions and the separations they enforce must surely be renounced. They are, after all, impediments to the "coming of the messiah." Indeed, even some ancient rabbinic teachings would agree that, in the time of the messiah, laws such as these will be annulled. So, if this is the messianic era, then the negation undertaken in the Platform is a genuinely Jewish act. Of course, the Platform as a whole is a re-reading of Judaism for modernity, an act of affirmation, not rejection. Hence, the statement on the dietary laws, and the change in practice it reflects, must be viewed in the same light. These rabbis, and those for whom they speak, are acting in what they believe to be a genuine Jewish spirit. For them, the identity of the modern Jew is best reflected in a thoroughly open dietary regimen. Though they are now eating as others, they are still eating as Jews.

In fact, I would argue that the major flaw in common discussion of "assimilatory" changes in Jewish eating practices in modernity is its failure to recognize the ways that these new practices are affirmations of the Jewishness of those who assume them. When Jews in twentieth-century America chose to eat in "kosher-style" delis, for example, or even in Chinese restaurants (to take two well-recognized and much commented upon examples), they were—*despite their literal neglect of the traditional laws of kashrut*—making Jewish choices, and this in ways that have not been sufficiently appreciated.

What would soon become the "traditional" Jewish delicatessen began to proliferate on the Lower East Side of Manhattan in the early twentieth century. By virtue of the nature of the Jewish community residing in that neighborhood at the time, the first delis were kosher, offering a canonical menu of *fleishig* items ("hot spiced corned beef, pastrami, rolled beef, hard salami, soft salami, chicken salami, bologna, frankfurter 'specials' and the thinner, wrinkled hot dogs always taken with mustard and relish and sauerkraut").[23] At this early stage, their kashrut was a significant part of their attraction, for, as Alfred Kazin recalls, when a Jew entered a delicatessen marked with a sign that declared "JEWISH NATIONAL DELICATESSEN" (or some other such marker—including the ubiquitous "Kosher" sign, in Hebrew characters), "it was as if we had entered into our rightful heritage" (Kazin, 34). But as delis followed Jews to other neighborhoods and to the suburbs—where populations were more diverse—and as the observance level of many Jews changed, these kosher delis soon gave way to "kosher-style" delis, where "kosher" was no longer required but where the "taste" was in significant respects the same.

Describing her father's choice to open a non-kosher delicatessen in his "new community in Long Island" sometime in the 1920s or 1930s (she doesn't provide a date, but she is writing in 1946 of her father's choice "when I was sixteen"), Ruth Glazer emphasizes the importance of maintaining the "taste" of the kosher deli. She writes that "the non-kosher but Jewish deli...differs, deliberately, in only the most subtle ways from the kosher deli. It looks exactly the same, smells exactly the same...But the neon kosher sign is missing from the window."[24] The meats in such establishments continued to be mostly (and sometimes exclusively) kosher. The primary difference between this and the kosher deli, therefore, was the presence of dairy foods: "you can get coffee with cream, and butter on your bread *if you insist on it.* But the resistance of the proprietors has been fierce..." (Glazer, 60; emphasis added). Dairy was available, in other words, but, even in the context of "kosher-style," it had its proper place.

Dairy transformed the deli menu in a notable way. As Glazer elaborates: "Since dairy dishes are not forbidden to the kosher-style store, a full selection of salads, fruit with sour cream, cheese and fish dishes are featured" (61). But Glazer, it seems, fails to appreciate the significance of what she has described. The addition of dairy to the menu of the deli is restricted by two considerations. First, dairy is not a promiscuous presence in the non-kosher Jewish delicatessen; it should have its own place even though it might be mixed with meat by the customer (hence her father's resistance). Second, not just any dairy will do. Crucially, the sorts of dairy foods that Glazer describes as being commonly available are precisely the foods offered on the menu of a Jewish dairy restaurant. Both of these points require elaboration.

Though both dairy and meat were (and are) available in the kosher-style delicatessen, they were typically not mixed indiscriminately. Each had its own display case and counter, often side-by-side but sometimes spatially removed from one another (I recall one such deli, in Jacksonville, Florida, where the meat case was to the right as you entered and the dairy case to the left, with tables in the middle). Of course, the customer could order from either menu (meat and dairy were separated on the menu as well), and the two categories of food could be mixed at the table. But the symbolic associations of the institutional separation of these categories were unmistakable. Remarkably, even when the reasons for this separation were long since lost, as delicatessens became "specialty stores" serving a far more diverse clientele, the categorical separation of dairy and meat was considered so "natural" that it was taken as a given. One need only visit the famous Zabar's on the Upper West Side of Manhattan to appreciate the stubbornness of this separation. There one will find smoked fishes, creamed herrings, and specialty cream cheeses behind one display case, and the meats—including everything from kosher salamis specially prepared for the establishment to gourmet hams—behind another, on the opposite side of the room. Such a separation of meat and dairy is "natural" only against the background of the separation required by traditional Jewish practice. Pragmatically speaking, it might make a lot more sense to locate the ham next to the cheese with which it will be combined in a sandwich.

That the dairy foods offered in the non-kosher delicatessen were typically of the same sort served in Jewish dairy restaurants is also significant. Jewish dairy restaurants developed in the same neighborhoods (mainly Manhattan's Lower East Side) and at the same time as the Jewish delicatessen. In fact, such restaurants were a mainstay—even a landmark—on the Lower East Side throughout the twentieth century, until the recent demise of Ratner's on Delancey Street. From the perspective of kashrut, these establishments were the other side of the Jewish restaurant coin from the kosher deli; one was where the Jew would eat meat, the other where he would eat dairy. Furthermore, the menu at these restaurants was every bit as "canonical" as that of the delicatessen. It featured such dishes as smoked fishes, blintzes, borscht, and dairy or parve soups; not cheese fondue or lasagna (though the latter would appear on some menus in later decades). Thus, when such dairy selections found their place by the side of pastrami and corned beef on the deli menu, the Jewish delicatessen was transformed into the Jewish restaurant *par excellence*. It embodied all of the culinary markers, both *milchig* and *fleishig*, that declared "Jewish!"

Even latter-day delicatessens, which have left kashrut far behind (even the meats are not kosher), often wear their Jewishness on their sleeves. The proprietor of "Artie's Delicatessen," on the Upper West Side of Manhattan, understands the idiom and semiotics of the Jewish deli perfectly. The awning above the entrance to the establishment announces "traditional specialties." The take-out menu, available outside the door (summer, 2004), pictures, on one side, a basket of bagels and, on the other, a platter piled high with pastrami, turkey, and other such sandwiches. It advertises not once, but twice, that it prepares "shiva platters." On the menu, one may find a long list of combination, "specialty sandwiches," none of which (even combination K, with "Turkey, Bacon, Lettuce, Tomato, Mayo") includes dairy (K is also the only sandwich with "Mayo;" all the rest are dressed with Russian Dressing). The section marked "Traditional Favorites" includes "Flanken in the Pot," stuffed cabbage, tongue, and cheese blintzes. Dairy favorites include nova on bagel, whitefish, and herring in cream sauce. Chopped liver and potato pancakes are found among the appetizers, and kasha and kugels are included among the "Sides." Needless to say, desserts include rugelach, "N.Y. [= Jewish, following Lenny Bruce's perceptive interpretation] Cheese Cake," hamentaschen and Jello (shades of the suburban Jewish kitchen in mid-century). And among the beverage choices are Dr. Brown's sodas and the "New York Classic Egg Cream." Anyone familiar with the idiom will immediately understand that this is the classic vocabulary of the Jewish deli. But, in case a customer is among the uninitiated, sometimes the implicit is made explicit: "Sides" include *Israeli* salad, the only beer available is "Maccabee *Israeli* Beer," Hero sandwiches include "The Moshe Dyan [sic] *Jewish* Hero...On a Giant Hand-made 3 ft. Long Twisted Chalah," and "Emergency Chicken Soup" (labeled as "*Jewish* Penicilin" [sic]) is available for delivery.

The profound Jewishness of these kosher-style restaurants has been recognized by some writers. For example, Jenna Weissman Joselit writes that "Deli...became an established part of American Jewish cuisine, a treat as hallowed and highly regarded in some quarters as the Sabbath was in others."[25] In view of the devotion of many "culinary Jews" to this way of eating—often once a week, at special, appointed times (Sunday evening, for example)—the term "hallowed" is hardly an exaggeration. And Hasia Diner, speaking of the "style" part of "kosher style," writes that "The Jewishness of style reminded [them] of who they were, and that counted more than *Halachah*." [26] Since, by the second generation of eastern European Jews in America, these restaurants were well-established centers of Jewish cuisine *and* culture, their reinforcement of the Jewishness of the Jews who chose to eat in them was unavoidable. In these establishments, the Jew would find him- or herself in the company of other *landsmann*, whatever the nature of his company at other times.

But what these writers, as others, have failed to appreciate is the degree to which the kosher-style delis represent a negotiation by their proprietors and clientele with *kashrut* itself. Ruth Glazer's words, describing her father's hesitation, even in his non-kosher deli, to serve buttered bread or coffee and cream with meat, already makes this clear. In her estimation, the resistance of proprietors to serving this prohibited combination was "fierce." The practice of serving one with the other was considered "obscene" (p. 60). So the boundaries were to be renegotiated, but this did not mean that all restrictions could be abandoned. Thus, even though meat or dairy could be ordered, the meat would be (mostly) kosher. Meat and dairy could come into contact on the tables, but, as anyone raised in the system of kashrut would know, cold contacting cold, or one category following the other, created only relatively minor problems according to traditional standards. And even when the deli assumed its most "assimilated" form, that is, when the meat was no longer actually kosher, most (if not all) of the meats were from "kosher" species. Thus, one could eat in these establishments and still observe what some would call "biblical kashrut" (= avoiding the biblically forbidden species while ignoring later elaborations of the eating laws). In the more traditional (culturally, not religiously) delis, an observant person could eat a bagel, lox, and cream cheese sandwich or a kosher pastrami sandwich—both cold—with little guilt, recognizing that, technically speaking, he had probably transgressed no prohibition. To be sure, the kosher-style deli represented a rejection of some traditional details by modern Jews for whom the kashrut of their parents or grandparents no longer made sense. Ironically, however, what they preserved was often as significant as what they abandoned.

Interpreting the eating patterns of twentieth-century Jews in America, Diner offers that "They wanted to have broad access to all the good stuff America had to offer and still be good Jews. Most looked for ways to do both. They divided the world in half: keeping a kosher home, but eating non-kosher food in restaurants. Rather than strictly adhering to law, they opted for Jewish tastes and flavors, creating a food system which they called 'kosher style'....They did not see their desire to become Americans...as antithetical to being Jewish. They wanted to have and be both" (185). She is quite right that relatively new American Jews, wanting to become as much American as they were Jewish, sought to negotiate a way to be both. But in her allusion to the commonplace dichotomy of "kosher at home, non-kosher out" ("be a Jew at home and a man abroad"), she seems to imply that "non-kosher" is American and therefore on the other side of the dichotomy from Jewish. But, in the case of the deli, the dichotomy doesn't work that way. If we refuse to succumb to the dichotomy created by kashrut itself, we will recognize that not only is the delicatessen Jewish—and this profoundly so—but it is also *selectively kosher*. By creating and eating in such culinary institutions, Jews were, to be sure, asserting the modernity of their identities (which, as Diner remarks, they did not view as being antithetical to the Jewishness of their identities). But they were also declaring their desire to preserve the tradition *on their own, newly negotiated terms*. They were holding on when they might be abandoning. They were maintaining inherited categories when they might have destroyed them.

From the perspective of this interpretation, we might view the other "Jewish" eating development we hinted at above—"eating Chinese"—as an act of abandonment and erasure. But a more careful interpretation of this phenomenon will reveal that this is far from being the case.

In a much-cited article on the phenomenon of New York Jews and Chinese food—a phenomenon that was noted in Jewish publications as early as the late nineteenth century (Diner, 205)—Gaye Tuchman and Harry Gene Levine characterize this eating pattern as "a part of Jewish culture in New York."[27] "New York Jews," they write, "love Chinese restaurant food so much that they have made it a second cuisine" (383). How is this phenomenon to be understood? Tuchman and Levine propose that Chinese food attracted and symbolized Jewish meanings in three ways: (1) Chinese food was cosmopolitan, urbane and sophisticated—not provincial or parochial. The former was what first generation Jewish Americans aspired to be, the latter was what they sought to distance themselves from. (2) Chinese food was "unkosher and therefore non-Jewish." But it was prepared in a way (cutting, chopping, mincing) that disguised its forbidden ingredients, thus making it "safe treyf." (3) By the second generation, eating Chinese was recognized "as something that modern American Jews, and especially New York Jews, did together," allowing second generation American Jews to eat as Jews by eating Chinese food (385–86). In an ironic twist of fate, this association became so powerful in the minds of many that the authors found a few Jews who, seeking to distance themselves from their Jewish identities, refused to eat in Chinese restaurants (398–99).

It seems to me that, as far as they go, Tuchman and Levine are largely correct in their interpretation. But their second observation embeds a contradiction that suggests they do not go far enough. Simply put, if unkosher is equated in the minds of Jews with non-Jewish, then why do they seek out "safe treyf?" The authors claim to answer this question by arguing that "a culture spawns the terms of its own rejection…a food-oriented rebellion cannot be accomplished, with just any forbidden substance. It cannot be food that looks so like prohibited fare that it automatically triggers revulsion…" (389). But, we must insist, why not? Jews could (and some did) just as easily have chosen to eat veal parmesan or Italian ham as Chinese food. Why prefer the latter over the former? A rebel, too, must choose the terms of his or her rebellion. The symbol of rebellion can symbolize "modest" or "radical." Jews chose Chinese not because they could not have chosen another cuisine, with its own Jewishly-relevant associations and resonances, but because Chinese food worked better. The question is, in what way?

To appreciate the significance of the "timidity" of the Jewish choice of Chinese cuisine, which minces its ingredients to the point that individual substances are no longer evident to the eye, we must return to the halakhic sources. In his codification of Jewish law, the Tur, R. Jacob b. Asher explains that one need not wash one's hands between a cooked dish containing meat ingredients and a cooked dish containing dairy ingredients (even when eating the latter immediately after the former) "since the meat *is not visible*, and it has only the taste [of the meat], and also the second [dish] has only the taste of the cheese" (O.H. 173, emphasis added). In his commentary on this same ruling, R. Joseph Caro quotes Rabbenu Tam who similarly suggests that the reason for the leniency is that "the meat is not visible and there is only [its] taste." Clearly, then, it matters (or, more correctly, once mattered), according to the terms of the kashrut system, whether a substance can be seen, and this is so whether or not it contributes a taste. If it cannot be seen, it is as though not there, and for this reason normal restrictions or limitations do not apply. According to the opinion recorded here, after eating a stew in which pieces of meat are visible, one may not eat a dairy food unless one waits some period of time. But after eating vegetable soup made with meat stock, one may eat dairy immediately, with or without washing one's hands, depending upon whether the dairy ingredient is visible.

I do not mean to suggest that Jews who ate Chinese food were familiar with the halakhic opinions described here—though some may well have been. And there is a difference between permitted foods (meat or dairy) which may not be mixed and prohibited foods such as pork or shellfish. But if "a culture spawns the terms of its own rejection," then it is crucial to recognize that these terms are spawned by the halakhic system itself. In other words, we might say that Jews who choose Chinese food because the prohibited substance may not easily be seen are making a kind of "halakhic" decision. They are choosing to go only so far, but no further. They are choosing to "rebel" in Jewish terms, and are thus, in significant respects, not rebelling at all. It is, by analogy, like the Jewish child who "rebels" against his traditional parents by choosing to go to college so that he may become a doctor or lawyer. The former, like Maimonides, devotes his life to the mitzvah of *pikuach nefesh* (saving lives), the latter, like the rabbi, undertakes the business of engaging the law to further the cause of justice. All "rebel" against earlier models and standards, but all appropriate Jewish terms or values to do so. Chinese food might, therefore, be "safe treyf," but it is, at the same time, "new Jewish." Few Jews who grew up in Greater New York in the middle decades of the twentieth century could fail to recognize this reality.

Jews, as others, have always recognized that the foods they eat, and the ways they eat them, symbolize who they are *over and against who they are not*. The foods and eating practices say, in other words, "I am a Jew and not a gentile." But Jews have often not wanted to be "not gentile" in the extreme sense, for they have recognized what they and their gentile neighbors have in common. For this reason, the question "how am I like the gentile and how different?" always had to be asked.

What we have seen in this chapter is that the answers of Jewish communities through the ages to this question were often found in their eating practices. They were intimated in the degree to which Jews crossed boundaries that had earlier been assumed. Some crossings were modest and some quite extreme. But the distance the Jew would go always involved a negotiation, and the partners to the negotiation were always the "Jewish identity" and the "general identity." Crucially, both sides always made claims. Those who erected strong fences at the boundaries also allowed for openings, even when they did not recognize them. And those who destroyed inherited fences erected new signposts of Jewishness, even when they were unaware of them. In modest or significant ways, transgressive eating was always a part of Jewish tradition.

10 "Bugs in the system" (The Kashrut Wars)

On Tuesday, June 1, 2004, readers of the *New York Times,* opened their morning papers to the first page of the second (Metro) section to find an article entitled "There's Something in the Water, And It May Not Be Strictly Kosher." The article went on to describe the discovery in New York City drinking water of millimeter-long zooplankton called copepods. These creatures, when viewed under a microscope (they are virtually invisible to the naked eye), look like crustaceans or oddly shaped bugs, which would clearly not be kosher if they were larger. The question, for the Orthodox Jewish community in Brooklyn, was what to do about the water now that copepods were known to be present. Could the water still be drunk without hesitation? Did it require prior filtering? Not surprisingly, different segments of the Orthodox and ultra-Orthodox community responded in different ways. But, whatever a particular group decided to do, New York City tap water would—for the observant Jew, at least—never again be the same.

How is it that water that had been drunk for generations without hesitation or compunction was all of a sudden suspect, and even "non-kosher?" Examined by itself, this chapter in the development of modern kashrut practices is a study in different interpretations of detailed legal sources. But studied in context, the copepod incident is the culmination of a not-so-long history of increasing alarm and accusation over kashrut in the Orthodox community and beyond.

Young (thirty-something) Orthodox Jews might be surprised to discover that, at around the time of their birth, there was not much public controversy—or even discussion—about kashrut in the Orthodox community, let alone beyond it. For example, scanning the pages of *The Jewish Press,* a weekly Jewish newspaper published in Brooklyn, representing Orthodox viewpoints, from the early 1970s, one finds scant mention of kashrut as a concern. Here and there one finds ads for kosher products, but otherwise kashrut seems barely to have been on the radar screen.

Later in the same decade, one finds evidence of emerging tensions over kashrut in the Orthodox community, but it is spoken in a whisper. Writing in the pages of *The Jewish Homemaker,* a publication of the Chabad Lubavitch (Hasidic) organization, Rabbi Bernard Levy warns his readers that "Kaf K," "diamond K," and "triangle K" are not kosher symbols indicating "our" endorsement. Only the "OK" symbol can relied upon to indicate Lubavitch approval.[1] But it should occasion no surprise that this kind of warning emerges from a Hasidic group, even if that group is the more "modern" and out-reaching Lubavitch. Hasidic groups have been notoriously separatist—from other Hasidic sects and from the rest of Orthodoxy—since their early history. It is important to note the proliferation of Kashrut organizations, therefore, but such divisions, in themselves, tell us little about more widespread developments in the world of Jewish eating.

More interesting is the appearance in the same issue of a notice permitting the use of peanuts and peanut oil on Passover, accompanied by a supporting written opinion by the greatest halakhic authority of the generation, R. Moshe Feinstein.[2] In fact, during this period it was commonplace to find peanut oil, marked with proper rabbinic approval, available for sale on the "Kosher for Passover" shelves of local supermarkets. Yet before too many years had passed, the "Kosher for Passover" peanut oil was no longer to be found, replaced with olive or, more commonly, flaxseed oil.

Of course, if R. Moshe Feinstein approved of the kashrut of peanut oil on Passover, there is no question that it is kosher. Yet today, less than a generation after this notice in *The Jewish Homemaker*, it is no longer considered to be so. What, in the passage of these few years, makes kosher not kosher? What makes water impure? For an answer to these questions, we look to the mid-1980s, when rhetoric relating to kashrut reached a boiling point.

To illustrate, let us return to the pages of the *The Jewish Press*. From March, 1985 through May, 1986, there are no fewer than ten editorials devoted to kashrut concerns. Consider the titles of these editorials: March 8, 1985—"Kashruth—A Return to Basics;" March 29, 1985 (lead editorial) — "Mounting Concern in Jewish Community Over Kashruth Violations;" May 10, 1985 (lead editorial) — "We Are For Traditional Kashruth;" January 3, 1986— "Kashruth: A Mounting Concern;" and so forth. What is the substance of the concern expressed in these editorials? The March 8 editorial questions "the integrity of the *shochet* [ritual slaughterer], the issue of whether the proprietor is *shomer shabbos* [observant of the Sabbath] . . ." (p. 5). The March 29 editorial similarly expresses its concern about the "lifestyle" of the proprietor. An editorial on November 8 of the same year declares that "we support the campaign by the consumers group that Glatt Kosher establishments should be owned by those who strictly observe the tenets of our Torah" (p. 54).

Most explicit is the editorial of January 3, 1986. In that piece, the editors deplore the "total disregard by some proprietors of their consumers." They continue: "It is no coincidence that these businessmen are so removed from *Yiddishkeit* [Jewishness] in their personal lives. We also welcome the continuing campaign by the Concerned Group of Glatt Kosher Consumers…Unfortunately, we can no longer say that kosher is kosher" (p. 43).

Notably, little is said in these pieces about the kashrut of the food itself, though that concern clearly lurks in the background. Time and again, the focus of the editorialist is the quality of religious observance on the part of the kosher butcher—does he "strictly observe the tenets of *our* Torah?" (emphasis added). There is certainly some truth to the observation that many kosher butchers at this time were not strictly *shomer mitzvos* (observant of the Torah's requirements). Many had inherited (or were in the course of inheriting) their butcher shops from immigrant fathers, and, as many second generation Jews in the United States, they were no longer as strictly observant as their parents. But this does not necessarily mean they compromised the standards of their shops. Furthermore, this shift had begun before the mid-1980s. So something else must have been going on which would explain this turn in focus in the observant world. What this was we will consider in due course. It is first necessary for us to appreciate the full extent of the phenomenon we are seeking to interpret.

The editorials noted above are of a piece with scattered news regarding reported violations of kashrut standards or regulations by kosher establishments and producers. During this same period, *The Jewish Press* featured a regular column informing readers of "kosher law violators." Occasionally, the violation would merit independent reporting in a dedicated article. On April 18, 1986, for example, the front page featured three separate articles on violations of New York State's Kashruth law (enhancements of which were then making their way through the state legislature).

But more than the mere "violations," which seem to have been so common (at least according to the *Press*'s reporting), were the variety of "crises" or "scandals" that shook the kosher world beginning in this period. One of the earliest, and certainly one of the most divisive of these, was the much-reported "vinegar scandal."

The Jewish Press of February 28, 1986, carries an article on its front page reporting that "Kosher Food Inspectors Get Death Threats." The article suggests that the threats were motivated by the fear that the inspectors were "on the brink of uncovering a Kosher food scandal of major proportions." What that scandal might be is not indicated, but the timing of this report suggests that the reporter was referring to the soon-to-break story of a kashrut approval (*hekhsher*) issued by the experienced and well-respected OK organization to a French company, attesting to the kashrut of alcohol *derived from non-kosher wine* used in the production of vinegar. Unfortunately, the French manufacturer had recently changed its manufacturing process and had failed to report this change to the kashrut supervisor. But the fact that an unreported change led to the problem evidently mattered little. Unkosher is unkosher, and there is no describing how calamitous this was deemed to be in the Orthodox world.

Perhaps the most alarmist of alarms regarding this incident was sounded by the president of Young Israel (a centrist Orthodox organization) in *The*

Young Israel Viewpoint (May, 1986).[3] There he declares that the tragedy precipitated by the carelessness of the kashrut supervisors should be compared to none other than the Chernobyl nuclear meltdown disaster (of April 25, 1986). A month later, according to a *Jewish Press* report, he called for "Full Kashruth Disclosure in Wake of [the] Scandal," criticizing, in particular what he believed to be the slow disclosure of the problem on the part of the responsible parties.[4]

Even after the disclosure of the "scandal," it did not go away. Competing kashrut organizations continued to make accusations and counter-accusations, creating a poisonous atmosphere. Several organizations sought to wrest responsibility for oversight of the kashrut of certain foods and companies from OK, the alleged offending party, making it appear that the ongoing dispute was as much about the business of kashrut as it was about assuring kashrut itself. These developments finally led Rabbi Bernard Levy, the head of OK, to issue a lengthy defense of his standards, published in the February-March (1987) issue of *The Jewish Homemaker* (p. 15). Most interesting in this piece is Rabbi Levy's characterization of the relationship between the competing kashrut organizations. He speaks of the present exchanges as a "battle." He insists that he and his agency "have always been ready for peace." He warns that the involved parties are giving voice to *"sinnas chinam"* —baseless hatred—the sin for which, according to the Talmud, the second Jerusalem Temple was destroyed (see b. Yoma 9b). Whether comparable to Chernobyl or *churban bais hamikdash* (the destruction of the Temple), the vinegar scandal and its consequences were thought to be a world-ending catastrophe.

The inflated rhetoric that typifies descriptions of the "vinegar scandal" extends to other kashrut crisis commentaries as well. So, writing in *The Jewish Press* in December, 1985, Rabbi I. Harold Sharfman declares that "Kashrut Quakes Jolt Jewry" (p. 26a). The specifics? Many kosher butchers, he says, cannot be trusted, and it is thus essential that the kosher consumer search out a butcher who is a *"yoreh shamayim"* —a God Fearer. And how will he be identified? By the fact that he covers his head. There is nothing out of the ordinary here; this is one of many expressions of distrust of butchers who are judged not sufficiently pious, accompanied by an insistence that the butcher be "one of us" (more on this below). What makes this case noteworthy is simply the language: unstable kashrut standards are nothing less than an earthquake.

Or take another, somewhat later example. *The Jewish Press*, in April 1993, prints a commentary on a recent "Catering Calamity." What is the "calamity?" Perceived misrepresentations in the use of the term "glatt" ("smooth") when describing a caterer's services for a "kosher" as opposed to "glatt kosher" affair. Originally, "glatt" was a term applied to a greater level of checking the lungs of slaughtered kosher animals. But, as the commentator indicates, the caterer used precisely the same kind of glatt kosher meat for all affairs, whether described as "glatt kosher" or merely "kosher."

The actual difference, the writer notes, is the type of supervision used in the different affairs. In other words, certain kosher supervisors produce "glatt" affairs while other supervisors produce merely "kosher" affairs, despite the fact that the meat is glatt at both.

Nor was such alarmist rhetoric confined to the English language press. In the March, 1989 issue of *Hapardes*, a Hebrew rabbinic journal of halakha published by the haredi (ultra-Orthodox) Agudath Israel, a notice by the *agudath hamasgichim* ("union of kashrut supervisors") warns of serious laxity and neglect when it comes to the observance of kashrut; the notice describes the situation as being "truly tragic."[5] What is the problem? The representation by caterers of their food as "glatt kosher" cannot be trusted. Why not? Because, before a "glatt" representation can be accepted, we must know the identity of the kashrut supervisors. As in *The Jewish Press* piece described above, the concern is for the people involved, not the food itself.

So, we see, according to the common rhetoric of the period, confusion is not merely confusion, it is a "calamity." A mistake is not merely a mistake, it is a "scandal." And the introduction of possibly unkosher food into the kosher food chain is not merely unfortunate, it is catastrophic. Given the quality of this rhetoric, it is clear that there must be something at stake here beyond kashrut itself. What might that "something" be? The beginning of an answer, at least, will emerge from the cries of common Orthodox folk who must negotiate their lives (and their stomachs) in such an atmosphere.

Earlier, we saw mention of a grass-roots group calling themselves "The Concerned Group of Glatt Kosher Consumer." It will surprise no one that such a group would arise in the atmosphere we have described. The first reported evidence of this group is found in the March 15, 1985, issue of *The Jewish Press*, on the heels of a March 8 editorial calling for "A Return to Basics" in kashrut. These basics are said to include "the integrity of the *shochet* (the slaughterer)" and "the issue of whether the proprietor is *shomer shabbos*" (p. 5). The very next week, an ad appears in the same paper (p. 56D) in anticipation of the upcoming Passover holiday. The ad, sponsored by this self-identified "Concerned Committee of 'Glatt Kosher' Consumers," directs the reader to "Ask Yourself 4 'Glatt Kosher' Questions" this Passover (playing on the Four Questions of the Passover seder). Included among the four are (1) whether the butcher or proprietor observes the "*strictest* interpretations of halacha" (emphasis added) and (4—according to their numbering) whether the proprietor is Sabbath observant.

Never do they–or anyone else in the same pages–explain why the strictest interpretation is the preferred one. Indeed, there is little precedent for such a notion, and the Talmud even goes so far as to say that the "power of the lenient [interpretation] is preferred" (see b. Gittin 41b and elsewhere). Nor do they explain what the Sabbath observance of the proprietor (as opposed to the slaughterer himself) has to do with the kashrut of the food. What is clear here—as it has been before—is that the standards being applied to kashrut are standards that separate one type of Jew from another, not one type of meat from another. These standards will assure that the proprietor of the store from which you (the Orthodox or haredi Jew) buy will be just like you. Indeed, there is more than good reason to believe that this is precisely the purpose of these new standards, and several contemporary reports or commentaries make this perfectly explicit.

In a report entitled "Accountability in Kashrus: A New Twist", Yehiel Mayer portrays the activities of the "Concerned Group . . ." against a background of suspicion and (intimated) laxity.[6] "Aren't there many *Glatt Kosher* establishments," he asks, "that are in fact owned by non-observant Jews?" Crucially, his concern is for the owners that might be non-observant, not the slaughterers or the standards applied to the meat. He continues, "How can I be sure they observe standards in Kashruth? . . . Your grandparents . . . would never consider patronizing a concern that is run by a *Mechalel Shabbos* [= one who breaks the Sabbath]." Whether this is true or not (it is quite possible that the grandparents' generation was far less suspicious), the call to the guilty heart is unambiguous. How can you claim to uphold the tradition when you fail to do what your grandparents did? So how is a glatt kosher consumer to be sure? Mayer recommends patronizing only butcher shops which display the decal distributed by the Concerned Group of Glatt Kosher Consumers that identifies the proprietor as a *"Shomer Torah* and *mitzvos"* (an observer of the Torah and the commandments). Non-observant proprietors are to be avoided. Only those who bear the sign of pious approval may serve the needs of the glatt kosher consumer.

Just a few years later (September, 1990), in the pages of *Kashrus Magazine*, Rabbi Eli Teitelbaum makes the intention of the exclusion of the non-Orthodox explicit. Teitelbaum asks the reader to join him on a trip to his *"frum* Boro Park supermarket," where he discovers, much to his alarm, marshmallows manufactured with gelatin. He reports: "checking out the name of the supervising rabbi, I found that he serves in the pulpit of a Conservative congregation in Syracuse, N.Y." As a result, he adds, the *"hechsher* is *extremely* unreliable" (38–39). Teitelbaum does not say that the rabbi is Conservative, only that the congregation is. In small cities such as Syracuse, where Jewish populations have commonly been on the decline, it has not been uncommon for Orthodox rabbis to accept pulpits at non-Orthodox synagogues. In fact, the rabbi to whom he is referring is R. David Sheinkopf, an Orthodox rabbi, and the synagogue he served was not actually a Conservative congregation. It was Beth El, a formerly Orthodox congregation that had accepted the practice of "mixed seating" (of men and women) in some of its pews and was not at the time affiliated with any movement. But for Teitelbaum, any such compromise renders the synagogue Conservative and disqualifies the rabbi serving there—regardless of his training or technical expertise—from overseeing kashrut.

Again, it is important to emphasize that the merits of the case are not addressed by Teitelbaum. He surely knows that numerous prominent Orthodox authorities have argued for the kashrut of regular gelatin. True, others have argued that it is not kosher, but Teitelbaum doesn't involve himself in considering the different positions. He also doesn't respect the possibility that certain pious Jews might follow the permissive position.[7] He simply observes that the rabbi who provides oversight is tainted by his association with a "Conservative" synagogue. The food isn't necessarily *treif* (un-kosher), but the rabbi surely is.

The attitude expressed by Rabbi Teitelbaum is shared by lay people in the same communities as well. In a letter to the editor in *The Jewish Press* on December 13, 1985, one Abraham Kaspi of Philadelphia laments the state of kashrut in his city. The writer begins by remarking that "none of the butcher shops that are within city limits are run or owned by *shomer shabbos, shomer mitsvos* proprietors." He then adds, "the big joke of this so-called 'Orthodox' Philadelphia Rabbinical Council is their *rav hamach-shir* [rabbi who gives kashrut approval]. Previously he was a Young Israel rabbi in New York, and now he davens [= prays] in a Conservative shul [synagogue]. Others serve in 'Traditional' synagogues with microphone and mixed seating" (48). So, again, the problem is not kashrut but synagogue affiliation. Does the rabbi daven in a Conservative synagogue? No good. Does he serve in a synagogue where men and women sit together? If so, how can his integrity be trusted? Even someone who has served at a centrist Orthodox congregation, a Young Israel, is not to be relied upon. The *frum* (pious) must maintain their distance from the non-*frum*. Anything less would be sinful.

Given the penchant of contemporary Jews to separate into smaller and smaller groups, it will surprise few to discover that the divisions fought through kashrut divide not only Orthodox from "un-observant" (= Conservative, and how much more so Reform, etc.) Jews. Perhaps even more pointedly, they divide one Orthodox group from another. For example, an article on "Kashrus Standards in Israel" (*Kashrus Magazine*, April 1994) reports that

> many charedim [= ultra-Orthodox Jews], *whether for political* or kashrus reasons will use only some or one of these [supervisions]. For example, you cannot find many Eida Hacharedis products in Bnei Brak—it is Sheeris territory.... This is the way *politics and hashkafa [= religious worldview] dominate the kashrus scene in Eretz Yisroel [=* Israel]. The fact is, *although no one will publicly admit it*, at present there is basically universal acceptance of all Eida Hacharedis products as kosher.... [Nevertheless,] the food producer...must make special wrappers for as many as six or more different certifications and satisfy entire crews of rabbis and mashgichim [= supervisors]. The products

may or may not be the same, but the rabbinic certification must be different. (p. 40; emphasis added)

This author recognizes that the divisions are rarely about kashrut as such. What divides the groups of supervisors, and necessitates the proliferation of supervising organizations, packaging, etc., is the politics of religion—often motivated by fine differences in religious outlook, but also—no less significantly—by economic and other more worldly factors. Whatever the precipitating forces, the outcome is the same: as one writer quoted earlier commented, "kosher is no longer kosher" (and, we might add, observant is no longer observant, Orthodox is no longer Orthodox , and so forth). The Jewish world is divided against itself, and these divisions show up, first and foremost, in their grocery stores and on their tables.

The article just quoted also makes it clear that kosher may be one thing and the demands of specific communities something else. In fact, there is widespread recognition, at least among the learned in the Orthodox (as in the non-Orthodox) community, that there has been a profound shift toward increasing stringencies in kashrut—as in many other matters of observance—during the years we have been examining. I reported earlier on such developments in the kashrut of certain products (such as peanut oil) for Passover. There are many other examples, and it is not unusual for rabbis to comment on them, even in popular publications.

In a column in *Kashrus Magazine* (April 1995) advising the reader how to "Plan... Your Kosher Kitchen," the author remarks on the "separation frenzy" that has taken hold in the Orthodox community in recent years (p. 45). This "frenzy" has gone so far, he reports, that some now demand separate refrigerators for meat and dairy foods. For technical reasons, there is no problem if cold containers or packages from the different categories come in contact with one another (even if the foods themselves touch when cold, they merely need to be washed of the other substance). It is obvious, therefore, that there is no need for two refrigerators in a kosher kitchen. But, despite his recognition of the extremity of this tendency, the author aids and abets it by declaring, "Of course, the ideal solution is to have two of everything. That's because the person who is not familiar with the halacha will avoid any problems...." So, though there is admittedly no need for two refrigerators, why not have them (that is, if you can afford two refrigerators and a kitchen large enough to contain them)? Better that than worry about errors.

The same phenomenon characterizes kosher food production as well. In a simple and matter-of-fact news item in the April, 1999 issue of *The Jewish Homemaker*, the writer reports that the "tendency in recent years has been toward stricter overall standards. This fact was brought to light by a participant from a chemical company who said that products which in previous years were approved are now rejected" (p. 22). The writer, evidently, approves of the increasing strictness of the community—at least he expresses no reservations about it. But he does note that it is new and that it has consequences for food suppliers. The question we would have to ask is this: what makes an item that is kosher one year non-kosher the next? We are speaking, after all, about the identical product. Of course, one might argue that insisting on greater stringency is simply a matter of increased caution, doing no harm. But this is not precisely true. There are, at the very least, important economic consequences. But even more important, I would argue, is the symbolism of these developments, which is both powerful and potentially harmful, as we shall consider following.

Consider the following case: In the June, 1986 issue of *Kashrus Magazine*, Rav Shimon Schwab, writing on the "Inspection of Vegetables," protests the recent development within the ultra-Orthodox community of avoiding various greens and lettuces because of the fear that they are infested with extremely small bugs, bugs that, because of the shape and texture of the leaves, are virtually impossible to remove thoroughly. What is Rav Schwab's problem with this stringency? "As far as our Jewish people are concerned, our fathers and mothers have for centuries used lettuce for Morror ["bitter herbs"] on the Seder Night as well as parsley for Karpas [greens], and in those days they were no less infested with vermin than they are today. *So we have no right to make new Issurim [prohibitions] and to forbid the eating of any vegetables per se to the general public*" (p. 22; emphasis added). The argument supporting these new stringencies—that is, that eating certain kinds of vegetables inevitably involves transgression and must therefore be avoided—is problematic not only because it ignores precedent, but also because *it casts aspersions on the piety of the ancestors*. Is it possible that the pious and noble Jewish mothers and fathers of old, who committed their lives to Torah and mitzvot, regularly transgressed the law in this way? Is it possible that the Torah meant to prohibit insects so small that they could barely be detected? These are questions that are impossible to avoid. Hence Schwab's objection.

But this comment is the tip of the proverbial iceberg. The concern for bug-infested vegetables represents in a single example all of the issues we have been discussing in this chapter. We shall therefore spend some time trying to understand its details.

"BUGS IN THE SYSTEM"

Vegetables were coming to light as a kashrut problem in the mid-1980s, first in the ultra-Orthodox community and then beyond. An early discussion of this problem appears in a "Special Report" on "Kosher Vegetables" in the June, 1984 issue of *The Kashrus Newsletter* (= Magazine; pp. 13–15). The report, written by Rabbi Yosef Wikler of Yeshiva Birkas Reuven, begins by admitting (by intimation) the novelty of the issue: "Kosher Vegetables?" Wikler asks. Of course, he knows that his readers have long assumed that vegetables are kosher. So he sees it as his task to educate them.

How can vegetables be un-kosher? First, because they may be produced on non-kosher equipment (this has long been recognized, but fresh vegetables are unaffected by this concern) and, second, "they may contain insects." He goes on to admit that insects that are actually microscopic "are not forbidden by the Torah to ingest." But insects "that can be seen by the naked eye, even though they cannot be identified as an insect without benefit of a microscope...are forbidden to be eaten." Though no one, before modernity, would have identified them as insects, and no one, therefore, would have prohibited their consumption, the then emerging consensus in the (ultra-?) Orthodox world seems to be that they are forbidden.

The question is, simply, what is to be done with vegetables that are thus affected? In a special section of the same report (p. 15), Wikler lists the various positions regarding different vegetables articulated by authorities who have dealt with this question. Some are relatively lenient. So, for example, Rav Moshe Henemann, the Rabbinical Administrator of the Vaad Hakashrus of Baltimore, judges that, "with vegetables such as broccoli, spinach and the like," where "it is virtually impossible to detect insects visually by examining them without the aid of artificial means...these insects are not considered 'noticable' (*nikar*) and the rule of nullification— one in sixty—applies." In his judgment, in other words, the insects that infest broccoli and spinach are so small that they pose no concern. Such vegetables may be eaten without hesitation. On the other extreme is Rav Avrohom Blumenkrantz, Rabbi of Ateres Yisrael in Far Rockaway, New York. In his opinion, *which is featured in a special, very prominent chart on the top of the same page*, vegetables like asparagus, broccoli, brussels sprouts, and parsley present such enormous difficulties for anyone who would want to remove their bugs that it is virtually impossible to do it right. In his opinion, therefore, the florets of asparagus and broccoli must be cut off and discarded; only the stems may be eaten after proper washing. Brussels sprouts and parsley leaves should not be eaten at all.

The questions being addressed here are not exactly new. Magnifying lenses of various sorts had been around for centuries. The first useful microscopes were manufactured by Anton van Leeuwenhoek (1632–1723) in Holland in the second half of the seventeenth century. In 1674, for the first time, van Leeuwenhoek was able to use his microscope to describe bacteria, and he then reported his discovery of the teeming microscopic life to be found in a common drop of water. Of course, microscopes did not spread immediately to all corners of Europe, let alone beyond. But commercial manufacture of improved microscopes, with achromatic lenses, began in the early nineteenth century. Besides, word of the discoveries of van Leeuwenhoek and others spread long before the new viewing device did.

The moment Jews became aware of this microscopic reality, they could not ignore its possible halakhic consequences. The earliest discussion of the microscope and kashrut I was able to find appears in the writings of R. Avraham b. Yehiel Michal of Danzig (1748–1820, the relevant work was first published in 1814). A questioner asks Danzig what is to be done about the fact that, when one examines vinegar under a microscope, one discovers that it is filled with microscopic worms. Is it therefore forbidden to consume vinegar unless one first boils it and filters it, as one authority insists? Danzig responds to this question with impatience. It would be ridiculous, he declares, to forbid vinegar. Great and pious Jews have always eaten vinegar! No, he says, worms are forbidden only when they can be seen, and the worms in vinegar cannot be seen without the assistance of a microscope.[8]

A similar response, to a related question, is offered later in the century (1860) by R. Solomon b. Judah Aaron Kluger of Brody, Galicia. Kluger rejects the notion that foods must be checked for infestation with a magnifying glass (a demand which emerges from the fact that previously unseen insects have been discovered with such magnification). The halakha requires the sort of checking that can be done by anyone, regardless of their place or station in life, and magnifying glasses are available (in his day) only to the few. Besides, he writes, "experts say that if we look at water using such a [magnifying] glass [= microscope?], we will see the water swarming with worms."[9] Yet no one would ever imagine that water is forbidden. Or, at least this was the opinion of learned authorities in the nineteenth century.

Writing later in the century, R. Yehiel Michal Epstein expresses the same sentiment, again in connection to the discovery of microscopic bugs in water. It is worth listening to the way he formulates his remarks:

> I have heard that all sorts of water, and particularly rain water, is filled with small creatures that the eye cannot see. And when I was young I heard from someone far away that he saw, by way of a glass that magnifies greatly [= microscope], all sorts of creatures in water. And according to this [report], how do we drink water...? However, the truth is that the Torah did not prohibit what the naked eye cannot see, for *the Torah was not given to angels.*[10]

How could the Torah have prohibited these things? If we cannot see them, then how can God demand we avoid them? (On the other hand, once we have seen them, how can we pretend that they are not there?) The new technology upset the status quo. But the broad response, during the first years that this discovery became generally known, was to continue eating what and how Jews had "always" eaten. This was the way of tradition.

Even in recent years, some of the most prominent rabbinic authorities have supported this same moderate position. For example, R. Ovadia Yosef, former Sephardic Chief Rabbi of Israel, writes that one need not concern oneself with bugs that can be seen only by means of a microscope or even a magnifying glass.[11] Another authority expresses his agreement, adding that "it makes no sense that earlier generations, God forbid, failed in this matter, for it is not clear that what they say, that is, that this [condition of "infestation"] came about in our generation because of spraying and chemical fertilization, is true."[12] And even the eminent R. Moshe Feinstein insists that his inclination is to be lenient in this matter, adding that those who demand stringency cast aspersions on the piety of earlier generations and this, in his opinion, is forbidden.[13] Elsewhere, he gives voice to the same emotion by saying, "all of the kosher generations, the great scholars and the righteous ones and the pious ones, never used a microscope, and it is clear that they upheld all of the laws of the Torah and failed in nothing, even unwittingly (Y.D. 2, #146)."

So despite the new recognition (sparked by the new technology) that foods of all sorts are normally infested with microscopic bugs, moderation gained the upper hand with most authorities. Nor should this be all that surprising, for the truth is, before the advent of modern farming methods–including the use of pesticides–and before the invention of refrigeration for storage, most foods were regularly infested with bugs, worms and other pests of all kinds. Indeed, reading halakhic discussions of the status of bugs from the ancient world until modernity, one gets the clear impression that food was a veritable breeding ground for vermin. How can it have been otherwise?

Facing such an unavoidable reality, those who defined the standards of Jewish eating took a relatively realistic position, for, despite much of what has been written in recent years, not all bugs are prohibited. Maimonides' formulation of the relevant laws is clear and straightforward:

> Those species [of bugs or vermin] that are [believed by pre-modern science to be] created in fruits and other foods...if they have never separated [from the foods in which they grew] it is permissible to eat the fruit along with the worm that is in it. But this is only true if the food became wormy after it was picked.... And, so too, water, in vessels, that has become infested [with worms and the like], behold, it is permissible to drink those bugs along with the water.... Acquatic bugs that are [believed by pre-modern science to be] created in pits, ditches and caves, since the waters are not flowing and are stopped up, behold they are like water in vessels and [the bugs in them] are permitted. And a person may bend and drink from them, and he need not avoid it even though he swallows the small bugs when he drinks. (*Mishneh Torah*, Laws of Prohibited Foods, 2:14–18)

Of course certain bugs were permitted. Given the realities of that world, how can it have been otherwise? If all bugs on all foods were forbidden under all conditions, it would have been impossible to eat.

Yet, despite the reasoned moderation of modern authorities first dealing with the problem of bugs, many during the mid-1980s began to assume a more and more stringent position. As we saw earlier, the most extreme of these demanded that all asparagus and broccoli florets, brussels sprouts, and parsley leaves be discarded. Lettuce, romaine, endive, spinach, and cabbage had to be agitated in water, soaked, "and then examine[d] carefully under a bright light." Cauliflower had to be "soak[ed] in hot water [for] ½ hour. Split vertically in two places, soak[ed] in salt water solution ½ hour and then examine[d] visually."[14] Etc. Under these conditions, how could anyone find the time to eat vegetables at all?

The answer came in the shape of a new vegetable produce company named "Bodek ["check" or "examine"] Kosher Vegetables." According to the company's introductory announcement, in early 1992, "a recent breakthrough in the cultivation and processing of fresh produce has been achieved by a new entry into the food market: Bodek Kosher Produce, Inc." This company, with a gradually expanding line of products, assured its customers that all of its produce, conveniently available in the freezer of your local kosher butcher or grocery, was absolutely free of insect infestation of any kind. These customers, who had been taught since the mid-1980s that there were dangers lurking in their vegetables, needed worry no more. By choosing the Bodek line, they could eat vegetables without fear of the forbidden.

Which brings us back to the *New York Times* and the bugs in the water. According to the article, the discovery of bugs in New York City water began because bugs were found on vegetables shipped from Israel for consumption by Kosher consumers. The Israeli company insisted that they sent clean produce and that the bugs must have come from the water in which their product was washed when it came to the United States. Upon close and careful examination, their claim was found to be correct. Indeed, there were bugs in the water—the microscopic copepods.

Anyone who regularly drinks New York City tap water will affirm that there are no visible bugs in it, at least in most of it. This has led some to suggest that the copepods must grow in local pipes, affecting some local water but not other water (others insist that the copepods could only develop in reservoir-like conditions). Whatever the explanation of the reality, the reality is clear: copepods are problematic only in a few, narrow neighborhoods, not in the entire system. So the panicked avoidance that followed the discovery of bugs in isolated locations must be seen as being of the same cloth as the stringencies described earlier. Despite the rulings for moderation repeated from the earliest discovery of the microscopic aquatic reality to the present, the ultra-Orthodox community has embarked on a new direction (as we saw, it is admitted to be new even within the community) and chosen the path of stringent avoidance.

The question remains "why?" Why have vegetables all of a sudden become suspect? Why, wherever and whenever kashrut is discussed in these sections of the community, are dangers seen to lurk in all quarters? Why in the mid-1980s were there, all of a sudden, "bugs in the system?"

UNDERSTANDING THE CONTEXT

There is no single answer to these questions. A variety of factors affecting the complexion of Orthodoxy during these years would explain these developments in kashrut, both the bug problem in particular and the atmosphere of alarm more generally.

To begin with, the move toward greater stringency and the battles over the precise placement of the new boundaries are part of a far broader phenomenon. It has widely been observed that large parts of the Orthodox community were becoming increasingly *frum* ("pious" = strictly observant) during this period. A variety of observers have speculated on *why* this occurred. In an oft-quoted article, Haym Soloveitchik suggests that the move is the product of a new Orthodoxy whose practices emerge not from traditional observation and imitation but from reading the law as recorded in books published by ultra-Orthodox sources.[15] Samuel Heilman has recently painted a fuller, more complex picture of the forces that have led to this "slide to the right."[16] But whatever the precise explanations, there can be no question that this has, in fact, occurred. So, in circles where "mixed dancing" of men and women together was once permitted, it is now prohibited. Where the singing voices of women were once heard, they are now silenced. It is possible to see increasing stringencies in eating practices as but one kind of stringency among others.

Obviously, these developments are also spurred by the politics of religion and power within and between various Orthodox communities. As we saw earlier in this chapter, kashrut agencies fought with each other throughout this period, one group accusing the other of carelessness or laxity while the other sought to wrest control of kashrut supervision from the former. The community that respected the oversight of one authority refused to accept the oversight of another. Who is the recognized authority in religious matters? Who has the power in the legislative chambers (in Israel) and in the home? Who controls—and benefits from—the kosher consumer dollar (or shekel)? These are all battles that are being fought through the vicarious agency of food and its regulation.

But, it seems clear to me, there is another, less recognized but no less important factor that helps explain the phenomena we documented above, the hints of which may be discovered in other headlines that joined those on kashrut in *The Jewish Press* and elsewhere during this period. The early-to-mid-1980s were a particularly difficult and divisive time for the Jewish community (or communities) in North America and Israel, and these conditions led to a series of responses that would divide segments of the community one from the other for the following many years. One of the most profound of these responses was the gastronomic one we have traced above.

In 1972, Hebrew Union College ordained the first woman rabbi. This would be seen as absurd in Orthodox circles, but it had little practical consequence (after all, male Reform rabbis were not viewed as true rabbis by these same parties either). Of far greater moment was the increasing willingness of some Reform rabbis to officiate at mixed Jew-gentile marriages (and to co-officiate at such ceremonies with Christian clergy), and the official Reform decision, in 1983, to recognize children with Jewish fathers but non-Jewish mothers as Jewish. Whatever the opinion of Orthodox rabbis and their followers toward Reform rabbis or Reform "halakha" (the quotation marks represent their opinion, not mine), these moves would have had unavoidable consequences: if a Reform Jew became a *"ba'al teshuva"* (one who "returned" to traditional practice) and sought to marry a partner within the Orthodox community, it could no longer be taken for granted that the person who thought himself a Jew was in fact (= halakhically) one.

Still, Reform Judaism never claimed to be halakhic and had been long dismissed by Orthodoxy as "beyond the pale." Had these been the only developments, it is possible to imagine that Orthodox authorities might mostly have ignored them. But Conservative Judaism insisted that it was halakhic and, through the years, some in the Orthodox camp agreed that this was largely so. The arguments between at least Modern Orthodoxy and Conservatism had been mostly over fine points, mostly matters of degree. Certainly, given the learning of many of its scholars, Conservative opinions and decisions could not be so easily dismissed. So when The Jewish Theological Seminary decided, in October, 1983, to ordain women, and the first woman was ordained as a Conservative rabbi in 1985, this would indeed make waves. It would be far more difficult for Orthodoxy to ignore these developments. One way or another, there had to be a reaction.

At the same time as these events, the Jewish world was becoming embroiled in a fundamental question of identity, known universally as the "Who is a Jew?" question. This question was, of course, not new in the early 1980s. It would be fair to say, in fact, that the question went back to the very beginnings of Judaism. But for long periods of Jewish history, there was substantial consensus on the answer to this question. That consensus surely broke down with the arrival of modernity, but even in the modern period, there have been times characterized by a "live and let live" attitude and others characterized by division and accusation. The early 1980s fell into the latter category.

The tone of this period began with the election of Menahem Begin as Prime Minister of Israel in 1977. Empowered by inclusion in the new Israeli government and the desire of the Prime Minister to consolidate his support, religious parties began to seek legislation that would strengthen their religious positions. They sought, for example, to restrict the authority of non-Orthodox rabbis in Israel. They put pressure on Israelis not to attend Israel's few non-Orthodox synagogues. And then, in 1981, they began a campaign to amend Israel's Law of Return so that it would exclude converts to Judaism who had not been converted by Orthodox rabbis. This move was the proverbial "straw that broke the camel's back," and it energized non-Orthodox movements to resist forcefully.

To understand the emotion that was brought to this fight, it is necessary to comprehend the enormous historical *and symbolic* significance of the Law of Return. The Law of Return is one of Israel's earliest and most central "Basic Laws" (Israel does not have a formal constitution). It was formulated in response to the catastrophe of the Holocaust, promising that, as long as Israel exists, no Jew would ever lack a place to escape persecution. The law grants Israeli citizenship to any Jew who requests it. For purposes of the law, a Jew is defined as a person who has one Jewish grandparent (intentionally echoing Nazi racial laws, to which it is a response) or converted to Judaism. But the law doe not specify what sort of conversion.

The change that Orthodox parties sought would have reformulated the law to say "conversion *according to the halakha*"—according to the standards of traditional Jewish law. This would effectively have excluded individuals converted by non-Orthodox rabbis. Needless to say, this would have been an extremely significant change, disempowering non-Orthodox rabbis in important ways and nullifying the Jewishness of anyone who had been converted by them. In other words, this change would have declared as "non-Jewish" individuals who were thought by other movements (that is, the most populous and powerful movements in the United States) to be Jewish. Hence, this matter came to be known as the "Who is a Jew?" controversy.

Complicating matters further was the fact that in August, 1985, Israel saw a significant influx of Ethiopian Jews on the back of a major Israeli salvation effort. Ethiopian Jews had identified as Jews for many generations; in fact, they claimed to be the remnant of the ancient "Ten Lost Tribes." But historians challenged this claim, and nobody knew the truth. So the question for the religious in Israel was this: should the Ethiopians be accepted as Jews, despite the fact that their lineage was difficult to pin down, or should they require conversion? Again, a fundamental question of Jewish identity and its definitions was up for grabs. The controversy would not go away easily.

Of course, the attention of all religious parties in the United States was focused on this controversy throughout these years, and the pages of *The Jewish Press* leave no doubt concerning the opinion of the editors and the community they represent. Naturally, they supported the proposed amendment and lamented its repeated parliamentary failure. What is most telling is the way they characterized the Israeli dispute. Opponents were spoken of as being "anti-religious" (Dec. 6, 1985: 13), or, even more extremely, as "Religion Haters" (May 2, 1986: 17). The dispute itself was characterized as "religious strife" (June 20, 1986: 1) or even as a "Civil War" (also May 2, 1986: 17).

The pressure of events in Israel caused Orthodox spokespeople in the United States to seek to reinforce distinctions between traditional and more liberal Jewish movements. To accomplish this, they insisted, first and foremost, that only Orthodoxy could assure the survival of Judaism in America, while liberal streams would encourage assimilation and ultimate demise. Characterizing this attitude was a cartoon appearing in the January 31, 1986 issue of *The Jewish Press* (5). The cartoon portrays three lines of "Jewish Youth" headed toward a "Wasteland." The three lines are labeled "conversions" (away from Judaism), "interfaith marriages" and "parental indifference." The entire cartoon is entitled "The Lost Tribe."

The meaning of the cartoon was perfectly clear to the common reader of the paper. Jewish youth, unprotected by the "fence of Torah" = Orthodoxy, was headed in the wrong direction—that is, toward a wasteland and away, therefore, from the Promised Land. The causes of their loss of direction were assimilation, intermarriage and lack of parental guidance—all thought to be characteristic of the more liberal Jewish movements. The mid-1980s was the period during which these concerns, and particularly intermarriage, were coming to the fore in the Jewish community; the 1990 Jewish Population Study would soon warn the American Jewish community of a 52 percent intermarriage rate (most likely an exaggerated number, but indicative of the tenor of the time). So non-Orthodox Judaisms were the way of doom, Orthodoxy the way of survival. Obviously, the two could mix only at the risk of Judaism itself.

The same argument, in somewhat different terms, commenced several years before the appearance of this cartoon, when Haredi rabbis reacted vociferously to recent developments in the Reform and Conservative camps. In 1983, the ultra-Orthodox Agudath Ha-robonim sounded the alarm regarding "the danger of Reform and Conservative" moves, with specific concern expressed for Reform decisions to accept patrilineal Jews as Jews and no longer to insist on a *get* (Jewish writ of divorce) to effect divorce.[17] From this point onward, both the alarm and the rhetoric grew increasingly more extreme, to the point that non-Orthodox movements were described as "a plague" and "an illness," and Reform and Conservative rabbis were compared (implicitly, at least) to Nazis, who had wiped out 6,000,000 Jews; the former, termed "spiritual murderers," were, through policies that encouraged intermarriage and assimilation, causing the disappearance of even more Jews.[18]

Yet, despite this all, the religious leaders of non-Orthodox movements were insisting on the recognition of their legitimacy even in Israel, and if they had the chutzpah to insist, then the status of these leaders had to be challenged at its very foundation. Of course, the easiest and most obvious way of doing this was to reject and even ridicule the choices they had made, beginning with the ordination of women as rabbis (an innovation with no precedent in the historical tradition). So, in an editorial on "Orthodoxy and Conservatism" in the March 22, 1985, edition of *The Jewish Press*, Rabbi Louis Bernstein, president of the (Orthodox) Rabbinical Council of America, is quoted as saying, in a speech before "a Conservative Rabbinic Group" (that is, at the annual convention of the Rabbinical Assembly), that "such innovations as ordination of women by the Conservative movement has slammed the door between us even tighter" (5). Adopting a far more extreme tone, Rabbi I. Harold Sharfman (administrator of the Kosher Overseers of America) writes, later that year ("Conservative and Reform Judaism," Nov. 15, 1985: 10), that "In their striving for absolute parity between male and female rabbis, we await word that Conservative and Reform Seminarians *have ordained an androgynous or hermaphrodite....* Conservative and Reform Judaism is but a reincarnation of the extinct *minim...they follow in the footsteps of the Christian Church*" (emphasis added).

The rhetoric of this latter piece is actually quite extraordinary. The *minim* were ancient sectarians, often understood to be the early Christians. So Sharfman insists not once, but twice, that Conservative and Reform Judaism are the new Christianity. In view of the historical experience of Jews in Christian lands, and the continuing "othering" of Christians in traditional Jewish circles, it is hard to imagine a more extreme way of declaring that "they (Conservative and Reform) are not us (Jews)." But this is not enough. The sectarianism of the non-Orthodox branches is not merely in their ordination of women as rabbis, but in their desire to erase all gender distinctions of any kind (or so Sharfman argues). Because ordaining women, he insists, is only the first step. Then comes the ordination of androgynous individuals and hermaphrodites—persons of ambiguous or confusing sexual identity. So the challenge to identity represented in recent developments is far more than a challenge to religious identity. It is a challenge to identities of all sorts, including sexual.

R. Simcha Elberg, ultra-Orthodox editor of *Hapardes*, urged his community to translate their rhetoric into action. Elberg viewed Conservative Judaism as a far more dangerous force than Reform. In his words, "The latter [Reform] speak as gentiles, conduct themselves as gentiles, and [true] Jews know how to protect themselves from gentiles.... Between Jews and gentiles stands a tall and wide partition.... But Conservatism is different, because it speaks in the name of halakha, in name of Judaism, in the name of the unity of Jews and in the name of continuity...".[19] So how can such a threat—an "illness"—be protected against? Elberg proposes that anyone who is ordained by a yeshiva or a recognized Rav (a proper rabbi, to be distinguished from a Conservative or Reform "Rabbi") should be ordained on the explicit condition that he never serve in a Conservative synagogue (there is no need, in his opinion, even to mention Reform). And if the newly minted Orthodox Rav transgresses this limit? His ordination should be nullified immediately.

Not all of the Orthodox arguments were explicitly extreme or alarmist. *The Jewish Press*, for example, saw fit to publish a detailed report on the training of rabbis in different branches of American Judaism, concluding that the training of all but Orthodox rabbis was severely inadequate. The report by Dr. Manfred R. Lehmann, entitled "On the Qualifications of American Rabbis,"[20] compares the curricula of Hebrew Union College (Reform), The Jewish Theological Seminary (Conservative), and Yeshiva University (Orthodox), asking how many hours of training students at each of the schools have in Talmud and halakha. The author shows, to no one's surprise, that the Orthodox require far more hours of training in these subjects, the Reform far less, and the Conservative something in between. Stating his conclusions based upon these data, Lehman writes:

> The claim of legitimacy on an equal basis with Orthodox rabbis has...originated...with the rabbis themselves...motivated by factors of personal vanity and ambition [so that they may be]...heroes and prima donnas to their own congregants....it is obvious that the discrepancy in education and training, as well as piety before the law, is so horrendous between the Orthodox, Conservative and Reform, that the claim for equality and legitimacy cannot be taken seriously.

Of course, Lehmann assumes his conclusions before he does the analysis. In his view, being a rabbi means being able to decide matters of Jewish law based upon a detailed and in-depth learning of the sources of the halakhic tradition. So the training of legitimate rabbis will require extensive preparation in the analysis of these sources. He knows that Reform and even Conservative rabbinic training lags significantly on this count, so he cites the "objective evidence" to support the conclusion of which he is already sure. This is a fundamental challenge to the legitimacy of non-Orthodox rabbis, but from a specifically Orthodox perspective. Needless to say, Reform polemicists could turn the tables and compare the hours of pastoral training required in each movement, to the detriment of the Orthodox. But no matter—the point is to de-legitimate, to ridicule the claims for equality on the part of non-Orthodox rabbis, in Israel and elsewhere. It is us versus them, Jew versus Jew. To be sure of who we are, we must be sure we are not them.

Not surprisingly, boundary building of a similar kind was also in evidence within the Orthodox community, dividing between one Orthodox group and another. To take just one of many possible examples, in the spring of 1985, alarm over divisions in the Jewish community had risen sufficiently that certain groups were seeking to take steps to counter the tide. The president of the centrist Orthodox Rabbinical Council of America was invited to address the Conservative Rabbinical Assembly, and the president of the latter group was invited to address the former as well. This development was utterly unacceptable to right-wing Orthodox groups, who called upon the RCA to withdraw its invitation. A severe condemnation of this invitation was issued by "The Council of Torah Authorities in the United States" following the leadership of R. Moshe Feinstein, the recognized halakhic authority of the generation.[21] This division within Orthodoxy provoked the editorial page of *The Jewish Press* to beckon: "We respectfully urge the RCA to hearken to the call of such illustrious *Roshei Yeshivos* [rabbinic yeshiva heads] and *Chassidic* leaders and withdraw its invitation to the president of the Conservative Rabbinical Assembly of America to address the RCA convention this month" (March 29, 1985: 5). Not only was Jewry being divided over these fundamental questions of identity and practice, but so too was Orthodoxy. The solution? Unify Orthodoxy (the editorial was entitled "A Call for Orthodox Unity") at the expense of Jewry. If a fence had to be built, it was clear where it had to be.

The trends and tenor of this period motivated one Jewish organization, The National Jewish Resource Center (NJRC) to take extreme steps. The organization was under the leadership of Modern Orthodox Rabbi Yitz Greenberg. Greenberg was deeply committed to Jewish unity, and he viewed the pluralism of the Jewish community as a potential strength, if also a challenge. He therefore committed NJRC to a full-court press on behalf of his cause. To express this commitment, the organization changed its name to "CLAL," nominally an acrostic for "The National Jewish Center for Learning and Leadership." But it is clear that this acrostic connection is secondary; the primary statement is that the organization stands for *"clal yisrael,"* the unified people of Israel.

At the same time, CLAL took out an ad in a variety of publications (*The Jewish Press* ad appeared in the October 18, 1985, issue), Jewish and general, expressing its concern for the deep divisions that were plaguing the Jewish community. The ad featured a drawing of a large stone Star of David, split down the middle by a deep fissure. The star, obviously, represented the contemporary Jewish community. The illustration was accompanied by a large caption that declared, "The Last Time We Jews Were So Divided We Lost 10 Out Of 12 Tribes. Forever." Ignoring the historical correctness of the claim (the loss of the ten tribes was a consequence of the Assyrian conquest, not of internal "Jewish" divisions), the point was clearly to sound alarm. "You mean we are in danger of losing 10/12s of our people?!" the reader was intended to ask. "No! We can't allow that!" Along with the broad, public campaign, CLAL also launched more targeted events—a conference and related publications—that were united by the thematic question, "Will there be one Jewish people in the year 2000?" (Greenberg's essay by this title was first published in June, 1985.) The implied answer, obviously, was "no," that is, unless immediate and serious steps were taken to assure a different outcome.

In classes and lectures given during this period, Greenberg powerfully conveyed the sense that the Jewish community was experiencing a serious crisis. The divisions, in his view, were not only dangerous, but exponentially so. In his analysis, the estrangement of one Jewish group from another was rendered increasingly more pronounced through a kind of multiplier effect. As each group was dismissed by the other, growing more and more estranged, it had to take steps to protect its own flank, essentially ignoring how these steps might impact on other Jewish parties. Thus, Reform, during this period, decided to accept as Jewish children of mixed marriages in which only the father, but not the mother, was Jewish (on the condition that the child assume a Jewish identity upon growing up). This was contrary to traditional Jewish law, which defined Jewishness through the mother. When challenged for what such a move would do to Jewish unity, Reform leaders responded something to the effect that "they don't accept us anyway, so what's the point." Of course, such steps only reinforced Orthodox opinions regarding Reform, and so encouraged further acts of "fence construction." Whether or not Greenberg's prognosis for the year 2000 was accurate, the dynamic he identified was surely operative. If not a crisis, it was certainly a source of concern. Undeniably, Jewish identity was being debated and challenged in ways that were virtually unprecedented.

It was in precisely this setting that kashrut became a matter of acute concern in the Orthodox community. What is the connection?

The first answer is the most obvious. As we have noted many times in prior chapters, if you can't eat with someone, then it is more difficult to be in relationship with him or her. Pragmatically speaking, the new attention to the minute details of kashrut—and even, literally, to the bugs in the system—would divide between Jews who demanded such restrictions and those who did not. If non-Orthodox supervision was *by definition* suspect, then this would assure that Orthodox and non-Orthodox Jews would be forced apart in all stages of the production and consumption of food. So, if the non-Orthodox were "dangerous," because of their ordination of women rabbis and enfranchisement of gays and lesbians and who knows what else, then this redoubled commitment to the most stringent interpretations of kashrut would guarantee that the Orthodox would stay far from the danger. It would be hard to find a more effective boundary.

Indeed, the separation erected by the Orthodox was—and is—felt acutely by non-Orthodox Jews. Not long ago, I asked Conservative Rabbis to describe divisive experiences they have had in their communities relating to kashrut. I received many responses, often relating similar stories or themes. The following examples are representative.

One rabbi had been a Hillel (the Jewish student organization) rabbi at the University of Minnesota. He had responsibility for facilitating and supervising the Shabbat meals for students at Hillel. The meals themselves were prepared by a kosher caterer, under Orthodox supervision, at the local Jewish Community Center. The question was: could this Conservative Rabbi be trusted to care for the kashrut of a soup pot supplied by the caterer? To ascertain the answer, the Orthodox kashrut supervisor had only one question—does the Conservative Rabbi drive on Shabbat? The question was not a kashrut question. In this, as in several other cases, the issue was observance or piety independent of the immediate matter at hand. As in the campaign of the "Concerned Glatt Kosher Consumers," approval was contingent on a question of observance that carried a symbolic and very public weight.

Mostly, the stories were not about one detail or another—symbolic or otherwise—but simply about the exclusion of a rabbi because he was Conservative. One prominent example is particularly telling. There is a synagogue is Tokyo, Japan, whose rabbi is called upon to provide rabbinic supervision for the kashrut of foods produced throughout the Far East. For most of recent years, the rabbi of this synagogue has been Conservative. A recent rabbi from Tokyo reports that when OU (a mainstream Orthodox kashrut granting organization) found out that he, the supervising rabbi, was Conservative, products that for years had been deemed "kosher" were no longer accepted as such—despite the fact that *nothing* about their production changed. Non-Orthodox was, by definition, non-acceptable. The separation wall constituted by food was functioning very effectively.

As we saw earlier in this chapter, the wall built to divide between Orthodox and non-Orthodox was deployed to separate Orthodox from Orthodox as well, and the threat to place the wall here rather than there could be used for great religious-political gain. Orthodox rabbis who did not toe the line could quickly find themselves excluded from the community. So, according to the report of one respondent to my informal survey, a particular Orthodox rabbi was ejected from the local "*va'ad hakashrus*" ("kosher council") for having allowed women in his synagogue dance with the Torah on the Simhat Torah holiday. Notably, he did not allow men and women to mix in this dancing. Moreover, there is absolutely nothing halakhically wrong with women holding a Torah scroll. Again, the concern is one of symbolism: women dancing with the Torah could be construed as an empowerment of women, or as a tip of the hat to modern, "non-Jewish" sensibilities. Someone who succumbs to such influences can obviously not be trusted to guard the food store.

The message was simple: if you refused to submit to the stringencies of the ultra-Orthodox, you were in danger of finding yourself on the same side of the boundary line as the Conservative, a danger that few Orthodox authorities or their communities would be willing to risk. So if "glatt" was the standard demanded by "*gedolei hatorah*" (the "great sages of torah"), then glatt it would be. If vegetables were subject to new prohibitions, then it would be difficult to continue the laissez-faire approach that had earlier characterized the consumption of vegetables. The question, at its foundation, was whom you could eat with, so everyone would have to choose sides.

But we would be mistaken if we were to imagine that the only purpose of the increasing stringencies was pragmatic, that is, to separate the pious from the non-pious. As has always been the case, other means of separation were available. And though food might be particularly effective in accomplishing the desired ends, the choice to use food in this way is still a choice, and hence meaningful. Turning the lens on our own generations, we must ask the same questions we have asked of earlier generations. What is the symbolism of the new turns in kosher practice? What is the meaning of a system that discovers its own bugs?

INTERPRETING THE BUGS

I turn to the new concern with bugs because, though this is but one of a variety of new stringencies that have come to characterize Orthodox—and particularly *haredi*—practice in recent years, it has arguably become a "banner" issue, one that has drawn exceptional attention and energy. It has taken on the quality of a symbol the significance of which transcends the specific case. This development may, therefore, help us understand the growth of stringencies in eating practices more generally, and even serve as a key to understanding the broad move to the right in contemporary Orthodoxy.

No reader of this book will be surprised by the ease with which I have been able to take advantage of the phrase "bug in the system" as a metaphor for what has happened to contemporary kashrut. But the ease of use shows just how expressive the metaphor is. The bugs on the vegetables or in the water, to which contemporary authorities have turned what might be described as excessive attention, remind us of the colloquial English phrase that readily captures the state of affairs in contemporary kashrut. When different kashrut communities are in a constant state of suspicion, each refusing to rely on the trustworthiness of the other, then "there is a bug in the system." When foods previously thought to present little kashrut problem (raw vegetables or, even more recently, water) becomes a major source of kashrut anxiety, then there is surely a "bug in the system." The bugs, both literally and figuratively, are at the center of the story.

To interpret the bugs, we will be well served by recalling an earlier interpretation, one that helped us distinguish rabbinic from biblical eating laws. The biblical regulations, we saw, defined animals as being either "pure" (= inside) or "impure" (= outside), representing, ultimately, Israel and the nations. The rabbinic innovation, by contrast, prohibited the mixing of two permitted foods (dairy and meat), which I interpreted as representing (among other things) rabbinic and non-rabbinic Jews. The fact that both kinds of food were permitted represented the fact that both sorts of Jews were Jews, and therefore fundamentally "inside." But this did not mean they should mix. In the rabbis' view, it was better for rabbinic Jews to maintain their separation, by and large, from their non-rabbinic Jewish neighbors.

The greatly more stringent modern rulings go one step further. In the past, raw vegetables and water have been assumed to be relatively "safe" from the perspective of Jewish eating regulations. The worm or other insect on/in them *might* have been prohibited, but this was never considered a serious problem. Did the biblical Daniel, in the king's court, demand that his vegetables be checked or his water be strained? Of course not. But today, the concern is for insects so small that they are difficult to see. They can be discovered only through very careful and thorough inspection (though, technically speaking, they might not actually be "microscopic"). So what do we have here? An apparently kosher food that, upon closer inspection, turns out to be forbidden. A food that, though presumed to be kosher by earlier generations, might now be declared off-limits. Why, in this time and place, would the kosher be made "treif?" Why would Jews go searching for the barely visible blemish that renders the whole thing unacceptable?

The answer, I submit, lies in the condition of Jewish identity in our age. Once upon a time, a Jew was a Jew. That is to say, not long ago, someone who presented him- or herself as a Jew was generally assumed to be Jewish. You could, more or less, take his or her word for it. Unless you knew something that might suggest otherwise, there was no need to check.

But today, Jewishness has become much more complicated. Someone might have been converted by a Reform or Conservative rabbi. Such a person will consider him- or herself Jewish. But the Jewishness of this person might not be accepted by a Jew further to the right (that is, a Conservative rabbi might not accept a Reform conversion and even a Modern Orthodox rabbi probably won't accept either conversion). So if someone, by all appearances Jewish, presents her- or himself to you as a Jew, you probably have to ask a few questions. You probably have to check.

We also live in a world in which many Jews intermarry with non-Jews. And, statistics have shown, the more liberal the Jew, the more likely it is that she or he will intermarry. So the frequency of intermarriage among identifying Orthodox Jews is very low, among Conservative Jews higher, and among Reform Jews higher still. Yet an intermarried couple might decide to raise their children as Jewish, and those children might not know that—in cases where the father is Jewish but the mother not—other Jews might not accept their Jewish identity. Of course, things could get even more complicated in the next generation, when the child of the mixed marriage, identifying herself as a Jew, marries a Jewish man, and together they raise children both of whose parents identify as Jewish. Yet, according to traditional Jewish law, neither the mother nor her children will be Jewish. So, if you are a traditional Jew, you have to ask questions. You have to check—*carefully*. The blemish might be invisible from the surface, so you have to dig deep.

Allow me to illustrate the recent shift through a personal example. My own grandmother on my father's side was a non-Jewish woman (before her conversion), and my father, therefore, was not Jewish when he was married (he was born before my grandmother's conversion and himself converted long after his marriage). Yet the rabbi who married my parents never asked about their Jewishness—which they both, not knowing any better, would have affirmed—nor about the Jewishness of their respective sets of parents. Admittedly, the rabbi who married my parents was Conservative, not Orthodox. But in that day, Conservative rabbis were quite traditional, and Orthodox rabbis were mostly not asking such questions either. Given the relatively low rate of recognized intermarriage, nobody felt the need.

Lest you think that this was a unique case, let me add that my mother's best friend was also the daughter of an intermarriage, with a non-Jewish mother, yet she was raised a Jew and therefore assumed herself to be a Jew. She then married a Jewish man, and together they raised four children, all of whom assumed themselves to be Jewish. Yet, halakhically speaking, none are. And so through the generations it continues.

Today, as I said, things have only gotten more complex. Today there is more and more religious drift, more and more shifting of identities. Assimilated grandparents might find their grandchildren in Jewish day schools, and those grandchildren might affiliate with, and raise their children in, Orthodox communities. In such a generation, when little is clear, everything must be checked. Why? Because appearances are deceptive, and problems might be hidden. The bug in the system might not be easily seen, it might not be evident from the outside. Yet that minute, nearly invisible bug might mess up the whole thing. If we eat what we are, then even what appears "obviously" kosher must be checked carefully.

The power of the nearly invisible bug to serve as symbol is a product of its linguistic associations as well. The prohibited bug is, in biblical language, a type of "sheretz," a swarming or crawling creature. It is, in terms of both its legal status and its linguistic resonance, closely related to the "sheketz," the loathsome crawling creature. Notably, it is precisely this term, "sheketz," that was appropriated by Yiddish-speaking Jews (including the entire *haredi* community) to refer to non-Jews—the non-Jewish woman is the "shiksa" and (less commonly) the non-Jewish man is the "shaygitz" (both slightly different pronunciations of the biblical term). So it is fair to say that the prohibited bug stands in, in these circles, for the non-Jew, for the "other." This is, of course, precisely the fear that attaches to the unknown other who lives outside of your own observant community.

The bug, by virtue of its legal category, also carries the connotation of "prohibited" and even "loathsome," thus strengthening its symbolic power. Wittingly or unwittingly, ultra-Orthodox rabbis writing in *Hapardes* during the period we have been examining make this association between offensive foods, offensive practices and offensive Jews quite clear. Relatively early on in this period, a report on the alarm sounded by rabbis of Agudath Israel regarding the danger of Reform and Conservatism declares that the Reform "profane the Holy Sabbath and the Festivals, profane the holiness of Israel by conducting intermarriages, *and pollute the Jewish home with prohibited foods*".[22] The pollution of intermarriage and the pollution caused by disgusting foods go hand-in-hand. And, though many non-kosher foods might be thought to be disgusting, it is the swarming, crawling kind that conveys this quality with particular power.

Later in this period of intensive suspicion and accusation, Elberg again offers his views as a spokesperson of the *haredi* camp, and he again (unwittingly) makes the association of the (in his mind) repulsive Reform and Conservative movements and hard-to-see, prohibited crawling creatures. He comments: "It is unnecessary to prove how much the *cancer* of the Reform and the Conservative spreads more and more through the body of Judaism...[leading to] a demographic holocaust...[they aspire] to introduce the worst *impurity* into the greatest holiness."[23] The Hebrew word for cancer, *sartan*, means (like the English, following the Latin) "crab"—a perfect example of a prohibited creeping creature. But in its current usage, as cancer proper, we are speaking of an even more threatening creature, for this "crab" invades, at its most dangerous, on the microscopic level. It is precisely this quality that makes it so feared; it can barely be seen, it must be sought out with the most sophisticated technology, yet you can never be sure you have discovered it all. Making it even worse, the "cancer" Elberg is speaking of is impure, just like the crawling creature in the Torah's system. In fact, the "*sheretz*" represents, for the rabbis, the very embodiment of impurity, for they speak of one who pretends to repent while still sinning as comparable to one who descends into the purifying mikvah (the ritual bath) "with the *sheretz* still in his hand."

There can be no doubt that Jews on the left and the right of the bug divide understand the power of its symbolism, if only intuitively. Kosher caterers are judged "glatt" or "not glatt" by virtue of their practices in these matters. They are acceptable to this community but not to that one precisely over the question of whether and how they check for bugs. It is significant that the Jewish Theological Seminary cafeteria (JTS is the center for the training of Conservative rabbis), after initial hesitations when bugs were first recognized as a problem, now commonly serves broccoli and cauliflower florets. They cannot miss the fact that precisely these foods are deemed practically irretrievable (i.e., not sufficiently cleanable) by stringent Orthodox authorities. In those circles, they are at least "recommended against," and often outright banned. Yet the supervisors at JTS approve of serving these items, confident that they are kosher. There is a difference of opinion in the law here. But there is also a symbolic affirmation of difference. We are not you, JTS declares. We *do* serve broccoli and cauliflower, whatever you decide to do.

****

Once again, in our own day, our food and eating choices have served to signal who we are—*and who we are not*. Food practices bring us together, and food practices wedge us apart. Jews today are as gastronomic—as controlled by the law of the stomach—as they have always been. The details may have changed, but the fundamental dynamic has not.

Notes

CHAPTER 1

1. Claude Lévi-Strauss, *The Origin of Table Manners. Mythologiques*, v. 3 (Chicago: University of Chicago Press, 1990), p. 495. Trans. of *L'Origine des Manières de Table* (Paris: Librairie Plon, 1968).
2. Jean Soler, "The Semiotics of Food in the Bible," in Carole Counihan and Penny Van Esterik (eds.), *Food and Culture: A Reader* (New York and London: Routledge, 1997), p. 55.
3. Roland Barthes, "Toward a Psycho-Psychology of Contemporary Food Consumption," in Carole Counihan and Penny Van Esterik (eds.), *Food and Culture: A Reader* (New York and London: Routledge, 1997), pp. 20–21.
4. Mary Douglas, "Deciphering a Meal," in Carole Counihan and Penny Van Esterik (eds.), *Food and Culture: A Reader* (New York and London: Routledge, 1997), p. 36.
5. Foods prepared in special ways on account of Sabbath strictures, or ritually significant dishes prepared for Passover, are an obvious exception.
6. The literature on foodways, eating practices, and their interpretation is, by now, voluminous. The articles cited previously, along with others collected in *Food and Culture*, and the literature cited therein, constitute an excellent recent introduction to the field.
7. See, for example, John Cooper, *Eat and Be Satisfied: A Social History of Jewish Food* (Northvale, NJ and London: Jason Aronson, 1993); Hasia Diner, *Hungering for America: Italian, Irish and Jewish Foodways in the Age of Migration* (Cambridge and London: Harvard University Press, 2001); Ariel Toaff, *Mangiare alla giuda*, (Bologna: Società editrice il Mulino, 2000); Joel Hecker, *Mystical Bodies, Mystical Meals: Eating and Embodiment in Medieval Kabbalah* (Detroit, MI: Wayne State University Press, 2005); and the volume of essays edited by Leonard J. Greenspoon, Ronald A. Simkins, and Gerald Shapiro, *Food and Judaism* (Omaha and Lincoln, NB: Creighton University Press, 2005).
8. For a more detailed discussion of problems pertaining to the Mishnah, its character and interpretation, see David Kraemer, "Mishnah," in *The Cambridge History of Judaism*, vol. 4, ed. by Steven Katz (Cambridge: Cambridge University Press, 2006), pp. 299–315.
9. Recent scholarship suggests that the latter was more likely. See Seth Schwartz, *Imperialism and Jewish Society, 200 B.C.E. to 640 C.E.* (Princeton, NJ, and Oxford: Princeton University Press, 2001), especially pp. 101–61.

10. There are many discussions of the challenge of using the Talmud for historical research. For my view, see "Rabbinic Sources for Historical Study," in *Judaism in Late Antiquity*, part. 3, v. 1, *Where We Stand: Issues and Debates in Ancient Judaism*, ed. by J. Neusner and Alan J. Avery-Peck (Leiden: E.J. Brill, 1998): 201–12. A variety of other views, by Jacob Neusner, Ze'ev Safrai, Günter Stemberger, Richard Kalmin, and Louis H. Feldman, may be found in the same volume.

11. For a probing analytical discussion of the use of the halakhic (= legal) literature of this period for historical research, see Haym Soloveitchik, "Can Halakhic Texts Talk History?" *AJS Review*, 3 (1978): 153–96.

12. Important recent studies include Christine E. Hayes, *Gentile Impurities and Jewish Identities: Intermarriage and Conversion from the Bible to the Talmud* (New York and Oxford: Oxford University Press, 2002), and Jonathan Klawans, *Impurity and Sin in Ancient Judaism* (New York and Oxford: Oxford University Press, 2000).

13. See, in particular, David Biale, *Eros and the Jews: From Biblical Israel to Contemporary America* (New York: Basic Books, 1992) and Daniel Boyarin, *Carnal Israel: Reading Sex in Talmudic Culture* (Berkeley: University of California Press, 1993).

CHAPTER 2

1. Milgrom's argument can be found in Jacob Milgrom, *Leviticus 1-16, The Anchor Bible*, v. 3 (New York: Doubleday, 1991), pp. 3–13; hereafter cited in text. Milgrom cites the earlier literature in the course of his discussion.

2. This paragraph recapitulates Susan Niditch's cogent argument in *Oral World and Written Word: Ancient Israelite Literature* (Louisville, KY: Westminster John Knox Press, 1996). See especially pp. 110–34.

3. The translation is Milgrom's.

4. Mary Douglas, *Purity and Danger* (London: Routledge and Kegan Paul, 1966; Reprint, London and New York: Routledge Classics, 2002).

5. For a review of many of the critiques, see Milgrom, pp. 720–21. Douglas's critique of her own earlier work may be found in her preface to the Routledge Classics Edition, pp. x–xxi. For an extended exposition of her more recent views, see *Leviticus as Literature* (Oxford and New York: Oxford University Press, 1999), pp. 134–75. Despite its flaws, it seems to me that Douglas has, in her receptivity to her critics, been too quick to repudiate the analytical framework of her earlier study.

6. Peter Garnsey, *Food and Society in Classical Antiquity* (Cambridge: Cambridge University Press, 1999), pp. 16 and 123; hereafter cited in text.

7. Århem, Kaj. "Massai Food Symbolism: The Cultural Connotations of Milk, Meat, and Blood in the Pastoral Massai Diet" in *Anthropos*, 84 (1989), 1/3: 4.

8. John Cooper, *Eat and Be Satisfied: A Social History of Jewish Food* (Northvale, NJ and London: Jason Aronson, 1993), p. 3.

9. Veronika Grimm, *From Feasting to Fasting* (London and New York: Routledge, 1996), p. 16.

10. Brian Hesse and Paula Wapnish, "Urbanization and the Organization of Animal Production at Tell Jemmeh in the Middle Bronze Age Levant," in *Journal of Near Eastern Studies* 47, n. 2 (April, 1988): 88, 91; hereafter cited in text.

11. Brian Hesse, "Animal Use at Tel Miqne-Ekron in the Bronze Age and Iron Age," *ASOR Bulletin* 264 (1986): 23.
12. Howard Eilberg-Schwartz, *The Savage in Judaism: An Anthropology of Israelite Religion and Ancient Judaism* (Bloomington and Indianapolis: Indiana University Press, 1990), p. 119; hereafter cited in text.
13. See *Oral World and Written Word*, especially pp. 131–34.
14. Robert R. Wilson, *Sociological Approaches to the Old Testament* (Philadelphia: Fortress Press, 1984), p. 251.

CHAPTER 3

1. There is an abundant literature on the history of Jews and Judea during this period. Particularly to be recommended is Seth Schwartz's *Imperialism and Jewish Society*, 200 B.C.E. to 640 C. E. (Princeton, NJ, and Oxford: Princeton University Press, 2001), pp. 19–99; hereafter cited in text.
2. A comprehensive accounting of Jewish works produced during this period may be found in George W.E. Nickelsburg, *Jewish Literature Between the Bible and the Mishnah* (Philadelphia: Fortress Press, 1981); hereafter cited in text.
3. There are several other, mostly brief discussions of Jewish eating practices as reflected in the literature of this period. One fine review of this material is E. P. Sanders, *Jewish Law from Jesus to the Mishnah* (London: SCM Press, and Philadelphia: Trinity Press International, 1990), pp. 272–83. Christine E. Hayes's more recent discussion is flawed by anachronistic and untested assumptions; she writes, for example: "the biblical laws of *kashrut* (and their postbiblical development) are sufficient to explain this abstention, and one need not resort to a theory of Gentile impurity." The term "kashrut," and much that it implies with respect to the specifics of observance, are unattested during this period. Hayes's discussion also ignores the eating habits of Jews and others during the biblical and Second Temple periods; consideration of these habits would (or should) affect her judgments in significant ways. See Christine E. Hayes, *Gentile Impurities and Jewish Identities: Intermarriage and Conversion from the Bible to the Talmud* (New York and Oxford: Oxford University Press, 2002), pp. 47–50.
4. For a discussion of the dating of this work, see Louis F. Hartman and Alexander A. Di Lella, *The Book of Daniel, The Anchor Bible*, v. 23 (Garden City, NY: Doubleday and Co., 1977), pp. 9–18.
5. The formulation here supports Hayes's observation that gentile impurity during this period is seen as originating in gentile actions; it is neither a ritual impurity nor one that is inherent in being a gentile. However, once the gentile is marked as impure, the distinction between types of impurity (ritual, ethical, or otherwise) is likely to be lost, at least on the common Jew. The evidence, from contemporary as well as from later rabbinic sources, suggests that the taboos designated by "impurity" effectively bleed from one source to another in the perception of most participants in the system. Hence, the gentile, once deemed impure, will communicate that "impurity" to his or her food, and for this reason it will be improper to eat with him. In other words, the distinction drawn by Hayes (following Jonathan Klawans) is of primarily academic interest and thus largely irrelevant in the context in which these impurities were deployed. See Hayes, pp. 45–67, and Jonathan Klawans, *Impurity and Sin in Ancient Judaism* (New York and Oxford: Oxford University Press, 2000), passim.

6. For the essentials of Hellenization during the Hasmonean period, see Schwartz, pp. 34–39.

7. See Louis Feldman, *Jew and Gentile in the Ancient World* (Princeton, NJ: Princeton University Press, 1993), p. 125–31.

8. This situation would change in the years immediately following the period we are now discussing, when separate tables and Jewish misanthropy are connected explicitly by various writers. See Sanders' discussion, pp. 277–83.

9. See Menahem Stern, *Greek and Latin Authors on Jews and Judaism,* Volume One: *From Herodotus to Plutarch* (Jerusalem: The Israel Academy of Sciences and Humanities, 1976), p. 415; hereafter cited in text.

10. Jacob Milgrom, *Leviticus 1-16, The Anchor Bible,* v. 3 (New York: Doubleday, 1991), p. 652; hereafter cited in text.

11. Peter Garnsey, *Food and Society in Classical Antiquity* (Cambridge: Cambridge University Press, 1999), pp. 16–17; see also Phyllis Pray Bober, *Art, Culture, and Cuisine: Ancient and Medieval Gastronomy* (Chicago and London: University of Chicago Press, 1999), p. 181.

12. Jean-Louis Flandrin and Massimo Montanari, *Food: A Culinary History.* Trans. by Albert Sonnenfeld (New York: Columbia University Press, 1999), p. 197; hereafter cited in text.

13. Stephen Mennell, *All Manners of Food: Eating and Taste in England and France from the Middle Ages to the Present* (Urbana and Chicago: University of Illinois Press, 1996), p. 42.

14. Brian Hesse, "Pig Lovers and Pig Haters: Patterns of Palestinian Pork Production," in *Journal of Ethnobiology,* v. 10, n. 2 (Winter 1990): 218.

15. Brian Hesse and Paula Wapnish, "Can Pig Remains Be Used for Ethnic Diagnosis in the Ancient Near East?," in Neil Asher Silberman and David Small, eds., *The Archaeology of Israel: Constructing the Past, Interpreting the Present,* JSOT Supplement Series, 237 (Sheffield, U.K.: Sheffield Academic Press, 1997), p. 262; hereafter cited in text.

16. *The Works of Philo,* trans. by C.D. Yonge (Peabody, MA: Hendrickson Publishers, 1993), p. 626.

17. The literature representing this shift is now voluminous. On the limits of rabbinic influence and authority even in subsequent centuries, see Schwartz, pp. 103–28 (especially pp. 110–23) and the literature cited there.

18. See Sanders discussion, 277–83, for a related but somewhat more affirmative view of Jewish eating self-restriction during this period. I am inclined to support a more agnostic position.

CHAPTER 4

1. The essays collected in Lee I. Levine, ed., *The Galilee in Late Antiquity* (New York and Jerusalem: The Jewish Theological Seminary of America, 1992), together document the complexity described in this paragraph. On Sepphoris in particular, see the essays by Eric M. Meyers and James F. Strange, pp. 321–55. Despite his overly credulous use of rabbinic sources, leading to a picture that grants the rabbis too much influence on the contours of Galilean society during this period, Martin Goodman's work also serves to document much of this diversity; see his *State and Society in Roman Galilee, A.D. 132–212* (Totowa, NJ: Rowman and Allanheld, 1983).

2. On the various claims of this paragraph, see Seth Schwartz, *Imperialism and Jewish Society, 200 B.C.E. to 640 C.E.* (Princeton, NJ, and Oxford: Princeton University Press, 2001), pp. 103–23.

3. In my reading of the Mishnah, as in my reading of all rabbinic texts, from Late Antiquity through the Middle Ages, I have consulted manuscripts for variants. I reference such variants only when they are pertinent to my interpretation and discussion. Furthermore, in my reading of ancient texts, I avoid relying on singular versions or isolated, specific textual details out of recognition of the fact that (a) very few manuscripts of classical rabbinic texts survived the Medieval world, (b) all preserved manuscripts are individual (= personal) copies of said texts, and (c) the "travels" of rabbinic teachings from purported "originals" to even the earliest surviving manuscripts makes it impossible to be confident of such specific teachings. Only larger patterns, attested in multiple texts, give us relatively firmer evidence.

4. The section in parentheses is unsupported by manuscripts and is most likely a later gloss.

5. See Tosafot, Hullin 104b, s.v. "'of ugevinah...."

6. I am arguing here that the gemara anticipates our reading and assumes us to be critically-minded advanced students of its teachings. If this is the case, then the rejected view, which we will view as rejected but nevertheless reasonable, remains part of the gemara's teaching. For a detailed elaboration of this approach and its theory, see David Kraemer, *Reading the Rabbis: The Talmud as Literature* (New York and Oxford: Oxford University Press, 1996), pp. 3–17.

7. "Dietary Separation of Meat and Milk: A Cultural-Geographical Inquiry," *Ecology of Food and Nutrition* 9 (1980): 203–17; hereafter cited in text.

8. "Massai Food Symbolism: The Cultural Connotations of Milk, Meat and Blood in the Pastoral Massai Diet," *Anthropos* 84 (1989): 1–23.

9. Jacob Milgrom, *Leviticus 1-16, The Anchor Bible*, v. 3 (New York: Doubleday, 1991), pp. 741–42.

10. The biblical term for the unit that will consume the lamb is literally "the house of the fathers" (Ex. 12:3).

11. I do not use the term "sectarian" here in any formal sense. My intent is to describe the many divisions that characterized Palestinian Jewish society during this period, including the sects proper but also including priests with their supporters and opponents, zealots and collaborators, wealthy and poor, Hellenized Jews and pietistic opponents, and so forth. See Shaye J.D. Cohen, *From the Maccabees to the Mishnah* (Philadelphia: The Westminster Press, 1987), pp. 115–23, and Schwartz, pp. 91–98.

12. See Shaye J.D. Cohen, "The Significance of Yavneh: Pharisees, Rabbis, and the end of Jewish Sectarianism," *HUCA* 55 (1984): 27–53.

13. Shaw, Brent D. "Eaters of Flesh, Drinkers of Milk." *Ancient Society,* 13/14 (1982/3): 5–31; hereafter cited in text.

14. Though the extent to which particular Jewish populations participated in Greco-Roman culture has been much debated. Still crucial in this connection are Saul Lieberman's *Greek in Jewish Palestine* (New York: Jewish Theological Seminary of America, 1942) and *Hellenism in Jewish Palestine* (New York: Jewish Theological Seminary of America, 1950). More recently, see Seth Schwartz's assessment, *Imperialism and Jewish Society*, pp. 129–61.

15. Peter Garnsey, *Food and Society in Classical Antiquity* (Cambridge: Cambridge University Press, 1999), p. 86, hereafter cited in text.

16. Howard Eilberg-Schwartz, *The Savage in Judaism: An Anthropology of Israelite Religion and Ancient Judaism* (Bloomington and Indianapolis: Indiana University Press, 1990), p. 119.

CHAPTER 5

1. The phrase "it is prohibited," though appearing in printed editions, is not supported by manuscripts. It is, however, implied.
2. See David Kraemer, "The Spirit of the Rabbinic Sabbath," *Conservative Judaism* 49, n. 4 (Summer, 1997): 42–49; reprinted in D. Kraemer, ed., *Exploring Judaism* (Atlanta: Scholars Press, 1999), pp. 295–304.
3. See Charlotte Elisheva Fonrobert, "Yalta's Ruse: Resistance Against Rabbinic Menstrual Authority in Talmudic Literature," in Rahel W. Wasserfall, ed., *Women and Water: Menstruation in Jewish Life and Law* (Hanover and London: Brandeis University Press, 1999), pp. 60–81.
4. This was as true outside of Israel as it was in Israel. See E.P. Sanders, *Jewish Law From Jesus to the Mishnah* (London and Philadelphia: SCM Press and Trinity Press International, 1990), pp. 278–81.
5. There are numerous examples of this appropriation of the historical priestly function or perspective by lay-people in early rabbinic Judaism. For instructive discussions, see Jacob Neusner, *Method and Meaning in Ancient Judaism* (Missoula: Scholars Press, 1979), 145–50, and, with respect to tractate Hullin in particular, *A History of the Mishnaic Law of Holy Things*, pt. 6 (Leiden: E.J. Brill, 1980), p. 109. See also Baruch Bokser, "*Ma'al* and Blessings Over Food: Rabbinic Transformation of Rabbinic Terminology and Alternative Modes of Piety," *Journal of Biblical Literature*, v. 100, n. 4 (December, 1981): 557–74; "Rabbinic Responses to Catastrophe: From Continuity to Discontinuity," *Proceedings of the American Academy for Jewish Research*, v. 50 (1983): 37–61; and *The Origins of the Seder* (Berkeley: University of California Press, 1984), pp. 84–100.
6. The idealized view of women as restricted to and largely responsible for the domestic realm, including food preparation, is found in both rabbinic and nonrabbinic (and Jewish and non-Jewish) sources. See Tal Ilan, *Jewish Women in Greco-Roman Palestine* (Peabody, MA: Hendrickson Publishers, 1996), pp. 184–90, and Miriam B. Peskowitz, *Spinning Fantasies: Rabbis, Gender, and History* (Berkeley: University of California Press, 1997), pp. 66–72 and 96–101.
7. See Isaiah M. Gafni, *The Jews of Babylonia in the Talmudic Era* (Hebrew) (Jerusalem: The Zalman Shazar Center for Jewish History, 1990), pp. 149–76.
8. This section in parentheses is a later addition to the Mishnah, taken from the Tosefta. See Epstein, p. 949. The sage whose enactment is recorded here is probably R. Judah the grandson of Rabbi Judah the Patriarch; see b. Avodah Zarah 37a.
9. Manuscripts preserve some significant variants in these texts; problematic sections have been omitted in the above translation.
10. In her discussion of these texts, Christine Hayes elides the difference between foods where kashrut is a real concern and cases where it is not, as in these cases. It seems to me that her omission of this distinction and its implications is a product of her apologetic project, a project which seeks to deny the rabbis' "othering" by arguing that "The Mishnah Avodah Zarah is best understood as a set of regulations that make it possible to deal with Gentiles with the confidence that one is not violating any religious prescriptions...." To make this argument, she not only ignores the present distinctions, but she gives short shrift to texts in the same chapter that restrict contact with gentiles because "they are suspected of bestiality...they are suspected of adultery...[and] they are suspected of murder" (m. A.Z. 2:1). She also ignores the

Mishnaic teaching, found in the same context, forbidding a Jewish woman to serve as a midwife or wet-nurse for a gentile because she would be bringing idolaters into the world. See her discussion in *Gentile Impurities and Jewish Identities* (Oxford and New York: Oxford University Press, 2002), p. 141.

11. See Hayes, pp. 130, 134, 142 and passim. Hayes makes entirely too much of the fact that gentile impurity is described by the rabbis as being of rabbinic as opposed to scriptural origin. In the rabbinic system, rabbinic laws are often stricter, and certainly harder to bend or break, than scriptural laws (a close reading of the talmudic sources leads none other than Maimonides to conclude that scriptural laws may be reinterpreted by any court in any generation, whereas rabbinic laws may only be changed by courts that are "greater in wisdom and number;" see *Mishneh Torah*, Laws of Rebels, ch. 2). Surely the rabbis do not admit that their own laws are to be less scrupulously observed than scriptural laws. Furthermore, the rabbis' confession that these laws are "merely" rabbinic is found in elitist texts of their own invention, communications of rabbis to rabbis and their disciples. So even if common people were less scrupulous about rabbinic laws (that is, if they observed them at all), it is doubtful that they would have known this rabbinic definition of their status.

12. This is my critique of Hayes's project seeking to determine "what kind" of impurity gentiles are marked with at the various stages of ancient Judaism. Particularly in the rabbinic period, after the destruction of the sanctum (where impurity has real consequences), the creation or extension of impurity would have had rhetorical consequences, seeking to persuade the observer to keep his or her distance from that which is marked as impure. This would replicate the intent of the prophets of Israel when they spoke of sinful Israel as impure (menstrually or otherwise). Hayes's distinctions are academic, not actual.

13. The rhetoric of these sources would reinforce attitudinally the legal boundaries erected by the rabbis in their ascription of impurity to the gentile, a process well-characterized by Hayes in these words: "Jewish ascriptions of impurity to Gentiles both constructed and reinforced the boundary needed to preserve group identity;" p. 162.

14. Obviously, therefore, and contra Hayes, they do not consider kashrut as such to be the operative concern.

15. This same tension is discovered by Hayes in the gentile-impurity laws themselves. On the one hand, ascription of impurity to gentiles seeks to "maximize disincentives for intimate contact" (p. 130), one the other hand, it "was not intended to establish an impermeable boundary between Jews and Gentiles" (p. 143). My explanation of the dynamic leading to this tension/balance is different from hers.

CHAPTER 6

1. Catherine Bell, *Ritual Theory, Ritual Practice* (New York and Oxford: Oxford University Press, 1992), p. 74. I am also particularly persuaded by Jonathan Smith's theory of ritual, as well as his interpretive application of that theory, in *To Take Place* (Chicago and London: University of Chicago Press, 1987), esp. pp. 103–05.

2. All of the teachings defining the ritual as outlined here are found in the Talmud, b. Shabbat 21b–23a.

3. Lawrence A. Hoffman, *Covenant of Blood* (Chicago and London: University of Chicago Press, 1996), pp. 159–60 (emphasis in the original); cited hereafter in text. Baruch Bokser also analyzes the blessings and their underlying ideology at length, with reference to the relevant rabbinic sources and with special attention to their terminology. See Bokser, *"Ma'al* and Blessings Over Food: Rabbinic Transformation of Rabbinic Terminology and Alternative Modes of Piety," *Journal of Biblical Literature*, v. 100, n. 4 (December, 1981): 557–74.

4. This claim is elaborated at length and in detail by Daniel Boyarin in his *Carnal Israel: Reading Sex in Talmudic Culture* (Berkeley: University of California Press, 1993). For a concise statement of his central thesis, see p. 5.

CHAPTER 7

1. See Tosafot at b. Hullin 104b, s.v. "fowl and cheese;" and *Sefer Hayashar, novellae* #472.

2. Jacob ben Asher was the son of the renowned authority, Asher ben Yehiel ("the Rosh"), whom he joined when he fled Germany to settle in Toledo in 1303. At that point, ben Asher effectively joined the Spanish (Sephardic) tradition, where he became extremely influential. For a discussion of the consequences of this resettlement for the relationship between the two traditions, see Benjamin Gampel, "A Letter to a Wayward Teacher," in *Cultures of the Jews*, ed. by David Biale (New York: Schocken Books, 2002), pp. 399–402.

3. Caro resided in Safed, Palestine, among other Jews whose families had fled Spain upon the expulsion of that community in 1492.

4. Jean-Louis Flandrin and Massimo Montanari, *Food: A Culinary History*, trans. by Albert Sonnenfeld (New York: Columbia University Press, 1999), p. 249; hereafter cited in text.

5. Stephen Mennell, *All Manners of Food: Eating and Taste in England and France from the Middle Ages to the Present* (Urbana and Chicago: University of Illinois Press, 1996), pp. 41–42; hereafter cited in text.

6. See Salo Wittmayer Baron, *A Social and Religious History of the Jews*, vol. xvi, *Poland-Lithuania 1500–1650* (New York, London and Philadelphia: Columbia University Press and The Jewish Publication Society of America, 1976), pp. 231–32.

7. Much has been written on the Jewish experience in Poland during this period. Baron's volume on this period is a fine general statement. See also Jacob Goldberg, *The Jewish Society in the Polish Commonwealth* (Hebrew) (Jerusalem: The Zalman Shazar Center for Jewish History, 1999).

8. Bernard Weinryb, *The Jews of Poland* (Philadelphia: Jewish Publication Society, 1973), p. 125. Baron describes the Poles' "great admiration for everything Italian," p. 59.

9. See Antony Polonsky, Jakub Basista and Andrzej Link-Lenczowski, *The Jews in Old Poland 1000–1795* (London: I.B. Tauris and Co., 1993), p. 1.

10. See Baron, p. 56, Moses A. Shulvass, Jewish Culture in Eastern Europe: The Classical Period (New York: Ktav, 1975), p. 40, and Jacob Elbaum, *zemanim umegamot besifrut hamaḥshavah vehamusar* (Ph.D. dissertation, Hebrew University, 1977), p. 34.

11. Z. Pietrzyk, "Judaizers in Poland in the Second Half of the 16th Century," in Polonsky, Basista and Link-Lenczowski, pp. 23–24.

12. Responsa #16 , quoted in Edward Aaron Fram, *Jewish Law and Social and Economic Realities in Sixteenth and Seventeenth Century Poland* (Ph.D. dissertation, Columbia University, 1991), p. 101.

13. Johann Buxtorf, *Jüden Schül* (Basel, 1603), p. 562.

14. In his generally excellent book, *The Laws of Kashrus* (New York: Mesorah Publications, 1993), Rabbi Binyomin Forst cites "*Rabbeinu Yeruchum* (sic.): *Issur V'heter* no. 39" as an authoritative record of this custom (p. 198, n. 34). There are, however, two problems with this source. First, this work is mistakenly attributed to Rabbeinu Yerucham; see the work of Israel Ta-Shema in *Sinai* 64 (1968–69): 254–57. Second, and more important, the manuscript of this work I was able to check (it was first printed only in the nineteenth century) has not three hours (*shalosh*) but six (*sheish*). It is dubious, therefore, whether this represents a bona fide attestation of the practice at all. It is far more likely that the printer (or the scribe of the other manuscript, which was unavailable to me) made an error in recording "six."

The other interesting reference to a three-hour waiting period is found in the work of a Jewish convert to Christianity, Victor von Carben, who lived from 1442–1515 in Germany. In his book, *Juden Büchlein* (first printed 1550), we find the suggestion that pious Jews were supposed to wait nine hours while common Jews waited only three. But a nine-hour wait is unknown in any Jewish source or practice, casting doubt on this whole testimony. Moreover, it is possible that parts of the work were actually penned by a Dominican monk who had no direct familiarity with Jewish practice (see Elisheva Carlebach, *Divided Souls* [New Haven: Yale University Press, 2001], p. 178). On the other hand, we must wonder why anyone would have invented these numbers, and it is in any case noteworthy that later German Jewish custom follows the more lenient practice described in this work. Whether or not this is so, there remains no known *halakhic* source for this practice, and we must assume, therefore, that it developed within the living community of German Jewry, as a product of its own practices and compromises.

CHAPTER 8

1. *Kelim mitekufat ha-Mishnah v'ha-Talmud*, second edition (Tel-Aviv: Haaretz Museum and Ceramics Museum, 1979), pp. 62–71.

2. In mss: Nahman.

3. Ms Vatican Ebr. 120-1 makes this explicit.

4. S.D. Goitein, *A Mediterranean Society: The Jewish Communities of the Arab World as Portrayed in the Documents of the Cairo Geniza*, 6 vols. (Berkeley: University of California Press, 1967–1988), v. 4, p. 252.

5. The same opinion is expressed by Aderet, in longer and more complicated language, in his *Torat Habayit Ha-Arokh*, 4:4, and elsewhere.

6. Vol. 1, #76 (Bnei Barak, 1959); also quoted by R. Aaron Hakohen b. R. Jacob of Lunil (early fourteenth century) in his *Orḥot Ḥayyim*, Laws of Prohibited Foods 72.

7. Manuscript variants relating to this section do not change its substance. The notion that a negative taste is considered null and will not, therefore, create a prohibition is an early rabbinic rule.

8. Benjamin Richler, *Hebrew Manuscripts in the Biblioteca Palatina in Parma* (Jerusalem: Jewish National and University Library, 2001), p. 387.

9. Haym Soloveitchik, "Piety, Pietism and German Pietism: *Sefer Hasidim I* and the Influence of *Hasidei Ashkenaz,*" *The Jewish Quarterly Review*, XCII, nos. 3-4 (January-April, 2002): 465.

10. Elisheva Carlebach, *Divided Souls* (New Haven: Yale University Press, 2001), pp. 55–56, 180–81.

11. See *Kurzer Entwurf* (Branschweig, 1754), pp. 93–94.

12. Bernard Rosenberger, "Arab Cuisine and its Contribution to European Culture," in Jean-Louis Flandrin and Massimo Montanari, *Food: A Culinary History*, trans. by Albert Sonnenfeld (New York: Columbia University Press, 1999), pp. 208.

13. Miguel-Ángel Motis Dolader, "Mediterranean Jewish Diet and Traditions in the Middle Ages," in Flandrin and Montanari, p. 233.

14. Margaret Visser, *The Rituals of Dinner: The Origins, Evolution, Eccentricities, and Meaning of Table Manners* (New York: Penguin Books, 1992), pp. 189–91 (hereafter cited in text) and Giovanni Rebora, *Culture of the Fork: A Brief History of Food in Europe*, tran. by Albert Sonnenfeld (New York: Columbia University Press, 2001), pp. 14–17.

15. *Kelim mitekufat ha-Mishnah v'ha-Talmud*, second edition (Tel-Aviv: Haaretz Museum and Ceramics Museum, 1979), pp. 14–15.

16. Jodi Magness, *The Archaeology of Qumran and the Dead Sea Scrolls* (Grand Rapids, MI, and Cambridge, U.K.: William B. Eerdmans Publishing Company, 2002), p. 117.

17. Yigal Yadin, *Hamimtza'im miymei bar-kokhba b'mearat ha-igarot* (Jerusalem: 1963), pp. 132–35 and plates 39–40.

18. See Binyomin Forst, *The Laws of Kashrus* (New York: Mesorah Publications, 1993), pp. 258–62.

19. See also the many examples cited in Edward Aaron Fram, *Jewish Law and Social and Economic Realities in 16th and 17th Century Poland* (Ph.D. diss., Columbia University, 1991), pp. 55–57, 101, 116–17 and 225.

20. On the dynamics of the gendering of the kitchen in a later period (Europe, nineteenth century), see Ruth Ann Abusch-Magder, "Kashrut: The Possibility and Limits of Women's Domestic Power," in Leonard J. Greenspoon, Ronald A. Simpkins and Gerald Shapiro, eds., *Food and Judaism, A Special Issue of Studies in Jewish Civilization*, vol. 15 (Omaha and Lincoln, NB: Crieghton University Press, 2005).

CHAPTER 9

1. Louis Ginzberg, *Ginzei Schechter*, v. 2 (New York: The Jewish Theological Seminary of America, 1929), p. 560; hereafter cited in text.

2. A concise description of the status of Jews in early Islam may be found in Bernard Lewis, *the Jews of Islam* (Princeton: Princeton University Press, 1984), pp. 24–28 and following.

3. On the broad experience of Jews in Islam, see Lewis, pp. 74–90.

4. Mordecai Margulies, *The Differences Between Babylonian and Palestinian Jews* (Hebrew) (Jerusalem: Rubin Mass, 1937), p. 112.

5. See Seth Schwartz, *Imperialism and Jewish Society, 200 B.C.E. to 640 C.E.* (Princeton, NJ, and Oxford: Princeton University Press, 2001), pp. 129–61, esp. pp. 132–33 and 142–45.

6. This is not to say that Jews did not make their peace with foreign rule. But rabbinic prayer—which speaks to and seeks to speak for the popular sensibility—leaves no doubt of the hope for restoration of Jewish sovereignty. The

ubiquitous Jewish iconography from this period, consistently combining symbols of a restored Temple (ark, menorah, shofar, fire-pan, lulav and etrog), does the same.

7. See Jacob Neusner, *Transformations in Ancient Judaism* (Peabody, MA: Hendrickson Publishers, 2004), pp. 98–116.

8. The legal developments are detailed in Amnon Linder, *The Jews in Roman Imperial Legislation* (Detroit, MI, and Jerusalem: Wayne State University Press and The Israel Academy of Sciences and Humanities, 1987), p. 120 and following.

9. See Isaiah Gafni, *The Jews of Babylonia in the Talmudic Era: A Social and Cultural History* (Hebrew) (Jerusalem: The Zalman Shazar Center for Jewish History, 1990), pp. 117–25.

10. Leon Nemoy, ed., *Karaite Anthology* (New Haven: Yale University Press, 1952), p. 111.

11. Shmuel Assaf, *Teshuvot ha-Geonim* (Jerusalem: Hamadpis, 1927), p. 68; cited hereafter in text.

12. *Sefer Hamanhig* (Jerusalem: Mossad Harav Kook, 1978), pp. 660–61.

13. For an excellent accounting of the Jewish socio-religious experience in Islam during these centuries, see Raymond P. Scheindlin, "Merchants and Intellectuals, Rabbis and Poets: Judeo-Arabic Culture in the Golden Age of Islam," in D. Biale, ed., *Cultures of the Jews* (New York: Schocken Books, 2002), pp. 313–46 and following.

14. *Teshuvot ha-geonim*, Jerusalem, 1863, #163.

15. *Sefer Hamanhig*, p. 659.

16. Quoted in S. Grayzel, *The Church and the Jews in the Thirteenth Century* (Philadelphia: Dropsie, 1933), p. 107.

17. See Edward Aaron Fram, *Jewish Law and Social and Economic Realities in Sixteenth and Seventeenth Century Poland,* Ph.D. dissertation, Columbia University, 1991, p. 225.

18. Quoted in Ariel Toaff, *Love, Work, and Death: Jewish Life in Medieval Umbria* (London: The Littman Library of Jewish Civilization, 1996), p. 75; cited hereafter in text.

19. Cited in Gunther W. Plaut, *The Rise of Reform Judaism* (New York: World Union for Progressive Judaism, 1963), p. 213.

20. Quoted in Max Wiener, *Abraham Geiger and Liberal Judaism*, trans. by Ernst J. Schlochauer (Philadelphia: Jewish Publication Society, 1962), p. 114; emphasis added.

21. Quoted in D. Philipson, *The Reform Movement in Judaism* (New York: Macmillan, 1931), pp. 278–79; emphasis added.

22. The text of the Platform is quoted in full in Michael A. Meyer, *Response to Modernity: A History of the Reform Movement in Judaism* (New York and Oxford: Oxford University Press, 1988), pp. 387–88.

23. Alfred Kazin, *A Walker in the City* (New York: Harcourt, Brace and Co., 1951), pp. 33–34; cited hereafter in text.

24. Ruth Glazer, "The Jewish Delicatessen: The Evolution of an Institution," *Commentary*, March, 1946: 60; cited hereafter in text.

25. Jenna Weissman Joselit, *The Wonders of America* (New York: Hill and Wang, 1994), p. 204.

26. Hasia Diner, *Hungering for America* (Cambridge and London: Harvard University Press, 2001), p. 185; cited hereafter in text.

27. Gaye Tuchman and Harry Gene Levine, "New York Jews and Chinese Food: The Social Construction of an Ethnic Pattern," *Journal of Contemporary Ethnography*, 22, n. 3 (October 1993): 384; cited hereafter in text.

CHAPTER 10

1. *The Jewish Homemaker*, v. 10, n. 1 (February-March, 1978): 18.
2. P. 19.
3. Quoted also in *Kashrus Magazine*, June, 1986: 18.
4. *Jewish Press*, June 13, 1986: 56D.
5. The notice appears at the opening of the volume.
6. *The Jewish Press*, August 16, 1985: 50.
7. Respect of different positions, each halakhically defended by reputable authorities, has ample precedent within the tradition; for the Talmudic foundation of this approach, see b. Yevamot 13b–14b.
8. See *Binat Adam, issur veheter*, #34.
9. *Tuv ta'am veda'at* II, *quntres aharon*, #53.
10. *Arukh Hashulchan, Yoreh Deah*, 84, 36; emphasis added.
11. *Yabi'ah omer*, pt. 4, Y.D. 20, 2.
12. *Minchat shelomo* II, 63.
13. *Iggarot moshe*, Y.D. 4, #2; cited hereafter in text.
14. *The Kashrus Newsletter* (June, 1984): 15.
15. Haym Soloveitchik, "Rupture and Reconstruction: The Transformation of Contemporary Orthodoxy," *Tradition* 28 (1994): 64–130.
16. Samuel C. Heilman, *Sliding to the Right: The Contest for the Future of American Jewish Orthodoxy* (Berkeley, Los Angeles and London: University of California Press, 2006).
17. *Hapardes*, May, 1983 (57, 8): 29.
18. *Hapardes*, December, 1985 (60, 4): 2–4, and January, 1986 (60, 5): 2–3.
19. *Hapardes* 60, 4 (December, 1985):2–3; my translation.
20. July 4, 1986: 21.
21. See *Hapardes* 59, 9 (May, 1985): 24.
22. 57, 8 (May, 1983): 29; emphasis added.
23. *Hapardes* 60, 5 (January, 1986): 2; emphasis added.

Bibliography

Adan-Bayewitz, David. *Common Pottery in Roman Galilee*. Tel-Aviv: Bar Ilan U., 1993.

Antons, Carl. *Kurzer Entwurf*. Branschweig, 1754.

Århem, Kaj. "Massai Food Symbolism: The Cultural Connotations of Milk, Meat, and Blood in the Pastoral Massai Diet." *Anthropos*, 84 (1989), 1/3: 1–23.

Assaf, Shmuel. *Teshuvot ha-Geonim*. Jerusalem: Hamadpis, 1927.

Baer, Yitzhak. *A History of the Jews in Christian Spain*. Philadelphia: Jewish Publication Society, 1966.

Baron, Salo Wittmayer. *A Social and Religious History of the Jews*, vol. xvi, *Poland-Lithuania 1500–1650*. New York, London, and Philadelphia: Columbia University Press and The Jewish Publication Society of America, 1976.

Barthes, Roland. "Toward a Psycho-Psychology of Contemporary Food consumption." In Counihan, Carole, and Van Esterik, Penny, eds., *Food and Culture: A Reader*. New York and London: Routledge, 1997.

Bell, Catherine. *Ritual Theory, Ritual Practice*. New York and Oxford: Oxford University Press, 1992.

Bleich, J. David. "Survey of Recent Halakhic Periodical Literature: New York City Water." *Tradition* 38:4 (2004): 70–103.

Bober, Phyllis Pray. *Art, Culture, and Cuisine: Ancient and Medieval Gastronomy*. Chicago and London: University of Chicago Press, 1999.

Bokser, Baruch. "*Ma'al* and Blessings Over Food: Rabbinic Transformation of Rabbinic Terminology and Alternative Modes of Piety." *Journal of Biblical Literature*, v. 100, n. 4 (December, 1981): 557–74.

———. *The Origins of the Seder*. Berkeley: University of California Press, 1984.

———. "Rabbinic Responses to Catastrophe: From Continuity to Discontinuity." *Proceedings of the American Academy for Jewish Research*, v. 50 (1983): 37–61.

Bokser, Ben Zion. "The Future of the American Jewish Community." *Proceedings of the Rabbinical Assembly*, 12 (1948): 193–206.

Boyarin, Daniel. *Carnal Israel: Reading Sex in Talmudic Culture*. Berkeley: University of California Press, 1993.

Brand, Joshua. *Kelei ha-cheres b'sifrut ha-Talmud*. Jerusalem: Mossad haRav Kook, 1953.

———. *Kelei zekhukhit b'sifrut ha-Talmud*. Jerusalem: Mossad haRav Kook, 1978.

Bresciani, Edda. "Food Culture in Ancient Egypt." In Flandrin, Jean-Louis, and Montanari, Massimo. *Food: A Culinary History*. Trans. by Albert Sonnenfeld. New York: Columbia University Press, 1999.

Brothwell, Don, and Brothwell, Patricia. *Food in Antiquity: A Survey of the Diet of Early Peoples.* Baltimore and London: The Johns Hopkins University Press, 1998.

Buxtorf, Johann. *Jüden Schül.* Basel, 1603.

Carlebach, Elisheva. *Divided Souls.* New Haven: Yale University Press, 2001.

Chotzinoff, Samuel. *A Lost Paradise.* New York: Arno Press, 1975.

Cohen, Shaye J.D. *From the Maccabees to the Mishnah.* Philadelphia: The Westminster Press, 1987.

———. "The Significance of Yavneh: Pharisees, Rabbis, and the end of Jewish Sectarianism." *HUCA* 55 (1984): 27–53.

Cooper, John. *Eat and Be Satisfied: A Social History of Jewish Food.* Northvale, NJ and London: Jason Aronson, 1993.

Corbier, Mireille. "The Broad Bean and the Moray: Social Hierarchies and Food in Rome." In Flandrin, Jean-Louis, and Montanari, Massimo, *Food: A Culinary History.* Trans. by Albert Sonnenfeld. New York: Columbia University Press, 1999.

Counihan, Carole, and Van Esterik, Penny, eds., *Food and Culture: A Reader.* New York and London: Routledge, 1997.

Da Modena, Leon. *Historia de' Riti Hebraici.* Venice: Apresso Benedetto Miloco, 1678.

Diner, Hasia. *Hungering for America.* Cambridge and London: Harvard University Press, 2001.

Miguel-Ángel Motis Dolader, "Mediterranean Jewish Diet and Traditions in the Middle Ages." In Flandrin, Jean-Louis, and Montanari, Massimo, *Food: A Culinary History.* Trans. by Albert Sonnenfeld. New York: Columbia University Press, 1999.

Douglas, Mary. "Deciphering a Meal." In Counihan, Carole, and Van Esterik, Penny, eds., *Food and Culture: A Reader.* New York and London: Routledge, 1997.

———. *Leviticus as Literature.* Oxford and New York: Oxford University Press, 1999.

———. *Purity and Danger.* London: Routledge and Kegan Paul, 1966. Reprint, London and New York: Routledge Classics, 2002.

Dupont, Florence. "The Grammar of Roman Dining." In Flandrin, Jean-Louis, and Montanari, Massimo, *Food: A Culinary History.* Trans. by Albert Sonnenfeld. New York: Columbia University Press, 1999.

Eilberg-Schwartz, Howard. *The Savage in Judaism: An Anthropology of Israelite Religion and Ancient Judaism.* Bloomington and Indianapolis: Indiana University Press, 1990.

Elbaum, Jacob. *Zemanim umegamot besifrut hamaḥshavah vehamusar.* Ph.D. dissertation, Hebrew University, 1977.

Feely-Harnik, Gillian. *The Lord's Table: The Meaning of Food in Early Judaism and Christianity.* Washington, D.C., and London: Smithsonian Institution Press, 1981.

Feldman, Louis. *Jew and Gentile in the Ancient World.* Princeton, NJ: Princeton University Press, 1993.

Flandrin, Jean-Louis, and Montanari, Massimo. *Food: A Culinary History.* Trans. by Albert Sonnenfeld. New York: Columbia University Press, 1999.

Fonrobert, Charlotte Elisheva. "Yalta's Ruse: Resistance Against Rabbinic Menstrual Authority in Talmudic Literature," In Wasserfall, Rahel W., ed., *Women and Water: Menstruation in Jewish Life and Law.* Hanover, NH and London: Brandeis University Press, 1999.

Forst, Rabbi Binyomin. *The Laws of Kashrus.* New York: Mesorah Publications, 1993.

Fram, Edward Aaron. *Ideals Face Reality: Jewish Law and Life in Poland, 1550–1655*. Cincinnati, OH: Hebrew Union College Press, 1997.

——. *Jewish Law and Social and Economic Realities in Sixteenth and Seventeenth Century Poland*. Ph.D. dissertation, Columbia University, 1991.

Gafni, Isaiah M. *The Jews of Babylonia in the Talmudic Era* (Hebrew). Jerusalem: The Zalman Shazar Center for Jewish History, 1990.

Garnsey, Peter. *Food and Society in Classical Antiquity*. Cambridge: Cambridge University Press, 1999.

Gampel, Benjamin. "A Letter to a Wayward Teacher." In Biale, David, ed. *Cultures of the Jews*. New York: Schocken Books, 2002.

Ginzberg, Louis. *Ginzei Schechter*, v. 2. New York: The Jewish Theological Seminary of America, 1929.

Glazer, Ruth. "The Jewish Delicatessen: The Evolution of an Institution." *Commentary*, March, 1946: 58–63.

Goitein, S.D. *A Mediterranean Society: The Jewish Communities of the Arab World as Portrayed in the Documents of the Cairo Geniza*, 6 vols. (Berkeley: University of California Press, 1967–988).

Goldberg, Jacob. *The Jewish Society in the Polish Commonwealth* (Hebrew). Jerusalem: The Zalman Shazar Center for Jewish History, 1999.

Goodman, Martin. *State and Society in Roman Galilee, A.D. 132–212*. Totowa, NJ: Rowman and Allanheld, 1983.

Goody, Jack. *Cooking, Cuisine and Class: A Study in Comparative Sociology*. Cambridge: Cambridge University Press, 1982.

Grantham, Billy J. *A Zooarchaeological Model for the Study of Ethnic Complexity at Sepphoris*. Ph.D. Dissertation, Northwestern University, 1996.

Grayzel, Solomon. *The Church and the Jews in the Thirteenth Century*. Philadelphia: Dropsie, 1933.

Greenspoon, Leonard J., Simpkins, Ronald A., and Shapiro, Gerald, eds. *Food and Judaism, A Special Issue of Studies in Jewish Civilization*, vol. 15. Omaha and Lincoln, NB: Crieghton University Press, 2005.

Greenstone, Julius H. "Report of the Committee on Jewish Law." *Proceedings of the Rabbinical Assembly*, 5 (1934): 100–03.

Grimm, Veronika. *From Feasting to Fasting*. London and New York: Routledge, 1996.

Grivetti, Louis Evan. "Dietary Separation of Milk and Meat: A Cultural-Geographical Inquiry." *Ecology of Food and Nutrition*, 9 (1980): 203–17.

Harris, Marvin. *Good to Eat: Riddles of Food and Culture*. Prospect Heights, IL: Waveland Press, 1998. Reprint of *The Sacred Cow and the Abominable Pig*, 1985.

Hartman, Louis F., and Di Lella, Alexander A. *The Book of Daniel, The Anchor Bible*, v. 23. Garden City, NY: Doubleday and Co., 1977.

Hayes, Christine E. *Gentile Impurities and Jewish Identities: Intermarriage and Conversion from the Bible to the Talmud*. New York and Oxford: Oxford University Press, 2002.

Hecker, Joel. *Mystical Bodies, Mystical Meals: Eating and Embodiment in Medieval Kabbalah*. Detroit: Wayne State University Press, 2005.

Heilman, Samuel C. *Sliding to the Right: The Contest for the Future of American Jewish Orthodoxy*. Berkeley, Los Angeles and London: University of California Press, 2006.

Herodotus. *The History*. Translated by David Greene. Chicago and London: University of Chicago Press, 1987.

Hesse, Brian. "Animal Use at Tel Miqne-Ekron in the Bronze Age and Iron Age," *ASOR Bulletin* 264 (1986): 17–27.

———. "Pig Lovers and Pig Haters: Patterns of Palestinian Pork Production." *Journal of Ethnobiology*, v. 10, n. 2 (Winter 1990).

Hesse, Brian, and Wapnish, Paula. "Can Pig Remains Be Used for Ethnic Diagnosis in the Ancient Near East?" In Silberman, Neil Asher, and Small, David, eds., *The Archaeology of Israel: Constructing the Past, Interpreting the Present*. JSOT Supplement Series, 237. Sheffield, U.K.: Sheffield Academic Press, 1997.

———. "Urbanization and the Organization of Animal Production at Tell Jemmeh in the Middle Bronze Age Levant." *Journal of Near Eastern Studies* 47, n. 2 (April, 1988): 81–94.

Hoffman, Lawrence A. *Covenant of Blood*. Chicago and London: University of Chicago Press, 1996.

Ilan, Tal. *Jewish Women in Greco-Roman Palestine*. Peabody, MA: Hendrickson Publishers, 1996.

Joannes, Francis. "The Social Function of Banquets in the Earliest Civilizations." In Flandrin, Jean-Louis, and Montanari, Massimo. *Food: A Culinary History*. Trans. by Albert Sonnenfeld. New York: Columbia University Press, 1999.

Joselit, Jenna Weissman. *The Wonders of America*. New York: Hill and Wang, 1994.

Kaj, Århem. "Massai Food Symbolism: The Cultural Connotations of Milk, Meat and Blood in the Pastoral Massai Diet." *Anthropos* 84 (1989): 1–23.

Kaplan, Mordechai. *Judaism as a Civilization*. New York: Macmillan, 1934.

Kazin, Alfred. *A Walker in the City*. New York: Harcourt, Brace and Co., 1951.

N.A. *Kelim mitekufat ha-Mishnah v'ha-Talmud*. Second edition. Tel-Aviv: Haaretz Museum and Ceramics Museum, 1979.

Klawans, Jonathan. *Impurity and Sin in Ancient Judaism*. New York and Oxford: Oxford University Press, 2000.

Kraemer, David. "Mishnah." In Katz, Steven, ed., *The Cambridge History of Judaism*, vol. 4. Cambridge: Cambridge University Press, 2006.

———. *Reading the Rabbis: The Talmud as Literature*. New York and Oxford: Oxford University Press, 1996.

———. "The Spirit of the Rabbinic Sabbath." *Conservative Judaism* 49, n. 4 (Summer, 1997): 42–49.

Levine, Hillel. *Economic Origins of Anti-Semitism: Poland and Its Jews in the Early Modern Period*. New Haven and London: Yale University Press, 1991.

Levine, Lee I., ed. *The Galilee in Late Antiquity*. New York and Jerusalem: The Jewish Theological Seminary of America, 1992.

Lévi-Strauss, Claude. "The Culinary Triangle." In Counihan, Carole, and Van Esterik, Penny, eds. *Food and Culture: A Reader*. New York and London: Routledge, 1997.

———. *The Origin of Table Manners. Mythologiques*, v. 3. Chicago: University of Chicago Press, 1990. Trans. of *L'Origine des Manières de Table*. Paris: Librairie Plon, 1968.

Lew, Myer S. *The Jews of Poland*. London: E. Gladstone, 1944.

Lewin, B.M. *Otzar Hilluf Minhagim (Thesaurus of Halachic Differences Between the Palestinian and Babylonian Schools)*. Jerusalem: Mossad Harav Kook, 1942.

Lewis, Bernard. *The Jews of Islam*. Princeton, NJ: Princeton University Press, 1984.

Lieberman, Saul. *Greek in Jewish Palestine*. New York: Jewish Theological Seminary of America, 1942.

———. *Hellenism in Jewish Palestine*. New York: Jewish Theological Seminary of America, 1950.

———. *Tosefta*. 5 vols. New York: Jewish Theological Seminary of America, 1955–88.

Magness, Jodi. *The Archaeology of Qumran and the Dead Sea Scrolls.* Grand Rapids, MI and Cambridge, U.K.: William B. Eerdmans Publishing Company, 2002.

Marcus, M. *The Ceremonies of the Present Jews.* London, 1728 and 1729.

Margulies, Mordecai. *The Differences Between Babylonian and Palestinian Jews* (Hebrew). Jerusalem: Rubin Mass, 1937.

Meigs, Anna. "Food as a Cultural Construction." In Counihan, Carole, and Van Esterik, Penny, eds. *Food and Culture: A Reader.* New York and London: Routledge, 1997, pp. 95–106.

Mennell, Stephen. *All Manners of Food: Eating and Taste in England and France from the Middle Ages to the Present.* Urbana and Chicago: University of Illinois Press, 1996.

Meyer, Michael A. *Response to Modernity: A History of the Reform Movement in Judaism.* New York and Oxford: Oxford University Press, 1988.

Milgrom, Jacob. *Leviticus 1–16. The Anchor Bible*, v. 3. New York: Doubleday, 1991.

Montanari, Massimo. "Food Models and Cultural Identity." In Flandrin, Jean-Louis, and Montanari, Massimo. *Food: A Culinary History.* Trans. by Albert Sonnenfeld. New York: Columbia University Press, 1999.

———. "Food Systems and Models of Civilization." In Flandrin, Jean-Louis, and Montanari, Massimo. *Food: A Culinary History.* Trans. by Albert Sonnenfeld. New York: Columbia University Press, 1999.

———. "Peasants, Warriors, Priests." In Flandrin, Jean-Louis, and Montanari, Massimo, *Food: A Culinary History.* Trans. by Albert Sonnenfeld. New York: Columbia University Press, 1999.

———. "Romans, Barbarians, Christians." In Flandrin, Jean-Louis, and Montanari, Massimo, *Food: A Culinary History.* Trans. by Albert Sonnenfeld. New York: Columbia University Press, 1999.

Nemoy, Leon, ed. *Karaite Anthology.* New Haven: Yale University Press, 1952.

Neusner, Jacob. *A History of the Mishnaic Law of Holy Things*, pt. 6. Leiden: E.J. Brill, 1980.

———. *Method and Meaning in Ancient Judaism.* Missoula, MT: Scholars Press, 1979.

———. *Transformations in Ancient Judaism.* Peabody, MA: Hendrickson Publishers, 2004.

Nickelsburg, George W.E. *Jewish Literature Between the Bible and the Mishnah.* Philadelphia: Fortress Press, 1981.

Niditch, Susan. *Oral World and Written Word: Ancient Israelite Literature.* Louisville, KY: Westminster John Knox Press, 1996.

Peskowitz, Miriam. *Spinning Fantasies: Rabbis, Gender, and History.* Berkeley: University of California Press, 1997.

Philipson, D. *The Reform Movement in Judaism.* New York: Macmillan, 1931.

Pietrzyk, Z. "Judaizers in Poland in the Second Half of the 16th Century." In Polonsky, A., Basista, J., and Link-Lenczowski, A., *The Jews in Old Poland 1000–1795.* London: I.B. Tauris and Co., 1993.

Plaut, W. Gunther. *The Rise of Reform Judaism.* New York: World Union for Progressive Judaism, 1963.

Pliny. *Natural History, with an English Translation by H. Rackham.* Cambridge: Harvard University Press, 1938.

Polonsky, A., Basista, J., and Link-Lenczowski, A. *The Jews in Old Poland 1000–1795.* London: I.B. Tauris and Co., 1993.

Rabinowitz, Louis. *The Social Life of the Jews of Northern France.* London: Edward Goldston, 1938.

Rebora, Giovanni. *Culture of the Fork: A Brief History of Food in Europe.* Trans. by Albert Sonnenfeld. New York: Columbia University Press, 2001.

Richler, Benjamin. *Hebrew Manuscripts in the Biblioteca Palatina in Parma.* Jerusalem: Jewish National and University Library, 2001.

Rosenberger Bernard. "Arab Cuisine and its Contribution to European Culture." In Flandrin, Jean-Louis, and Montanari, Massimo, *Food: A Culinary History.* Trans. by Albert Sonnenfeld. New York: Columbia University Press, 1999.

Sanders, E.P. *Jewish Law from Jesus to the Mishnah.* London: SCM Press, and Philadelphia: Trinity Press International, 1990.

Scheindlin, Raymond P. "Merchants and Intellectuals, Rabbis and Poets: Judeo-Arabic Culture in the Golden Age of Islam." In Biale, David, ed. *Cultures of the Jews.* New York: Schocken Books, 2002.

Schmitt-Pantel, Pauline. "Greek Meals: A Civic Ritual." In Flandrin, Jean-Louis, and Montanari, Massimo. *Food: A Culinary History.* Trans. by Albert Sonnenfeld. New York: Columbia University Press, 1999.

Scholliers, Peter, ed. *Food, Drink and Identity: Cooking, Eating and Drinking in Europe Since the Middle Ages.* Oxford and New York: Berg, 2001.

Schwartz, Seth. *Imperialism and Jewish Society, 200 B.C.E. to 640 C.E.* Princeton, NJ, and Oxford: Princeton University Press, 2001.

Shaw, Brent D. "Eaters of Flesh, Drinkers of Milk." *Ancient Society,* 13/14 (1982/3): 5–31.

Shulvass, Moses A. *Jewish Culture in Eastern Europe: The Classical Period.* New York: Ktav, 1975.

Simoons, Frederick J. *Eat Not This Flesh: Food Avoidances from Prehistory to the Present.* 2nd ed., revised and enlarged. Madison: University of Wisconsin Press, 1994.

Smith, Jonathan. *To Take Place.* Chicago and London: University of Chicago Press, 1987.

Soler, Jean. "The Semiotics of Food in the Bible." In Counihan, Carole, and Van Esterik, Penny, eds., *Food and Culture: A Reader.* New York and London: Routledge, 1997.

Soloveitchik, Haym. "Can Halakhic Texts Talk History?" *AJS Review,* 3 (1978): 152–96.

———. "Piety, Pietism and German Pietism: *Sefer Hasidim I* and the Influence of *Hasidei Ashkenaz.*" *The Jewish Quarterly Review,* XCII, nos. 3–4 (January–April, 2002): 455–493.

———. "Religious Law and Change: The Medieval Ashkenazic Example." *AJS Review,* 12, n. 2 (Fall, 1987): 205–21.

———. "Rupture and Reconstruction: The Transformation of Contemporary Orthodoxy." *Tradition* 28 (1994): 64–130.

———. *Yaynam (Principles and Pressures: Jewish Trade in Gentile Wine in the Middle Ages,* Hebrew). Tel-Aviv: Am Oved Publishers, Ltd., 2003.

Stern, Menahem. *Greek and Latin Authors on Jews and Judaism.* Volume One: *From Herodotus to Plutarch.* Jerusalem: The Israel Academy of Sciences and Humanities, 1976.

Toaff, Ariel. *Love, Work, and Death: Jewish Life in Medieval Umbria.* London: The Littman Library of Jewish Civilization, 1996.

———. *Mangiare alla giuda.* Bologna: Società editrice il Mulino, 2000.

Tollet, Daniel. "The Private Life of Polish Jews in the Vasa Period." In Polonsky, A., Basista, J., and Link-Lenczowski, A., *The Jews in Old Poland 1000–1795.* London: I.B. Tauris and Co., 1993.

Tuchman, Gaye, and Levine, Harry Gene. "New York Jews and Chinese Food: The Social Construction of an Ethnic Pattern." *Journal of Contemporary Ethnography*, 22, n. 3 (October 1993): 382–407.

Visser, Margaret. *The Rituals of Dinner: The Origins, Evolution, Eccentricities, and Meaning of Table Manners*. New York: Penguin Books, 1992.

Weiner, Max. *Abraham Geiger and Liberal Judaism*. Trans. by Ernst J. Schlochauer. Philadelphia: Jewish Publication Society, 1962.

Weinryb, Bernard. *The Jews of Poland*. Philadelphia: Jewish Publication Society, 1973.

Wilson, Robert R. *Sociological Approaches to the Old Testament*. Philadelphia: Fortress Press, 1984.

The Works of Philo. Trans. by C.D. Yonge. Peabody, MA: Hendrickson Publishers, 1993.

Yadin, Yigal. *Hamimtza'im miymei bar-kokhba b'mearat ha-igarot*. Jerusalem: 1963.

Index